Harriet Lamb has been Chief Executive Officer of the Fairtrade Foundation since 2001. Before this she worked at Fairtrade Labelling Organisations International (FLO) in Bonn – the global umbrella body for Fairtrade. She led the campaigns of the World Development Movement and has held a range of other roles, including campaigning for a minimum wage in Britain while at the Low Pay Unit.

Harriet has lived and travelled widely in the developing world, including time in India working with farmers and landless labourer co-operatives, and she is a highly experienced public speaker and media spokesperson. Her awards include a CBE in the New Year's Honours List 2006 for her contribution to Fairtrade, Cosmopolitan Ultimate Eco-Queen 2008 and Credit Suisse Outstanding Woman in Business 2008.

D0488421

Fighting the Banana Wars and Other Fairtrade Battles

How We Took on the Corporate Giants
to Change the World

Harriet Lamb

RIDER

LONDON · SYDNEY · AUCKLAND · JOHANNESBURG

1 3 5 7 9 10 8 6 4 2

First published in 2008 by Rider, an imprint of Ebury Publishing
This edition published by Rider in 2009

Ebury Publishing is a Random House Group company

Copyright © The Fairtrade Foundation 2008

Harriet Lamb has asserted her right to be identified as the author of this
Work in accordance with the Copyright, Designs and Patents Act 1988.

The Random House Group Limited Reg. No. 954009

Addresses for companies within the Random House Group can be found at
www.rbooks.co.uk

A CIP catalogue record for this book is available from the British Library

The Random House Group Limited supports The Forest Stewardship
Council (FSC), the leading international forest certification organisation.
All our titles that are printed on Greenpeace approved FSC certified paper
carry the FSC logo. Our paper procurement policy can be found at
www.rbooks.co.uk/environment

Line illustrations by Rodney Paull
Printed in the UK by CPI Cox & Wyman, Reading, RG1 8EX

ISBN 9781846040849

Copies are available at special rates for bulk orders. Contact the sales
development team on 020 7840 8487 for more information.

To buy books by your favourite authors and register for offers, visit
www.rbooks.co.uk

Royalties from the sale of this book will support the work of the
Fairtrade Foundation.

Contents

Acknowledgements

Firstly a huge heart-felt thank-you to Ben Jackson for editing this book, and to Simon Pare for additional research.

For their contributions I would like to thank Foundation staff and volunteers past and present, especially Barbara Crowther, Gemma Steptoe and Dave Goodyear, as well as Richard Anstead, Sara Barron, Ian Bretman, Bruce Crowther, Chris Davies, Frank Foo, Eileen Maybin, Nita Pillai, Julia Powell, Tamara Thomas, Mark Varney, Eileen Veitch-Clark, Jenny Tither and Phil Wells.

I would also like to thank all those who have given their time and told me their stories, including: Barry Coates, Peter Gaynor, Mike Gidney, Katharine Hamnett, Brad Hill, Joe Human, John Kanjagaile, Silver Kasoro Atwoki, Raymond Kimaro, Justin King, Steve Knapp, Jeroen Kroezen, Comfort Kumeah, Tadesse Meskela, Robin Murray, Penny Newman, Matt North, Noel Oettle, Merling Preza Ramos, Renwick Rose, Alistair Smith, Tammy Stewart-Jones, Sophi Tranchell, and Greg Valerio.

I am grateful to World Development Movement for opening up their banana archive and Bananalink for all their help.

Thanks also to Oxfam America (www.oxfamamerica.org) for the original idea upon which the diagram on page 235 is based.

Above all else, I would like to acknowledge those many, many people across the world who have played their part in putting Fairtrade on the map but whose stories could not all be included in this book.

Foreword

Every time a shopper picks a product with the FAIRTRADE Mark off a supermarket shelf that person is showing how profit and principle can go together. The story of Fairtrade is not about how we can buck the market but about how we can bend it, to serve the people who are at the bottom end of a supply chain that stretches from some of the poorest parts of the world to some of its richest regions.

As a foreign correspondent I have crossed that great divide myself many times. I took pictures of the destitute and diffident, and beamed them into sitting rooms across Britain. The places changed but the core of what I did remained the same: I described the problem, but didn't stay on to help find a solution. How often I wished I could offer help, how often I wanted to rail against the injustice I saw around me. But as a reporter you move on; the phone rings and you are on another plane to yet another story. The invitation to become Patron of the Fairtrade Foundation changed all that for me. Here was my chance to become a part of the solution. So many of the conflicts I had witnessed were rooted in poverty. It is when we have nothing in our back pockets that we are most tempted by the warlord who would place our children in harm's way or the politician who would persuade us that our situation is all about tribe or ethnicity. But when we know there is money to feed the family today and there is the promise of more to come to educate our children tomorrow we are much less likely to listen to the hate-mongers. That is precisely what Fairtrade does. Its offer of a stable income is the best protection against violence and insecurity. It is also one that the world's poorest desperately need, if they are to equip themselves to deal with the global crises of food and fuel price rises, and climate change. As the challenges faced by us all increase, through Fairtrade we can give the disadvantaged a fighting chance to cope with them.

Today 7 out of 10 households in Britain have bought a Fairtrade product in the last year. Every major supermarket and scores of independent shops and cafes, restaurants, workplaces and companies in Britain are now playing their part in making sure their customers can choose Fairtrade. It's not been easy. With honesty and insight, this book charts the journey of the Fairtrade movement, its high and lows, its successes and failures. It tells the story of Fairtrade from its hesitant but hopeful beginnings to what it is today – a mainstream option for millions of shoppers, and therefore also for farmers and workers.

Fighting the Banana Wars and Other Fairtrade Battles offers a compelling eye-witness account from someone at the heart of the campaign to make us re-think the way we do our shopping. From her encounters with farmers desperate for change, with activists who want it all and more, to boardroom executives with their bottom-line scepticism, Harriet Lamb has managed to get behind the facts and figures of Fairtrade; in this book she has revealed its soul. 'Soul' – what a word to use when all around you people are talking about markets and margins! What's 'soul' got to do with the business of buying and selling coffee, the world's second most traded commodity after oil? Who cares about 'soul' when share prices have to be kept buoyant and costs kept to a minimum? The Fairtrade movement – that's who cares.

I remember attending a meeting in London that brought together all the varied, and sometimes competing, players in the Fairtrade movement. The supermarket staff with their PowerPoint pie charts were there. They sat next to church-hall supporters from rural towns in Britain. Mingling with them were farmers from far-flung countries, twitching at collars too tight on necks more accustomed to the heat of a tropical sun. One speaker was talking about how the FAIRTRADE Mark was taking on the status of a brand logo, its blue and green symbol instantly conveying its own message. I was chairing the meeting and saw a hand go up – it was a farmer from South America. In halting English but in words I still remember, this man encapsulated the spirit of Fairtrade. 'I ask you, my friends, to remember one thing,' he said. 'Fairtrade is more than a brand, it is a people.'

Above all, *Fighting the Banana Wars and Other Fairtrade Battles* is about the farmers, workers and their families for whom Fairtrade has been a lifeline in a trading world that has yet to offer them the level playing field they have been promised for decades. This is the story of how they have helped create Fairtrade, with the support of shoppers overseas, and so brought tangible, measurable change to many people's lives – change with dignity because this is about a fair exchange. When you meet the farmers, their pride shines through: pride in their perfectly kept account books and neat plots, pride in their new warehouse or school, pride that they are themselves selling quality products on world markets, but above all else pride in their ambitions and their bold dreams for the future.

George Alagiah
Patron, Fairtrade Foundation
2008

Introduction

In 2002, my two children spent the cold February half-term holiday at their grandparents in the Somerset countryside, playing with their dog and getting very muddy. When I went to join them at the weekend, I was amazed to find the family and the whole village gripped by the women's curling event in the Winter Olympics. I was bemused. For the uninitiated, curling is a kind of bowls-on-ice, played with large rounded stones that players slide across the ice; they run in front of the stones furiously sweeping away ice particles that impede the rock's progress. Was it really such an all-absorbing sport?

And yet it was certainly the hot topic in the post office, on the street corner and in the village shop, with everyone rushing home to catch up on the fortunes of the British team. Swept along, I settled down to watch the TV coverage. Finally I understood the appeal. For here was a team of completely ordinary Scottish women. They didn't have athletic bodies or the ambitious, focused eyes of professional sports stars. They were mothers, sales reps, housewives, deputy managers, administrators. And here they were going for gold – and winning.

That too is the buzz of Fairtrade: perfectly ordinary people in their everyday lives reaching for the quite extraordinary ambition of transforming trade – and beginning, just beginning, to win. It is the making of a marvellous mosaic: millions of tiny pieces, millions of tiny steps, which in isolation may look like nothing much, but as they fall into place create something far, far greater. It is a way that you and I, whether in Britain or South Africa or the United States, can do something positive to challenge the deep injustices still disfiguring our divided world.

Which is perhaps why, for so many people in such very different circumstances right across the world, Fairtrade can become an addictive habit. You start by savouring a really good cup of Fairtrade coffee or some luscious chocolate; it's delicious and it's just basic common sense that farmers and workers should get paid a fair price for it. Why wouldn't you choose Fairtrade, all things being equal? Soon, when you're out shopping you find yourself scanning the shelves for tea or juice, nuts or bananas carrying the independent stamp of approval, the FAIRTRADE Mark. Before you know it, Fairtrade has become a part of your everyday life. Then you're asking the manager if they could stock some Fairtrade wine, or you're encouraging your workplace, school, college or place of worship to use Fairtrade goods. And suddenly there you are – part of a global network because people in Ireland, Australia or now the Baltic states are doing just the same. As Tadesse Meskela, General Manager of the Oromia Coffee Farmers' Co-operative Union in Ethiopia – and 'star' of the acclaimed documentary film about the coffee trade, *Black Gold* – puts it, 'Fairtrade is not just about buying and selling. It is about creating a global family.' One that links citizens in the rich world with farmers and workers in Peru or Burkina Faso or India – who are also, step by step, creating change. For them, as Merling Preza Ramos from Nicaragua describes in Chapter Four, 'Fairtrade is a whole way of life.' It is that bringing together of people which is a defining feature of Fairtrade – and one reason why so many people warm to it. Because it is putting people back into the heart of trade and chipping away at deeply ingrained injustices.

Fairtrade has grown and become much more visible in our shops, media and local communities. But I know that as more and more people hear about Fairtrade and support it, they also want to understand more about what lies behind it. And that's why I wrote this book. To explore why we need Fairtrade in the first place and how it got started; and to describe the scale of the challenges that have been overcome to date. To examine the difference Fairtrade can make. To assess where Fairtrade might go next and what you can do to help it grow and deepen around the world. And I wanted to do all this by sharing some of the rich stories of the hundreds of people who are creating, and fighting for, Fairtrade.

Because when you see Fairtrade oranges or coffee or nuts in your shop or café, you can be sure there's been quite a battle to get them there and that the farmers, companies and Fairtrade guardians have had to overcome huge problems. Making Fairtrade work is never easy. I've tried to sketch, in more detail than will fit on the average packet of tea or leaflet, just some of the battles we have had – and are still having. For, as Fairtrade becomes more widely available, it's easy to begin to take it for granted, and to forget that only a few years ago companies laughed in our faces at the very idea. And to forget there are still too many companies sneering or idly dismissing or actively undermining Fairtrade. The battle is far from won. As when we started, so today Fairtrade remains a tall order: to tackle injustice and poverty through trade. Usually it feels like swimming against the tide – surrounded by sharks!

But, for all that, Fairtrade is also great fun and, indeed, a joy because of the people across the world that turn Fairtrade from a nice idea into a living reality. I am constantly humbled and inspired – whether talking to an Indian rice farmer, or an active supporter in an English country town, or a hard-bitten supermarket buyer who seems to have caught the Fairtrade bug. Each of those very different people can tell their fascinating story about their involvement in Fairtrade – and I've tried to paint at least some glimpses of their lives.

I describe how I first got hooked on Fairtrade through bananas. Back then in 1999, you couldn't buy a Fairtrade banana in Britain – and there weren't any Fairtrade labelling initiatives at all in countries like Australia or Spain. But there were fledgling initiatives right across North America and Europe, led by the pioneers in the Netherlands and Switzerland, forging partnerships with coffee farmers in Mexico, Costa Rica and Tanzania. In country after country, people in towns and villages were talking to their friends and neighbours about Fairtrade. And they still are. This is the grass-roots movement that is blossoming into a phenomenon of our time.

For me, Fairtrade matters because it is creating change for over 7 million farmers, workers and their families across the developing world; but also because it is a living challenge to the injustices of world trade which shows that ordinary people can, when they take matters into own hands, make a difference. As the Indian author and activist Arundhati Roy has said, 'Another world is not only possible, she is on her way. On a quiet day, I can hear her breathing.' Fairtrade helps swell that growing sound.

1
Banana Battles

I was trudging wearily round a supermarket in Camberwell, south London after work one evening, wondering what on earth to cook for the family supper, when my eye was caught by a bright-eyed, ten-year-old boy tugging at his father's sleeve.

'Dad, Dad! Let's get this coffee, Dad. With this Mark on. It means the farmers get a fair deal,' he announces ever so slightly proudly, putting a packet of coffee in their trolley. 'I saw it on Blue Peter, on children's TV.'

His father is keen: the coffee, from the company Cafédirect, comes from Peru and has a picture of the ancient ruins of Machu Picchu on the front. He runs his finger over the photo and talks excitedly to his boy in Spanish. It's soon clear the family are themselves from Peru. The child scampers off to get some Fairtrade bananas too, still enthusing about how buying this fruit will help the children of banana farmers to go to school. Resisting the urge to try to recruit him to our promotion team on the spot, I watch him drag his smiling father round the end of the aisle.

'I think the farmers should get all the money, don't you?' the boy says, glancing up and hopefully adding, 'There's Fairtrade chocolate too, you know …'

As my kids would say: How cool is that? How cool that the next generation gets the idea of Fairtrade straightaway; no messing, no clever gainsaying or quibbling; to them, it is obviously right that the farmers who work day in, day out in the fields should get a fair price. How cool that they heard about it on the TV and then could find those bananas right there in the supermarket. When that child was born, Fairtrade bananas seemed a hopeless dream. Who would have thought that today around half of all bananas in Switzerland, one in four of those in Britain should now be Fairtrade; that they have become part of the fabric of our lives when recently they were contested so hotly, dismissed so coldly. There, surrounded by shoppers pushing past me, my mind rewound years to a painful memory of when I first went to the steamy, emerald green country of Costa Rica.

What could I say? There was nothing I could say. So I just sat next to Maria, held her hand, listened to her story and cried with her. I was in Costa Rica to find out about life for the workers who grow the bananas sold in Britain's shops. But suddenly I was just one mother listening to another talking about the most precious thing in the world – her child.[1]

Like so many local men, her husband, Juan, worked on a banana plantation. During the 1980s his job was to inject a chemical called DBCP into the ground with a hand-held machine to kill the worm-like parasites that attack the roots of banana plants. He prepared the chemical, carried it in an open container, and reloaded the machine from an open vat many times a day. As he worked he breathed in DBCP. It often went on his skin.

Juan knew nothing of its hidden dangers. But the chemical companies who made it did, and the banana companies that used it did. The US manufacturers knew DBCP caused sterility in rats as early as the 1950s but suppressed the information and pressured officials to approve its use. Then in 1977 it was revealed DBCP had made thirty-five workers sterile at a factory in California. The state quickly banned its use and the US Environmental Protection Agency stopped registering any products containing DBCP.[2] But the chemical manufacturers went on exporting it to poor countries like Costa Rica, where the banana companies continued using it on their plantations.

Day after day Juan's body absorbed the poison – slowly and silently. Only years later did it exact its toll. It was 16 November 1993. It should have been one of Juan and Maria's happiest days. But, Maria told me, after she had given birth to her son, the hospital staff seemed afraid to bring him to her. It had been a very difficult birth. In the end it was a caesarean.

'But now that was all over, I just wanted to see my child,' she said.

When she finally held him in her arms, she understood why it had been such a hard delivery and the staff had been reluctant to show her the baby. The boy was severely deformed. His head was four times bigger than his body. His eyes and nose were joined together. He had no proper eyelids. His skin was sickly green. Parts of his brain were missing. And it had all been caused by his father's exposure to DBCP.

Haltingly she told me – with her eyes filling up – how her baby could never sleep for more than two hours at a stretch, as his condition tortured him. Even now, years later, it makes me cry when I remember her telling me, as she gestured weakly to the room where he had lain, how she couldn't even cuddle the crying boy.

'I couldn't hold him because it seemed to make him cry more. So I just talked to him and cried with him. It's the worse thing that can ever happen to anyone. There are no words to explain what life is like.'[3]

When Maria and Juan went to their local doctor for advice about the cause of the deformities and what could be done to help him, he fobbed them off.

'The doctor is in the pay of the company,' the local priest later told me. A few months later the baby died. Maria was far from alone. The babies of over 3,500 women in Costa Rica alone suffered birth defects, we were told. Tens of thousands of workers in Central America and Asia say they have been left sterile by DBCP.[4] As we sat there, and she showed me pictures of her baby, rage bubbled up inside me because the companies knew of the dangers of this chemical but they ignored them. I have never, ever forgotten Maria.

As I walked away down the path from her small house, I felt a burning desire to tell supermarket shoppers the misery suffered by people like Maria and Juan in order to deliver ever cheaper and more spotless fruit into their shopping trolley. It was 1997. I was working for a British pressure group on world poverty, the World Development Movement (WDM). I was in Costa Rica's banana-growing Atlantic region with Alistair Smith – a tall, intense campaigner from the watchdog group Bananalink – to find out from the workers there how shoppers who ate their bananas could support their struggle for better wages and conditions. The emotions of my meeting with Maria were still churning inside me as he and I sat later in a smoky, ramshackle café in town sipping hot sweet coffees and long glasses of water. Nick Shaw, a somewhat dishevelled freelance journalist who was hoping to interest TV's *Channel Four News* in the issue, had just joined us.

We were discussing the companies' line that things had improved. 'Things are getting worse, not better,' Alistair interjected heatedly, looking up from rolling a cigarette. 'The price war between the supermarkets means the banana companies are squeezing workers so they can get the fruit cheaper. Sackings, union-busting, wage cuts, threats to move production to other countries, intimidation – you name it. They're clamping down everywhere.'

I'd felt this pressure among the staff of the country's embattled Plantation Workers Union, called SITRAP, when we'd visited earlier in the day. 'It's like a war now,' one of them had told me starkly.

Arriving during the still-gentle, pink, early sunlight we'd met Carlos Arguedas, a former 'bananero', banana worker, now working on environmental issues at SITRAP. His warm, avuncular face and drooping grey moustache belied the horrors he, too, had suffered.

'Yes, I'm one of the "burnts", as we're jokingly called,' he told me. 'I was affected by DBCP. I am unable to procreate. I have headaches, kidney problems, loss of sight. DBCP produces inflammation of the testicles, or the shrinking of testicles even to the point of being nearly eliminated. The worker who has reduced testicles has suffered less than those whose testicles have been inflamed or those who have had to have theirs amputated. There are co-workers affected by DBCP who don't have genitals any more now.'

By that time 16,000 banana workers from twelve countries were trying to take legal action in the US courts against the chemical companies Shell, Dow Chemical and Occidental Chemical as well as the three banana giants – Dole, Chiquita and Del Monte – that dominate the trade. Despite years of legal wrangling, none of these workers had yet received one single cent in compensation from US courts. Others had felt compelled to take offensively small, out-of-court settlements. Many have died young waiting for justice. In November 2007, however, after decades of doing everything to avoid justice in the US, Dow and Dole finally were proved guilty in a Los Angeles courtroom of making six Nicaraguan banana workers sterile through the use of DBCP and were ordered to pay out $3.3 million in compensation. Company letters from the 1960s and 1970s were used in court to show that 'Dole knew about the problems with DBCP, but wanted to continue using the chemical because the company feared not doing so would hurt their banana crops', reported Associated Press. Thousands of further cases of banana workers in Central America and West Africa who allege they have been affected by DBCP are waiting to come to court.[5]

As we sat in the union's cramped office, Carlos told me he'd eventually accepted an out-of-court settlement of $7,600 – no liability was admitted, but it was only enough for ten treatment sessions at a local clinic for a condition he'd have for the rest of his life. And yet, he says, some US workers affected by DBCP received $1 million compensation each.

He says of the pay out, 'It makes me angry when I think the multinationals come to our country, contaminate our men, take back their dollars, leaving mutilated men and women, and don't face up to their responsibilities afterwards.'

I asked Carlos if he'd like to give a message to people in the UK who buy Costa Rican bananas. His response was striking, 'Bananas carry a high cost in this country. We don't ask people in Britain to stop buying them. But we do ask they be mindful so that sooner, rather than later, we should have a banana industry that is in accord with nature and with humankind. We hope to have the strength to continue producing that dessert which is so popular in your country. But we hope to continue doing so in humane and ecologically sound living conditions.'

His vision of a fairer way of trading bananas could have sounded hopelessly naive. But from Carlos, who knew first-hand the brutal realities of the cut-throat trade and the power of the companies who controlled it, the words were powerful and inspiring. I felt then for the first time, as I feel now, that building this better type of trade *had* to be possible. And across the world – in Costa Rica, in Mexico, in tiny Caribbean Islands, in development organisations in Europe and North America – more and more people were thinking along the same lines. The beginnings of a global movement were stirring.

Today, when every banana in British supermarkets Sainsbury's or Waitrose carries that cheerful little blue and green FAIRTRADE Mark which embodies exactly that vision of a fairer, more environmentally sustainable trade, it is easy to forget that back then the idea was new. In fact, it was so new that most people saw it as mad or irrelevant – or dangerous enough to need stopping.

Before long, I was to be drawn into the long, hard battle to turn this vision into reality. For the dropped stone of Carlos's words spread ripples through my mind.

The next morning we drove into the plantation on a side-access road. After a while Carlos asked the driver to pull over and stop. And then the silence hit me. Apart from the occasional flapping from the great fraying leaves arching into the air around us, there wasn't a sound. No birds. No animals. I almost felt I had to whisper so as not to wake up the ranks of bowing green giants. It was eerie.

Nothing else lived in this lush desert – only the one Cavendish variety of bananas, growing in line after line, for mile after mile. The ripening bunches hung on the plants in translucent blue plastic bags impregnated with yet more insecticide. You could see why they needed such a constant chemical barrage – pests and diseases could spread like wildfire through such one-crop agricultural factories.

Cables were suspended at intervals above the rows with hooks to carry the bunches, ski-lift-like, to the packing sheds. There, workers slice each hand of bananas off, wash them in great baths of water, before checking them for exacting quality standards and packing them into boxes along lines of steel rollers. Often this job is done by women who, as they were later to tell me, had missing fingernails and damaged skin from working in the chemical-filled water.

As we stood awed by the vastness of the plantation, we suddenly heard a distant buzzing. It steadily grew louder, but we still couldn't make out where it was coming from. Then a small yellow plane started to appear over the horizon. As it came closer I could see, strung underneath the length of its wings, two pipes with dozens of nozzles pouring down an intense fine rain.

Nick rushed back to the car and climbed on to its roof to get into position. He steadied his camera and his nerve to get a shot of the plane roaring over us so low it seemed to touch the tops of the banana plants. The startled pilot momentarily caught this strange sight. We quickly jumped into the car as the foul-smelling cocktail of pesticides fell, our eyes and noses running from just this passing exposure.

Elsewhere 'marksmen' stood holding flags to guide the pilot to the bloc of bananas selected for spraying on that run. The process went on incessantly, with each section covered as often as every five days to keep at bay the black sigatoka fungus that is the dread of all banana growers. But, as Carlos told us, bananas were not the only things covered.

'Whole areas of the population get sprayed by the poison: schools, churches, wells, homes with children and the sick – all kinds of people are constantly contaminated by the poison which the planes and the wind carry long distances.'

Workers and their families in another part of the plantation complained of asthma and bronchitis, heart and skin ailments; while Carlos told us of the contamination of soil and rivers, coral reefs and wildlife killed by the run-off from the plantations.

The next day, Carlos introduced us to Dolores. A large woman, bustling round her wooden house, she straightened white crocheted doilies on the long table as she brought us tea and biscuits. She sighed as she said their wages had been cut yet again. The milk for her young children now used up more than half the wage packet.

'The rest goes on food – only vegetables. The water is bad here so my daughter has tapeworm and amoeba [that causes dysentery]. But we don't have money to treat it. It's really difficult if we need to buy clothes or shoes; we just don't have enough money.'

The connection was direct: cheaper bananas in our shops meant people like Dolores getting less to survive on. Any action by the workers to resist the wage cuts was blocked by the companies. Later in the evening we met some workers in secret who were trying to get better conditions by organising a trade union.

'The problem we face, not just on this plantation but on all plantations, is that we are not allowed to stand up for our own rights,' one worker told us. 'Union members are persecuted. Even just saying the word union is asking to be sacked.'[6] People wanted to talk and talk, but finally we had to leave. We drove off out of the sickly chemical air – knowing that most people could not escape so easily.

Back in London I worked furiously distilling the evidence from Costa Rica into briefing materials and campaign leaflets calling on people in the UK to write to one of the largest banana companies, Del Monte Fresh Produce.

To get things going, one hot day in August 1997 we paid a surprise visit to the Kent headquarters of Del Monte. And took a few banana skins with us. A tonne of them actually.

The Body Shop, who used bananas to make a lush shampoo, had a regular supply of the discarded skins and was happy to help. We filled a white van with banana skins at the Body Shop HQ in Littlehampton, and drove to Kent. Outside Del Monte's warehouses, our small group of protestors nervously readied themselves in the back of the warm, and by now smelly, van.

We weren't sure we'd have time to mount the protest before the security people stopped us. Nerves jangling, we drove into the yard, parked in front of a loading bay, opened the doors and shovelled the banana skins on to the tarmac. I squelched up the mound and triumphantly planted a placard on top declaring: 'Stop Del Monte Dumping on Banana Workers'. Stunned staff watched out of the windows as security guards wondered what to do. The journalists we'd tipped off took their pictures, and the management invited us in to explain our concerns.

That night on *Channel Four News*, the shots of the demonstration ran together with the footage of the plane spraying pesticides on the plantation in Costa Rica and a report on the conditions suffered by banana workers. I felt we had, at least, started to honour our promises to the banana workers to publicise their plight and build pressure for change. The battle was on.

As letters from the public piled in over coming months, Del Monte's management agreed to meet us with two Costa Rican trade unionists. We met in an anonymous, airless meeting room with flock wallpaper and lurid swirly carpets in a business hotel in Kent. As we left the reception we allowed ourselves some guarded smiles and celebration. The company had agreed to negotiate a deal with the union! And they did indeed sign an agreement allowing trades unions to organise freely on all their plantations. [7]

But it's a fact of life that change is hard won: two steps forwards are all too often followed by at least one-and-half back. At first, hundreds of workers started joining the union. But within a year, with a further banana price war breaking out, the deal was falling apart and the faxes from Costa Rica told grim news.

At the same time, the banana companies were seeking to protect themselves from future PR nightmares by trying to reassure consumers that their bananas were exploitation-free. Following the World Development Movement campaign, the Banana Group, representing the main banana importers and suppliers, announced plans to launch a Banana Code to 'prove to customers that we are taking these issues seriously'. [8]

I knew from other industries we'd worked on, such as the toy industry, that such codes are several sandwiches short of the full picnic. Codes lack teeth and have no independent monitoring so companies can make claims that might, or might not, be true: but how can the customer know? They might or they might not be doing a better job. The emphasis is too often on insulating the company's reputation from the reports of the worst excesses, and giving them tick-box reassurance – without investing the resources in enabling suppliers to make long-term change. Indeed, codes usually demand more and more of suppliers – at the very time that prices are being cut. I knew codes just weren't enough. We would keep supporting the unions so that they could represent workers' interests on a daily basis on the plantation and keep putting pressure on companies. But we were also convinced that, just as companies are governed at national level by national laws, so in the age of global companies, we needed global regulations. At the same time, I kept hearing about this 'Fairtrade banana' and thought of Carlos's appeal for a new vision of banana trading.

I remembered when I was a postgraduate student at the Institute for Development Studies at Sussex University how my tutor Robin Murray's brand of economics in action inspired me. He'd been an architect of the pioneering Fairtrade organisation TWIN, and was also behind the Fairtrade company Cafédirect they had set up along with Oxfam, Traidcraft and Equal Exchange. Its impressive debut was starting to make big waves in the coffee world and the supermarkets. So I went to see him. I wanted to know – could the model they had pioneered for coffee, work for bananas?

'We need "do-tanks" not "think-tanks",' he said as he explained their first steps in Fairtrade. 'We are', and now he cupped his hands in the air, 'trying to create a little bubble in the global economy where we do trade differently, where we show it can be done successfully by putting people first.'

His inspirational words were also grounded in realism. But he was distinctly less optimistic about Fairtrade in fresh fruit having already got his fingers burnt with one of the earliest experiments. Back in the 1980s a poverty-stricken Mozambican government under constant attack from apartheid South Africa, wanted to sell oranges to the UK and Sainsbury's had shown interest. But the entire consignment had gone rotten before it even reached the docks in Mozambique's capital, Maputo, and the venture collapsed. It was an expensive mistake that no one in Britain was in a hurry to repeat. But among Fairtrade pioneers in other countries moves were already well afoot to address the banana challenge.

Not long after, in 1998, I got the chance to help nurture the fledgling Fairtrade banana by taking up a job with the – embarrassingly comical – title of Banana Coordinator at the newly created Fairtrade Labelling Organisations International (FLO) in Bonn, Germany. The national Fairtrade groups in Europe and North America had pooled their efforts by recently establishing one international organisation. In each country, organisations like the Fairtrade Foundation, which is a charity set up by groups like Oxfam, would focus on building public support for Fairtrade and getting companies on board. FLO's brief was to avoid duplication in the international sphere – working with farmers and workers in developing countries to forge a common international system for awarding goods the Fairtrade stamp of approval so that if you went shopping and bought a banana with the FAIRTRADE Mark on it you'd know the producers had received a better deal.

The rules for bananas to carry the FAIRTRADE Mark had been hammered out before I arrived. It had been no mean feat getting all the producers from Costa Rica, Ecuador and Ghana, as well as activists and Fairtrade organisations from the Netherlands, Switzerland and Germany, to agree on when a banana could be labelled a 'Fairtrade banana'. As I ploughed through the detailed standards, I realised that this was Carlos's vision of a 'humane and ecologically sound' banana trade codified into a charter that any company could meet – if they had a mind to. Here, finally, was a scheme that went to the economic heart of the matter and was based upon empowerment of the farmers and workers.

My top priority after starting my new role was to visit the farmers and learn for myself how the system worked. Ecuador is king of bananas, selling more than any other country. The banana companies, in their relentless search for cheaper bananas, had been switching to non-unionised Ecuadorian plantations with even worse conditions than I'd seen in Costa Rica – including using child workers as young as eight.[9]

But some of the first Fairtrade bananas had come from a small farmers' association also in Ecuador, and so we travelled up from the coastal city of Guayaquil to the El Guabo Banana Co-operative in the south of the country.

The roads here are perfect, fast, wide and well tarred – and soon it becomes clear why. It's weekly harvest day, and long sleek lorries are pounding down the highway, boasting their branding of Dole, Del Monte, Chiquita and also Noboa, the name of Ecuador's own billionaire banana king and three times presidential candidate, Alvaro Noboa. The fact is that these companies – together with Fyffes, making the banana world's 'big five' – produce four out of every five bananas sold in the world, while also controlling much of the packing, transport, shipping, ripening and distribution too. It's a classic case of what economists call an oligopoly.

When we arrive at El Guabo we are greeted by Jorge Ramirez, the dignified manager of El Guabo and Jeroen Kroezen, then a Dutch volunteer supporting the group and today Director of the Dutch company which pioneered the sale of Fairtrade bananas in Europe, Agrofair. As we drive past the vast plantations on either side of the road, they start pointing out the little farms squeezed in between that belong to their members, all busy with the harvest but always ready to take a break and show us round. Grinning widely, they give us the idiot's guide to banana farming as we crunch over the dry leaves of their farms – on average about six hectares, though many are less. I make a mental note not to tell my children about the guinea pigs one farmer keeps, and breeds to eat, just as European farmers keep chickens.

The contrast between these small, lush farms tended by one family and the plantations was stark. As isolated individuals it was obvious the small farmers hadn't a hope of competing. But by joining together through the co-operative to meet quality and Fairtrade standards, arrange transport and sell their bananas overseas they had a fighting chance. Through being in a co-operative, families combine the responsibility and incentives of having their own small farm but also gain the advantages of being part of a bigger operation – and are able to export their produce themselves. Starting with just fourteen farmers in 1997, today there are now over 350 farms in the El Guabo co-operative.[10]

In the small town of El Oro, the centre for El Guabo's processing operation, a container lorry parked in a side street is acting like a magnet. From all directions, battered pick-up trucks are rumbling in with bananas the farmers have spent the day harvesting. The co-op's quality controller is doing rigorous checks and recording each farmer's harvest for the week, before loading them into the container, treating each box like glass to protect the precious quality. Everyone is working flat out into the night before racing down to the port and getting the bananas on to the boat for the morning's departure.

The Fairtrade rules are, first and foremost, for traders to meet. Most far-reaching, the standards say companies must pay the growers' organisation a guaranteed, fair and stable minimum price. For bananas, the prices are calculated for each country based on how much it costs farmers to produce bananas there in a sustainable way. So, for example, the Fairtrade minimum price is higher in the steep hills of the Windward Islands, than in the flatter banana zones of Ecuador. Importers must pay this minimum price even when the going market price sinks below it – as it usually does.

Bananas have been beset by a series of vicious price wars – which still go on. At one point, in June 2007, Asda and all the other big UK supermarkets cut the price of their loose bananas to 59p a kilo – 45 per cent lower than five years before. While by September they had put prices back up, such price cuts don't come free: someone somewhere pays the price and usually that's the growers – who often have to sell their fruit for less than it has cost them to grow it. So the Fairtrade minimum price is a huge boost, and a security, for producers.

The farmers explained to me animatedly that they used to get throwaway prices for their fruit. But they had no choice, they said: the local traders would come to their village and you either accepted their price, or watched your fruit rot by the side of the road. Now, via the Fairtrade system, their co-op was getting paid over half as much again per box compared with selling to the local traders.

Joining the tour was the tall, lanky Wilson Navarrete, then being trained up by Jorge, who had spotted his talent, and who is today Secretary of the co-op. He used to be a plantation worker without a secure income or social security. Today he's the owner of a farm he took out a debt to buy – only possible because of the

£1.08 per kg

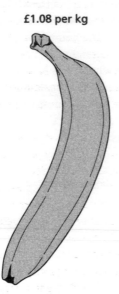

£0.68 per kg

November 2007

November 1997

The shrinking price of bananas in our shops

The retail price of bananas in main UK supermarkets in 1997 and 2007 (compiled by Bananalink from industry sources, November 2007)

secure Fairtrade income. Otherwise, he says, 'I would have gone to Spain to find work, just like so many others do. My case is similar to that of many producers over here.'

For the farmers, the minimum price guarantee was a lifeline. But what shone through was their pride in owning their own organisation where they were calling the shots. The rules state growers' organisations also get a 'Fairtrade premium' on top of the minimum price (or on top of the market rate if higher). This bonus was a substantial $1.75 a box of bananas at that time. The growers could decide democratically how to spend the premium on improving their business and the local community – from putting in irrigation or a packing shed to offering medical insurance for the workers, building new classrooms at the local school, or experimenting with more environmentally friendly ways of farming. As I listened to the farmers wrestle with the dilemmas – whether to support this or that village first, how to involve their workers more, whether to let more farmers join the co-op when they still weren't able to sell all their own fruit as Fairtrade as it was – I was struck by how the Fairtrade system was empowering farmers and communities to steer their own course of development.

The fair price guarantee is combined with a raft of standards traders have to meet such as buying as directly as possible, committing to long-term agreements and regular reports so that FLO can check they are selling the same number of Fairtrade bananas to the public as they have bought from growers.

The growers' side of the bargain means being organised into groups – with different rules for smallholders and workers on plantations. As long as farmers remain isolated smallholders, they have no choice but to sell to the local trader; it is impossible to change their position in global trade or ensure they get a fair price. But by coming together into associations, farmers can begin to take more control.

Jorge was a reserved, serious man – but with an underlying mettle. As we lent on the banana washing stations, talking to the farmers, he turned to me saying, 'Fairtrade is the reason the small farmers in our association still have a livelihood at all. The most important thing is the feeling we're no longer dependent on the big companies. We've proved we can sell directly and we're proud of that. We, the small producers, have shown that you don't need the multinationals. We've changed things and you can see the difference.'

On plantations, workers must be allowed to join a trade union if they wish, as the best means to improve their conditions, and they organise into committees to decide how to use the Fairtrade premium. That way it's the workers, not the plantation owners, who get the benefits of Fairtrade. Finally, there's a series of other standards to protect the health, safety and labour rights of plantation workers – and their environment.

In fact the farmers talked at length about the environmental standards. The standards do not demand fully organic growing, though Fairtrade helps many producers obtain organic certificates. Some of the El Guabo farmers were experimenting and hoping for organic certification. Others had trouble with chemicals drifting on to their small plots from nearby big farms, and they were unsure how to control some virulent pests if they went fully organic. But they'd all had to make big changes to the way they farmed already. Fairtrade bans the internationally recognised 'dirty dozen' most dangerous chemicals, for example. It sets clear rules to protect workers and the environment where chemicals are used – as well as a plan to cut their use over time. The rules also cover disposing of waste properly, ensuring nearby rivers and lakes are kept clean, protecting natural ecosystems, and preventing soil erosion.

It was, said the farmers, much harder work – for example they were weeding by hand instead of using chemicals. But they were all clear that the public want 'clean' bananas, and they all had tales to tell about how their health had improved since using fewer of them. 'Other companies don't care,' they told me, 'they just want the fruit.'

I was struck by how the system combined minimum standards, which farmers must meet, with 'progress standards' where they sign up to a plan to improve, say, levels of composting and recycling waste as the benefits of Fairtrade flow. The standards thus enable poorer, more vulnerable farmers to enter the system, while encouraging them to progress gradually as they learn more about how the trade works.

Meanwhile I was on my own steep learning curve about how the Fairtrade system worked in practice. Groups of farmers meeting the standards, like the El Guabo group in Ecuador, applied to an international committee in FLO. We would check if they met the standards, and if so they would be certified to join a register of Fairtrade suppliers. An importer wanting to sell Fairtrade bananas, in this case Agrofair, would also register with FLO, undertaking only to buy from producer groups on the register and to meet all the trade standards such as paying the set price. Once they'd signed a licence agreement, they could put the FAIRTRADE Mark on bananas they imported from Fairtrade producers. Consumers could then choose those bananas with confidence that they gave a better deal to the farmers and workers.

This new model of trade enshrined in the Fairtrade standards was very inspiring in theory; but could it actually work in a world of supermarket price wars and notoriously ruthless banana companies? It felt very fragile.

The start had been suspiciously bright. The first Fairtrade bananas had hit the Dutch shops with great success in 1996, taking a stunning 10 per cent of the Dutch market almost overnight. Switzerland followed swiftly, building on work by a group of women who had been raising awareness about the problems in the banana industry and selling 'Solidarity' bananas from Nicaragua, since 1985, following the then US embargo on the country. And they're still the world's benchmark. Over half of all bananas the Swiss eat are Fairtrade.

But problems followed swiftly. The startling Dutch debut soon slumped back to a shaky 1 per cent. There'd also been similar setbacks following launches in Denmark and, most disastrously, in Germany.

It was painfully clear that the whole project was permanently on a knife-edge. Back in Bonn, my phone never stopped ringing with urgent calls from producers and importers facing potentially catastrophic problems: a hurricane had wiped out all the bananas so the farmers faced ruin; the environmental standards were too hard for the farmers to meet and they faced a pest crisis; small-holders in the Dominican Republic didn't have enough water to irrigate in the summer; the banana boat had been delayed by customs in Miami, all the bananas were rotten and the insurance company refused to pay; the supermarket had cancelled an order and everyone in the chain argued it was everyone else's fault ... it never ended. And as we took those tentative early steps, every setback seemed to threaten the whole project as supermarket buyers became hopping mad and shook their heads, saying they couldn't make space for Fairtrade bananas unless we could fill them with top quality bananas on time, every time. I felt the weight of a huge responsibility and sometimes I could feel almost physically my brain whirring and my hair going grey as I tried to broker solutions.

The whole chain had to work and we faced challenges at every step. We had to: help banana producers meet the Fairtrade standards, and enable new groups to participate; work with importers to ensure the bananas got to Europe; persuade shops to stock Fairtrade bananas; and, the final acid test, ensure the public knew about Fairtrade and bought the bananas. Each strand presented its own set of problems – and progress on each strand was intimately dependent on the others.

There was no doubt about the need for bananas to follow on from the first Fairtrade ventures into coffee, tea and cocoa. The present trade was so starkly unjust and banana producers really needed Fairtrade. NGO campaigns highlighting the banana battles had created a public appetite for a positive alternative. And, with bananas having overtaken apples as Britain's top-selling fruit a decade ago, if Fairtrade could make in-roads here it would show we were serious about changing how we trade and shop.

But the obstacles were huge. Bananas – usually one of the first products you see on walking into a store – are one of those products where supermarkets use lower prices to entice shoppers into their store. Nowhere is the 'pile 'em high sell 'em cheap' philosophy starker. Persuading supermarkets that the public would pay more because their bananas were fairer meant rewriting all their rules. There were also the practical difficulties of getting delicate, perishable bananas from farm to shop.

The Dutch church-based group Solidaridad had been the mover and shaker behind setting up the world's first Fairtrade label, for coffee, in the Netherlands – where it's called Max Havelaar after a literary character who exposed the injustices of the nineteenth-century coffee trade from Indonesia. On Fairtrade bananas, they quickly concluded, the big companies weren't going to play ball. So they set up a new company, called Agrofair, which is now owned fifty–fifty between Solidaridad and the banana farmers – though the producers get 100 per cent of the profit. Their first partners were El Guabo and two unusual plantations in Ghana and Costa Rica.

Jorge was pleased to share the stories of those early days. Amidst the constant shouting and pressure as farmers jostled round the banana container, he had a calm, authoritative presence as he steered me towards his office. Jorge was from a farming family and one of the few local people to go to university. When the co-operative was set up he had been elected leader by the other farmers, putting his education at the service of the young co-op. Jorge's complete commitment, hard work and almost poetic sense of vision was an inspiration to many and his death in 2003 a loss to the whole Fairtrade movement.

He switched on the overhead fan that gave a very welcome cooling downblast and settled down to explain the endless problems they'd overcome. 'Even the weather seemed against us,' he said philosophically.

Just after the co-op started exporting directly, ferocious storms and flooding linked to the notorious El Niño weather system destroyed the banana farms.

'We were really worried we wouldn't have enough bananas for the supermarkets who'd committed to Fairtrade,' Jeroen Kroezen, the energetic Dutch volunteer, added. 'If we lost markets, we wouldn't get them back again. Drought hit another of our Fairtrade suppliers in Ghana. We had to have Fairtrade bananas unloaded at Antwerp every week, on the same day, to keep up the supply to the ripeners. Supermarkets wouldn't stock Fairtrade bananas if they were there one week but not the next.'

But unlike the big companies, they didn't own a banana boat and they found that most companies, perhaps sensing the threat of small farmers succeeding in selling direct, were keen to keep Fairtrade bananas off the 'reefers', the refrigerated ships used to keep bananas fresh in transit.

'So we just had to take whatever boats we could – often taking a slow, roundabout route.'

'It was really a transport glitch that gave us one of our biggest setbacks,' said Jeroen. 'A consignment of Fairtrade bananas had been unloaded in a container at Hamburg, but ended up waiting a day on the dockside before being transferred. Unfortunately it was a frosty January day. All the bananas were damaged. None would ripen. They had to be dumped. Eager supermarkets in the Netherlands were left without supplies just months after they'd launched.'

'Then things started to take an even darker turn,' said Jorge. Their boats suddenly started to suffer mysterious, repeated delays in the Panama Canal for 'their documents to be checked', he related with an ironical look.

'Other ship owners began to conclude that carrying our bananas meant trouble. It became harder and harder to find anyone willing to ship them.

'When we raised concerns with officials in the Netherlands, and it was taken up through diplomatic channels, the delays miraculously stopped,' Jeroen remarked raising an eyebrow (a trick I have tried and failed all my life to master). There was even a strange incident when the boat carrying their bananas had its rudder suddenly and violently broken one night right out in the Cuban Sea. No one could explain how that could happen unless it had been deliberate sabotage. The situation was so bad that Agrofair had considered developing its own fleet of banana boats but it was financially impossible.

Just then William came in, taking off a faded blue baseball cap and wiping his brow. 'Excuse me, friends,' he said to us. 'Jorge, we're packing up the container now.'

Jorge led us out into the dark evening. Under the ever-watchful eye of the co-op's quality controller, farmers were squeezing in the last boxes right up to the top. When they'd finished, we hopped into the cab. We sat closely packed beside the driver as he started up the engine.

'I still feel so proud when we load up our bananas,' Jorge said solemnly. 'Despite all the problems, we haven't given up.'

As we swung on to the main road to the port, we joined the long convoy of enormous, white articulated lorries, headlights on, heading down from the huge plantations with that week's harvest to the port at Machala. The scale of the multinational companies' operations was overwhelming. One by one they pulled into the humming dockside lit by vast yellow overhead lights shining down on containers being picked off the lorries and swung by crane into the waiting bellies of vast ships also owned by the companies. Chiquita's famous Great White Fleet, with its newly installed technology for controlling the atmosphere on board to suspend the ripening process, dwarfed the rather ancient Russian ship carrying a mixed bag of cargo into which the El Guabo fruit was eventually loaded.

Seeing what we were up against and the multiple hurdles for Fairtrade bananas, I did start to wonder whether they'd really be viable in the long-term – or just a valiant experiment. I was haunted by a bleak statistic: more than nine in ten new food and drink products fail. If that's the alarming statistic for mainstream trade, what hope had we? Conventional products with many times the resources behind them regularly suffered the fate we all feared for any Fairtrade product: 'delisting' from the supermarkets – the retail equivalent of excommunication.

For producers the stakes could not have been higher. There was much common cause, but any naive thoughts that all would be peace, love and solidarity were quickly brought down to earth. Fairtrade bananas still had only the shakiest toehold in Europe. If they did not succeed, they would be left without buyers for their fruit and by going with Fairtrade many had alienated their former importers who viewed the project with deep suspicion. At that time the producers had never met each other and each group feared bringing in new groups. I was pressed: 'Aren't we flooding a tiny, fragile market? Had I heard what this, that or the other group or company were up to?'

The debates were always hot. No sooner had I put the phone down to one group furiously arguing that we risked compromising our principles if this or that importer got involved, than another group were on the line impatient at the pace of growth, saying we were consigning ourselves to an ideologically pure, but irrelevant, bubble – that if we didn't increase sales faster, the producer groups could not survive.

I discovered that while every phone call was 'In total confidence, Harriet, do not tell anyone ...', everyone always seemed to know exactly what everyone else in the trade was up to. I soon got used to their shifting allegiances: one minute two importers would be sworn enemies, then I'd find they'd signed a partnership deal for the next ten years. I knew we had to get all the parties together to build understanding and find solutions. And we had to build the sales that would help knock down some obstacles.

That was when I first started to work closely with Ian Bretman at the Fairtrade Foundation. With a business background and a long stint at Oxfam Trading he'd been brought in as a consultant to clinch a deal to get Fairtrade bananas into British supermarkets. Ian is the brain of Fairtrade Britain. In fact, he has a brain the size of Britain, able to write policy papers more quickly than most of us can read them. And rarely among men of such prodigious talents, he's quietly unassuming. He left school young, went straight to work and has never stopped working flat out ever since, broken only by the odd fag break until he managed to kick the habit. His business nous, fierce intellect and dogged commitment to talk through problems to find a consensus solution made him ideal for the British banana challenge – and to be Deputy Director of the Fairtrade Foundation today.

One thing was clear to Ian straightaway: Fairtrade bananas wouldn't work in Britain unless they included the farmers of the Windward Islands in the Caribbean who had supplied Britain for

right **Key countries in the 'banana wars'**

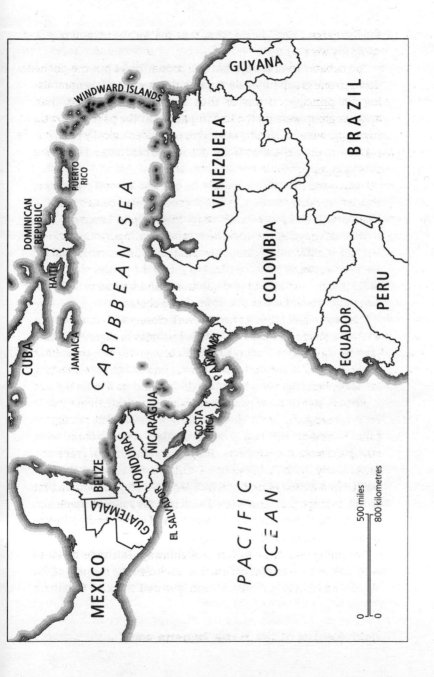

years but faced ruin with the ending of the special import deal they had with the European Union. The deal was under threat following intense lobbying and 'generous' political donations from the US-based banana giant Chiquita towards the incoming Clinton administration – which duly won a key ruling from the World Trade Organisation (WTO), the global body that polices trade rules.[11] The WTO decided the EU had to stop reserving a portion of Europe's banana imports for its former colonies such as the Windward Islands. The so-called 'banana war' between the US and EU was moving into a new phase. Faced with being wiped out by cheap bananas grown under the appalling conditions I'd seen on plantations in Latin America, the small banana farmers were in despair. Their plight had started to catch the attention of consumers increasingly concerned about where their food came from and how it was produced and traded. But at that time, Fairtrade was virtually unknown on the Windwards.

The lifelong champion of the small farmers' cause was Renwick Rose, founder and leader of the Windward Islands' Farmers Association (WINFA). One of the great privileges of being involved in Fairtrade is the opportunity to work alongside such great thinker-doers – people like Renwick and Jorge – each of whom, in their own way, was arriving at Fairtrade as a solution to the injustices of trade around them.

Renwick has a handsome face tired from a lifetime of struggle for the farmers. He recalls why he saw Fairtrade as so crucial long before the Windwards' banana industry woke up: 'You have to remember that bananas have been the mainstay of our economies since the British colonial administration engineered a switch from sugar cane to supplying banana-hungry post-war Britain,' he says. 'During the move to independence from Britain in the 1970s we campaigned for land reform to get the big plantations, often owned by white Britishers descended from the slave overseers of the past, transferred into the hands of the labourers who worked them. This move came at the same time as a banana boom – the "green gold" times as we called them.'

Even by the late 1990s, while banana production had fallen, it still accounted for half the islands' export earnings. Of the jobs on

St Vincent, one of the four islands, 70 per cent were in bananas.

Renwick explains, 'I visited Britain in 1992 and even then it was quite clear the Windwards were facing a catastrophe after the ruling from the WTO to take away their protected sales to Europe. We had to have a concrete solution for smallholders. So we began to look into Fairtrade. We were ridiculed by the islands' governments, the banana officials and the companies – even some farmers. They thought it was some foolish, crazy idea from Europe,' Renwick laughs.

Back in Bonn I was struggling to persuade colleagues from other European Fairtrade initiatives who thought banana farmers in the Windwards didn't need Fairtrade on top of the protected prices they got under the EU's banana import rules. And, in London, Ian was telling me, the retailers were making warm noises about Fairtrade bananas, but conspicuously avoiding any concrete commitment.

We were bogged down in circular arguments going nowhere. We needed to break the logjam – but time and money were running out. The Board of the cash-strapped Fairtrade Foundation had told Ian they could only give him a few more months to deliver some results before they'd have to pull the plug on the whole venture.

Just as the door seemed to be closing on Fairtrade bananas in Britain, Ian phoned, as excited as he gets in his understated way, to say his long-running discussions with the Co-operative chain of supermarkets had taken on a new feel. They were looking at making Fairtrade one plank in their strategy for renewing the business. They seemed to have an appetite for some major Fairtrade lines – including bananas.

Meanwhile, on the Windward Islands, Renwick was working to crack knotty issues like land records to help the first farmers there form a Fairtrade group.

'We walked up and down the villages, talking to farmers about Fairtrade,' Renwick recalls. 'And they always asked the same question: How much will you pay?! Then farmers started looking more and more at Fairtrade. But we still couldn't get the co-operation of the islands' banana industry associations. Finally in 1998 we started registering farmers for Fairtrade – the first hundred in St Vincent, then others in my native St Lucia.'

At last the moment came when I was presenting applications from the first hundred St Vincent farmers – each with probably no more than a couple of acres of bananas – to the next meeting of the FLO committee in Bonn. There was long and heated debate – with members raising all the familiar concerns. I was on tenter-hooks as I felt passionately this could be the first step in a whole new chapter for Fairtrade bananas, for the Fairtrade movement as a whole in Britain and – most importantly – for the banana farmers in the Windward Islands. The Committee finally gave the thumbs-up.

Then suddenly, like a mountain-bike ride, after the long, slow, hard climb to the top of the slope, we were shooting down very fast. Just before Christmas 1999 Ian emailed with the scary news that Co-op wanted to get Britain's first Fairtrade bananas in their shops; and they wanted them there by 20 January! Everyone worked day and night to get ready in time.

In the final run-down, somehow Sainsbury's heard about Co-op's plan and didn't want to be left behind. They wanted Fairtrade bananas in at least a few stores – and on the same day! In the end they had to send a special truck to Rotterdam to pick up some pallets of Fairtrade bananas. But we weren't complaining. If traditional supermarket rivalry could be harnessed in a competition on who offered more Fairtrade, it could be a real motor to extend the Fairtrade banana market. At that time, as our first few boxes crept onto the bottom shelves, we barely dared dream that by December 2006, Sainsbury's and Waitrose would be competing on who offered their customers *nothing but* Fairtrade bananas.

People from all walks of life joined the long-time campaigners to swing into action behind the new Fairtrade banana. Tammy Stewart-Jones was one. Though she's lived in Britain most of her life, she was born in St Vincent in the Windward Islands and witnessed rural poverty in West Africa while living there with her engineer husband, who she met, fittingly, at a Commonwealth

Institute 'Banana Ball'. So when she heard about the threat facing small banana farmers in her birthplace, she knew she had to act. She'd been an active member of her local Women's Institute for a decade and decided to mobilise the women there, whipping up support for Fairtrade bananas as soon as they came out. She spoke at Women's Institutes all across the country, winning strong support for her appeal to women to use their consumer power to press their local supermarkets to stock Fairtrade bananas. Her stance ruffled a few feathers among those who thought the issue 'too political' for the WI, but she was elected on to its National Committee.

'One lady asked me why I was always going on about bananas. "A banana is a banana is a banana," she said to me. I tried to explain if you're in St Vincent your bananas mean health and education for children. If people can't sell bananas any more, they'll start to turn to growing drugs in desperation – which end up on the streets of our towns and cities with our kids. We're all connected in the end; what goes around comes around.

'Most women I met saw that what a mother wants for her child here is just the same as a woman wants in a developing country. And Fairtrade is a way for them to realise their hopes for their kids.'

I have no doubt the support of Women's Institutes up and down Britain for Fairtrade bananas played a big role in getting the supermarkets to move. And Tammy's one-woman crusade was behind it. She's still active working to get her local area of Thanet in Kent behind Fairtrade and has set up links with women in St Vincent. 'They tell me Fairtrade has brought new energy. Farmers feel they're running their business through the co-op – not just growing bananas. We didn't have that when I was a girl queuing at the weighing station with our bananas.'

By the end of 2000, people in Britain had bought nearly £8 million worth of Fairtrade bananas – and the following year nearly twice that. The long drag followed by the frenzied launch of Fairtrade bananas in Britain had been an enormous step. But it was, of course, just the starting point. Now we had to prise open the door to the market beyond that first tiny gap. And this was in spite of the fact that not all the supermarkets were exactly rushing to stock the bananas. Far from it. At one point, one retailer's banana buyer wanted to take the bananas, but threatened not to put the FAIRTRADE Mark on them. Ian gently explained that the whole system was based on the shopper knowing if a product was Fairtrade because of the presence of the Mark. 'I'll give you two choices in this matter,' said the buyer in a rage. 'You can take it or you can leave it.' Ian replied nervously that we would have to leave it then. Slam went the phone, as the buyer's response. Worried that he'd blown it and we had just lost a major partner, Ian phoned the Foundation's Chair. By the time he finished that call, the buyer was back on the line, picking up the conversation as if it had never ended and talking about stocking Fairtrade bananas, Mark and all.

My chance to join this campaign came when I landed my dream job – as Director of the Fairtrade Foundation back in London. Although sad to be leaving Germany and the international arena, I relished being back working directly with the public again.

After I took up the post I approached British broadcaster and writer George Alagiah who agreed to become Patron of the Fairtrade Foundation and soon we were discussing how to move Fairtrade bananas up a gear. We agreed that if we wanted to go for scale, we needed Fairtrade to be widely available in the shops used by the most people and that meant Britain's number one retailer, Tesco – which now accounts for nearly a third of the country's supermarket sales – offering more Fairtrade bananas.[12]

So George wrote to the most powerful man in British retailing, Tesco Chief Executive, Sir Terry Leahy. To our amazement, he agreed to meet. George, Ian and I went to see him and his ex-senior civil servant Corporate Affairs Director, Lucy Neville-Rolfe, at their surprisingly low-key Cheshunt HQ. They dissected our proposal for them to scale up sales of Fairtrade bananas. Tesco had wrestled to its place at the top by 'creating value for customers' – and low prices for products like bananas were at the heart of this. Now they were engaged in a new price war with Asda, after its recent takeover by the US giant Wal-Mart. But Tesco was also in touch with its customers, constantly checking what they thought and what they wanted, seeking to win every 'floating shopper' – the informed consumer prepared to move their whole regular weekly shop to the supermarket that offers the products they are looking for. A section of the public clearly wanted Fairtrade. So, much detailed focus group and consumer research later, Fairtrade bananas from one of the Windward Islands, Dominica, hit their shelves in September 2002. By 2004 they were shifting 8,000 boxes a week literally transforming that island's economy.[13]

That June a fax whirred through from the government of St Vincent inviting me to address a major conference on the future of the Windward Islands' banana industry – the very next week! I knew I had to be there. The writing was on the wall for the endangered banana quotas into Europe. A total market free-for-all was looming where only the cheapest banana producers would survive. And while Fairtrade had become more and more important to the Windwards, they still only added up to less than one in five of the islands' output.

I hurriedly rearranged my diary, organising the usual complex schedule of last-minute childcare for my two kids, and jumped on a plane. Supermarket representatives were going too – but they, for all their keenness on cost-cutting for others, were enjoying the pleasures of first class so we didn't meet up until we got to the tiny St Vincent airport. There even the official on passport control knew about Fairtrade and the conference. There was no doubting the importance of bananas in this economy!

I was met by the warm, broad smile of Amos Wiltshire. A cheerful, round man, he is himself a banana smallholder with four acres, as well the National Fairtrade Co-ordinator for neighbouring Dominica. His head is shaved apart from a long plait at the base of his neck matched by the neat, pointy pigtail into which his beard is shaped.

'Oh welcome, welcome, welcome,' he beamed giving me a bearhug. 'I want you to come and see why I really believe Fairtrade bananas are the future of these islands.'

We set off in the car, along the coast, then making our way up steep winding roads through small hamlets and banana farms until we reached Spring Village. We turned off down a small bumpy track and stopped. Among the banana trees which grew all around her house stood a redoubtable lady in a floral print dress and wellington boots, trimming the peeling brown fibres off the stem of a plant. Her lined face and gap-toothed smile lit up under the shade of her white pork-pie hat.

'Welcome to my farm,' boomed Miss Jocelyn Trumpet, as, swinging her machete by her side and swiping at the odd weed, she clumped off up the muddy track to show me the banana trees, the orange trees, the compost heap, the water. 'I come here early in the morning. I love to watch the sun rise,' she murmured pointing out her little billy can and Primus stove for a cup of tea.

Filled with passion, she expounded on her love for this hilly little plot where she'd changed many ways of farming to meet the Fairtrade standards. She was pleased to be using fewer chemicals, she said, but it was much harder work. Now she was having to do all the weeding herself instead of spraying them.

She understood very clearly how the recent series of decisions in Brussels, Geneva and London threatened total devastation for her community. She proclaimed in her rich, defiant Caribbean accent, 'I love farming. I love Fairtrade. I ain't going down with no banana boat. I staying and I fighting all the way.'

As we left Spring Village to drive back into the capital Kingstown, Amos suggested we take the opportunity to catch up.

'I know just the place,' he said with a mischievous look.

We pulled into a place held in a time warp. One minute we were on the tarmac road passing trucks, the next we were outside a centuries-old tall wooden warehouse, upturned barrels scattered across the dusty ground, a wooden cart on its side.

'This is where they shot *Pirates of the Caribbean*,' Amos laughed. 'After filming finished, they kept the set and opened a bar here.'

As the sun set over the black volcanic sand and we sipped a rum punch, Amos sketched out his plans to bring Fairtrade on further. Surreal as it was, this mock-up of the time when plunder, slavery and sugar marked European contact with this island was strangely appropriate. We sat discussing how the long and bitter legacy of unjust trade could be refashioned into a more equal and balanced relationship. How thousands of small banana farmers on these islands could secure a decent livelihood through a new Fairtrade partnership with consumers in the old colonial power, Britain. Fairtrade had not come a moment too soon, he said. In the 1980s, there were 11,000 banana farmers in Dominica; but that number had fallen to less than 700.

'When prices dropped farmers lost interest and trust in the industry,' Amos said of Dominica. 'The economy went down to zero because bananas are the heartbeat of the country. Everything was going haywire: increasing crime, youth violence, delinquency. We even had families torn apart because there was no income, nothing coming in. Husbands couldn't maintain their families. There was an exodus from the country because things were so bad.'

And then, he related, Tesco's Fairtrade orders started coming in. It transformed their situation. Farmers started tending their plots again. As the premiums came in, they bought a 'grasscutter' (which I worked out must be what we call a lawnmower), cut a field and created football and cricket pitches. The Fairtrade footie teams were soon attracting young people. As money built up from more sales, they were able to install street lighting in the village most affected by youth violence. The gangs started to melt away as the whole island picked up.

'Fairtrade has been the saviour of the farmers in Dominica – of agriculture and the whole economy,' he said. 'With Fairtrade, small farmers have been transformed from marginalised farmers into businessmen.'

In the dim half-light behind the bar, the owner flicked on the TV news and called Amos over to watch a report on the conference. The hosting Prime Minister of St Vincent, Ralph Gonsalves, a larger than life charismatic bear of a man, was giving an impassioned speech condemning the 'almost suicidal price war' in bananas between British supermarkets. He described how farmers across the islands were trying to survive despite 'the contemporary international political economy with its ideological focus on trade liberalisation and a "don't care" attitude for the people who become its victims.'

At the conference the next day, it was the Prime Minister of

Dominica whose speech struck me most. He was the world's youngest prime minister at thirty-two – and with his good looks and charm, also considered the islands' most eligible bachelor. He gave a stark warning that the industry had to recognise that – however unjust – the old protection of their bananas in the EU market was ending, and that all energy must be thrown behind Fairtrade. This is what farmers like Amos had been saying literally for years and now, at last, the governments were beginning, not only to agree, but to back them up.

Fired up by the vision of the banana farmers and their leaders, I returned keen to increase the sale of Fairtrade bananas by persuading a supermarket to switch all their bananas. The Co-op had pioneered this type of step when they switched, firstly, all their own-brand chocolate and then all their own-brand coffee to Fairtrade. Yet the idea of achieving this for the number one grocery item, fought over so ruthlessly on price by retailers, was daunting. Every time we floated the idea, UK retailers dismissed it with a string of impossible Herculean tasks that would need completing first. But we knew that if two leading Swiss supermarkets had made the switch on bananas, then it had to be possible in Britain too.

Ian and I decided to go to the top again and requested a meeting with the man credited with reversing Sainsbury's previously sliding fortunes, Chief Executive Justin King. He was interested in differentiating Sainsbury's from its competitors and reconnecting with the traditional, classic Sainsbury's shopper. 'The people who used to collect milk-bottle tops for Blue Peter and could see them changing into guide dogs for the blind,' as he put it. He could see Fairtrade making that practical connection between the consumer and the producer. He had a lot of questions about the challenges of switching a whole category to Fairtrade. It was a big call for Sainsbury's and the Fairtrade Foundation.

It was a tough session and I left deflated. His questions went round and round in my mind as I thought now, too late, of the perfect answers. On my bike going home, I kept kicking myself wishing I'd given this or that answer. But over the next few months Ian and his team worked through all the problems one by tricky one with Sainsbury's. And then came the green light! Sainsbury's, who sell a fifth of all supermarket bananas in Britain, wanted to switch to 100 per cent Fairtrade. Shrouded in the utmost secrecy under their codename 'Operation Perry', we mapped out a plan to help them achieve this. It would cost them some £4 million a year in lost profit margins and take at least six months to complete. But we were off.

In December 2006 Justin King went on *BBC Breakfast* to announce their move. It was the biggest ever commitment to Fairtrade by a single company anywhere in the world. With sales of 10 million bananas a week, the prize for banana farmers and workers was huge. It also marked a sea change with retailers moving from battling purely on price to competing on their ethical credentials. And, indeed, the moment Sainsbury's went public, Waitrose announced a similar pledge. We reckon 25 per cent of the 7 billion bananas eaten in the UK every year are now Fairtrade. The Sainsbury's announcement, together with wider growing Fairtrade sales in the UK market, means that in 2007 the Windward Islands were selling nearly all of their bananas under Fairtrade terms.

What's more this was part of a wider international trend. In Finland, for example, one of the major supermarket chains, Siwa, switched to all Fairtrade bananas, helping overall national Fairtrade sales swell to 11 per cent of all bananas sold in 2006.[14] Worldwide sales of Fairtrade bananas grew by nearly a third in 2006 and at least some Fairtrade bananas are now sold throughout Europe and North America – in fact in every market with a Fairtrade label apart from Mexico and Australia.

The Australian case is particularly sensitive because there is a total ban on banana imports to protect the 2,000-odd Australian growers in Queensland and New South Wales. This has been a continual bugbear in Australia's relations with the Philippines (the region's largest banana producer which stole the number two spot in world banana exports from Costa Rica in 2005). The Australian authorities and growers' federation say the import ban is necessary to protect them from diseases that could destroy their plantations; the Philippines say that this is a trade barrier and have brought the matter before the World Trade Organisation to force Australia to practise the free trade it preaches so aggressively elsewhere. There is some chance that the Philippines will eventually win, but this may take a long time.

Pressure for imports only intensified when Hurricane Larry destroyed 90 per cent of the Australian crop in March 2006 – blogs went crazy comparing skyrocketing prices and cases of banana rustling were even reported.[15] Steve Knapp, Director of the Fair Trade Association of Australia and New Zealand, acknowledges Fairtrade bananas may be some way off there, but that sourcing them from producers in the Pacific could be one way to gain momentum.

Filipino producers interested in Fairtrade are also eyeing up the Japanese market which imports over 85 per cent of its conventional bananas from the Philippines and where Fairtrade bananas have only just been launched.

The United States is the world's largest banana market, but also one of the most difficult to break into for Fairtrade as it is the homeland of the three biggest banana multinationals – Dole, Chiquita and Del Monte – who dominate logistics and shipping routes to Latin America. The US Fairtrade group TransFair has been able to gain a foothold with organic Fairtrade bananas in natural food stores, reinforced by the founding of Agrofair USA, and work continues to get Fairtrade bananas into mainstream supermarkets.

So there's certainly no room to rest. Most bananas in Britain, let alone across the world, are of course still not Fairtrade. However, the story of the rise of Fairtrade bananas is one of people working together to make that vision, in Carlos's words, of a more humane and ecologically sustainable form of trade, a reality against all the odds.

When I went back to Costa Rica in 1999, I visited one of the first Fairtrade banana farmer groups, Coopetrabasur, a tongue-twister of a name which all English speakers find impossible to pronounce. It was founded by former Chiquita workers who lost their jobs when Chiquita pulled out of the area in response to a strike. As land was distributed, the workers had the foresight to pool their tiny plots into co-operatively owned plantations. But the cut-throat market killed them all off one by one so that today, only Coopetrabasur, which went with Fairtrade, remains. I always remember the wiry, sardonic founder member and poet, Arturo Gomez, telling me what switching to Fairtrade meant to him.

'Traditionally the banana worker is the poorest person in our society, managed and exploited by multinational corporations,' he told me. 'I hope that with Fairtrade, we will become an example for governments and multinational companies. Maybe we are only farmers, but we have a right to dream and to think, and to plan for our children. Before I was someone that took a box and loaded it on to a train. That was my only responsibility. In this new system, I have become an international businessman.'

2
You'll Never Make it Work

We were buffeted by the icy November wind as Bruce Crowther, bearded local vet and enthusiastic Oxfam campaigner, led me down a pretty street of old stone shops. The wet road widened into a marketplace dominated by a weathered market cross, erected to celebrate Queen Victoria's diamond jubilee. Set in the Wyre Valley's lush dairy pastures, Garstang is the epitome of a traditional Lancashire market town in the north of England. It doesn't seem the obvious place to spawn a burgeoning international grass-roots movement.

Bruce was taking me shopping. Bruce is always proud to show people round. First stop is the Co-op supermarket and its small, bustling manager Betty Whitham. This was back in 2001 and she boasted one of the largest Fairtrade ranges I'd seen anywhere. She'd insisted on an especially large order of Fairtrade bananas when they were first introduced into selected Co-op supermarkets and had kept it that way ever since.

A few doors down and Bruce pointed at a gift shop's old-fashioned window with a green sticker declaring: 'We support Fairtrade and local produce'.

'People say to me charity begins at home – that we should support our own farmers before those miles away. That's why we make it clear we don't see a conflict between the two.'

Local farmers were struggling as the EU cut the quotas of milk they were allowed to produce and the supermarkets squeezed the prices they paid them.

'But when people start to understand the extreme pressures on poor farmers in the Third World, it makes them support Fairtrade,' Bruce says.

No sooner noted, than we're off again. Even the Kwik Kutz hairdressers had the sticker up. Bruce explains: 'They serve Fairtrade coffee and tea to their customers while they wait. The extra sales may not be huge, but it's a place where people meet and talk – and it spreads the Fairtrade message.'

It was a glimpse of how Fairtrade can become an ordinary part of everyday life woven into the fabric of the nation. All down the street, it was the same. In fact 90 per cent of businesses in Garstang had signed a pledge to support Fairtrade. The schools and churches had switched to serving Fairtrade hot drinks too.

We ended up in the Coffee Pot café. It wasn't the fashionable latté bar or wholefood café sometimes seen as the home of Fairtrade. It was a cosy place serving home cooking and the large floury barm cakes typical of the north of England. Its proprietor, Avis Jones, was equally straightforward about switching to Fairtrade.

'It's just a practical way you can make a difference,' she tells anyone visiting. 'Anyone can do it, with just a bit of effort. My customers have given it a warm welcome – and that's worth a lot.'

I was in Garstang for a ceremony to declare it the world's first 'Fairtrade Town'. After our walk around, we joined local business people, church leaders, the mayor in his chains of office, and secondary school pupils in the community centre as they crowded round our celebrity guest, comedy actor and TV presenter Tony Robinson.

'When I asked my son what he associated with Fairtrade, he said crap chocolate wrapped in cardboard,' he joked. 'I remember the days when buying fairly traded coffee was a kind of macho activist badge of honour because the stuff tasted so vile only the most committed would actually drink it. But I think the Fairtrade movement is now coming of age. It's breaking into the mainstream.'

Dotted around the audience I could spot the hardcore supporters – the paid-up Oxfam campaigners and churchgoers who'd handed in their till receipts to the supermarkets asking them to stock Fairtrade goods in the early days. But there were people here from all walks of life in the town. We needed just this movement of all types of people to back Fairtrade if we were to change how the food industry and supermarkets did business. Conventional companies pour millions into persuading us to buy their products. For example, Cadbury's spent an astonishing £10 million to convince us to take up chewing its new Trident chewing gum when launched in the UK in 2007.[1] We couldn't beat them at that game. We couldn't even afford a single advert back then. We did once get special funding for one advert, one day, in one paper, the *Financial Times*, which was designed for free by Saatchi and Saatchi. But anyone can tell you that despite the frightening sums of money such an advert costs to place in a newspaper, it only works as part of a long sustained advertising campaign and we couldn't afford that.

So we had to use a very different strategy to build public demand for Fairtrade. What I saw in this room was worth its weight in gold – ordinary people prepared to act together as *organised* consumers to bring about change. This unique alliance of organised consumers with organised producers is the beating heart of Fairtrade, which gives it its strength to create change.

Some people portray Fairtrade as a way to live 'guilt-free' – as just another choice in the great consumer society. And for millions of people who have busy, pressed lives and are barely coping day to day, but aren't happy with the poverty afflicting the world, I think it's great that Fairtrade offers them an easy way to play their part in creating a better world. But to me and thousands of supporters it's much more. The legendary US campaigner Saul Alinsky once observed that 'tactics mean doing what you can with what you have'.[2] Fairtrade turns the fact that we all go shopping into a new tactic for us to act together to tell those who run trade, that we not only don't like the way they do it at the moment, but that we also want them to back a fairer alternative.

However, from the beginning we were painfully aware that just setting up the Fairtrade system and hoping it would catch on wasn't enough. People had to know about Fairtrade and then buy the products if it was going to make any difference to farmers in developing countries. And that's why Fairtrade Towns are so important in building awareness and mobilising people behind Fairtrade – starting in their own backyard. And having some fun along the way.

All movements have their legends. Bruce Crowther is a Fairtrade legend. What had happened in Garstang hadn't just been a spontaneous coming together of the community. It had taken vision, persistence and a lot of hard work to get people organised.

After the ceremony I went to Bruce's house to find out more. Children were milling around tucking into celebratory Fairtrade Dubble chocolate bars. We took our cups of tea through to sit by the fire, the greying hills of the Trough of Bowland rising in the distance through the window.

Bruce tilts his animated face forward as he speaks intently and always with deep personal feeling, 'I first moved here when I got married. I'd been living in Liverpool and was very involved in the Oxfam group there. In Garstang I thought, "What can I do in a small market town like Garstang?" This wasn't Liverpool. To be honest, I thought maybe it was time just to retire from campaigning and settle down.'

However, inspired by a harvest festival talk at a local school, he formed the Garstang Oxfam group and started plugging away on Fairtrade and other Oxfam campaigns. But with little joy. For years, they trudged round local shops asking them to stock Fairtrade products, mounted stunts to get the local paper to cover the issue, tried to win over dyed-in-the-wool town councillors who'd been in office for years, with little success. Everywhere he met the same responses: 'we're perfectly happy with our current coffee, thank you', 'it won't taste as good', 'it won't make any difference anyway'. One church in the town had set up a small shop selling

Traidcraft and other fairly traded goods. But, in other cases, Bruce observed, 'Churches would hold coffee mornings to raise money for Third World aid projects but use coffee from the large companies that pay coffee growers in the same countries a pittance.'

Here, it seemed, Fairtrade was 'too political'.

I wondered why he hadn't given up. Bruce doesn't wear his Quaker convictions on his sleeve. But they smoulder behind the unflinching connection he makes between belief and action.

'I don't think you *can* give up. Our children will look back and ask us how we could live in prosperity while over a billion people live in abject poverty – including many who produce things we use every day. How could we know this and *not* do what we could to stop it? I just can't accept we have to live in world like that. I believe everyone wants to do the right thing when faced with the facts. It's just they don't know what they can do. Fairtrade gives everyone a way to do something to change things.'

He draws parallels between Fairtrade and the movement to abolish the British slave trade.

'People realised that by buying slave-grown sugar or cotton they were complicit in a system that was wrong. They started to say, we don't want to be part of that. It's the same today. When you realise the existing system of trade is totally unacceptable, then you don't have a choice. Every time you buy a Fairtrade product you're not only helping 7 million farmers and their families you're also sending a signal that you don't agree with the current system.'

Bruce loves telling stories, waving his arms about as he does so, and describes with relish how change crept into his community.

'All on the same day I got a card saying Cafédirect was running a competition for best local Fairtrade campaign; the vet nurse gave me a recipe for chocolate banana pancakes – *and* I realised Pancake Day fell in Fairtrade Fortnight. I knew we had a winning entry: a Fairtrade banana chocolate pancake party!'

Before long this mushroomed into a full-blown meal to which they invited all the local community representatives they'd been trying – but failing – to get interested in Fairtrade. Then two days before the event Bruce woke up in the middle of the night.

'I suddenly thought, if we succeed in getting everybody at the meal to sign up to using Fairtrade, we'd be a community that all supported Fairtrade and, well, Garstang would be a Fairtrade Town. I jumped out of bed and wrote it down so I wouldn't forget it in the morning!

'The evening of the meal, I was working at a vet's right over in Blackpool and rushed back,' Bruce recalls. 'I find speaking in public really hard. But I made our case while people actually listened for once. As it shows – and as I always say to people – don't give up trying. The evening was a triumph. Everyone attending signed up to support Fairtrade. Of course, we had to follow up to make sure people acted on their promise. But what you can see when you walk around Garstang today all started that evening.'

During the meal Bruce got the chance to float his idea of Garstang becoming the world's first Fairtrade Town with the Mayor. The Mayor looked wary.

'Would no one be allowed to sell Nescafé in Garstang then?' he asked.

Bruce reassured him it wouldn't mean that – it was about offering people a choice.

So a few weeks later the Mayor invited him to address the once-a-year public Parish Council meeting.

'This is all very well – but what's the Council actually going to do about it?' said someone at the back, after Bruce had spoken and they were just about to adjourn.

The councillors would consider the matter at their next meeting, the Mayor replied.

But then the Council Clerk – there to advise on the proceedings – spoke up, 'Mr Mayor, you don't have to wait until then. This is a public Council meeting. It can discuss it now and make a decision today if it wants.'

A slightly stunned Mayor looked at the councillors and asked, 'So, what do you think?'

Bruce grinned as he savoured the moment again in his mind, 'I'll never forget the look on their faces – followed by silence as they looked awkwardly at the floor. It was clear they didn't want to take this dangerously subversive step!'

'Members of the public have the right of the vote at this meeting,' intervened the Clerk again. 'Councillors don't even have to be here for it to agree something.'

'We had no idea about this,' said Bruce. 'We were absolutely gobsmacked!'

Immediately a woman stood up, 'I propose we make Garstang a Fairtrade Town!'

'I second that,' said another woman leaping to her feet.

It went to the vote and the motion was carried virtually unanimously. I pictured the scene of democracy triumphant and reflected how such turning points in the life of a movement so often combine careful planning with the totally unexpected.

When Garstang informed the Fairtrade Foundation office that they had in fact declared themselves a Fairtrade Town, some eyebrows were raised pretty high. The Foundation was nurturing a certification Mark, battling to establish its credibility as a stamp of approval for companies' products which meant they had met a rigorous set of standards. We were always fighting to convince companies that they had to meet our rules about using the Mark – putting it on the front of the packaging so the public could see it clearly, not changing the shape, not claiming their whole company was Fairtrade certified – only the products. In fact, treating it with the serious respect they happily accord to everyday corporate brand-marks such as Disney. And now here were a bunch of campaigners saying a whole town had become Fairtrade and starting to use the Mark as a campaigning tool – on town signs, flower beds grown in the shape of the Mark, chocolate art, wool badges ... It was a branding-controllers' nightmare. And a campaigners' dream come true.

We decided that despite this tension, we would back the Fairtrade Towns movement as the most effective way to raise local awareness of Fairtrade. So we agreed with Bruce a set of goals around increasing local awareness and availability of Fairtrade that a town or village or city has to meet. (There's more on this in the What You Can Do section at the back of this book.)

Launching the Fairtrade Towns pack, the then junior international development minister George Foulkes said, 'I think this is starting something that could spread through the United Kingdom and beyond. I hope that the beacon that has started in Garstang can spread like wildfire through the whole of the country.'

And spread it has. Before long the *Guardian* newspaper called it 'one of Britain's most active grass-roots social movements'.[3] Within seven years the movement has grown to 400 Fairtrade places – from the appropriately named Fair Isle in the far north to the island of Jersey in the far south – right across the UK, with Wales pipping Scotland to the post to become the first Fair Trade nation. For all Fairtrade is based on co-operation, we've clearly unleashed the ruthless competitive spirit that lurks in every town as people seek to become Fairtrade before the rival town over the river, or first in the county or to be Britain's first Fairtrade sea-resort. Even London has, borough by borough, become a Fairtrade city. It was great to see then Mayor Ken Livingstone – who'd sponsored the setting up of a unit pioneering early solidarity trade deals when he was leader of the since-abolished Greater London Council years ago – launch the start of London's long campaign for Fairtrade status during Fairtrade Fortnight 2003. And we're hoping the city could host the first Olympic Games where Fairtrade goods are served in 2012. Who knows, there could even be medals made of Fairtrade gold awarded too?

Bruce, who now advises towns going for Fairtrade status, was taken aback when he got a call saying Gordon Brown wanted to include him in his book *Britain's Everyday Heroes*. The Prime Minister writes, 'It is a special kind of empathy that makes someone devote themselves to changing the lives of people they have never met or to fighting for the rights of communities on the other side of the world. This is what moved me about Bruce. Our world has got very much smaller, and the problems facing people far away from us can no longer feel like far-away problems.'[4]

Now the movement has picked up globally. People are organising Fairtrade Towns in Belgium, France, Italy, Norway, Sweden; Ireland has notched up twenty-four. When Wolfville in Nova Scotia became Canada's first Fairtrade Town in April 2007, Mayor Bob Stead said it was the 'conscience of the community speaking'. This was where Jeff and Debbie Moore set up Just Us! Coffee Roasters, whose Fairtrade coffee is now found across Canada, and is also home to a museum on Fairtrade. There is a growing network of Fairtrade Communities in Australia and New Zealand. Yarra in Victoria became 'the first Fairtrade municipality in the Southern Hemisphere' in 2006. Others are in the pipeline in Australia and they are to be joined by Auckland and Wellington in New Zealand.

In the United States a network of local Fairtrade coalitions is picking up pace. The group in New York, for example, persuaded the City Council to pass a resolution supporting Fairtrade after hearing testimony from the Gillies Coffee Company, the American Jewish World Service and the trade union representing shop workers in the city. As the rabbis of the B'nai Jeshurun synagogue also argued in a letter to the Mayor, the move would 'contribute significantly to the welfare of millions of often-exploited farmers, and enable them to earn a decent living without having to abandon their homes and seek their fortunes in more prosperous lands.' The coalition has been lobbying the city to use its considerable procurement budget to support Fairtrade – delivering its message to the Mayor with Fairtrade flowers and chocolates on Valentine's Day.

The idea is spreading among producers too. A representative of a Sri Lankan tea plantation was inspired to consider using the Fairtrade premium to build a whole village to replace people's dilapidated housing. Getting into the friendly rivalry, he joked: 'Now that really would be the world's first Fairtrade village.'

The Fairtrade Towns idea captures people's imagination because it provides a connection between the big global issues of poverty and trade – which can seem so overwhelmingly impossible to you and me – and our own school or office or local community organisation down the road. We can all persuade them to use Fairtrade – it's a step-by-step approach, but it's deeply empowering because such small local steps are achievable.

Time and again, such local action has a knock-on effect across the country. When I went to award Leighton Buzzard their Fairtrade certificate, a cycling dynamo of a grandmother, Angela Feaviour, told me how she'd asked the manager of her local pub in Leighton Buzzard to stock Fairtrade tea and coffee.

'Sorry', came the reply, 'it's not my decision. Try head office.'

So Angela called the headquarters of the Slug and Lettuce pub chain. Not only did they agree that her local pub would offer Fairtrade, the whole chain would try it too.

'I found the right man, in the right place, at the right time, in the right frame of mind,' Angela recalls. 'It's not usually that easy!'

Shortly afterwards the chain's parent group SFI adopted Fairtrade and, by March 2006, was reporting double-digit increases in sales.

The movement has wings and keeps flying on to new ideas. Fairtrade Towns have morphed into Fairtrade universities, schools, churches, synagogues ... you name it, they're at it. Soon, people set their sights on workplaces – where we all consume more and more food and drinks but where Fairtrade is only just beginning. The giant accountants KPMG were one of the first companies to move their tea and coffee to Fairtrade for staff drinks and hospitality but lots of others have gone the same way, including Microsoft, Orange and the Nationwide building society, along with scores of small businesses. At British Telecom a member of the trade union Connect and some supportive managers first got the company to pilot Fairtrade in four staff cafés by circulating a petition signed by 700 workers. Staff support grew so much that the company switched completely in 2006 – and now gets through 3 million cups of Fairtrade coffee a year.

Sometimes it takes years. An early foray came in 1994 when Glenda Jackson MP led a call by 200 MPs for the House of Commons to serve Fairtrade tea and coffee. But it was four years and plenty of letters later that it followed the lead of the European, Belgian and Dutch parliaments by going Fairtrade. The 'mother of parliaments' now drinks 2,500 cups of Fairtrade coffee a day. In 2007, the newly elected Irish government set the pace by pledging to make Fairtrade part of all government purchasing policy wherever possible.

Of course, overall, the amount the British government spends on products is huge – imagine all the tea and coffee the army or the National Health Service must get through. So we've a long way to go.

Behind each of these shifts, there's usually an individual who has warmed to Fairtrade because it shines a light on the people behind the product. People increasingly want this personal connection instead of the anonymous, sterile, industrial food system. In turn, Fairtrade gives those farmers a greater understanding of the people who buy their crops. For generations farmers have grown and sold their goods with no idea what happens to them. With Fairtrade that all begins to change. And producers keep the best of their crop for their best customers – those who buy through Fairtrade. The closer relationship with the customer has boosted the drive for quality.

During Fairtrade Fortnight 2007 we invited over Conrad James, a banana farmer from St Lucia in the Windward Islands. First stop was a Waitrose supermarket. And there, by chance, were bags of his very own bananas. He could tell from the two-letter code stamped on the plastic fastening on the neck of the bag! He said he'd never forget standing there and watching, for the first time in his life, as customers walked past him and picked his bananas off the shelf and put them into their baskets.

When Sainsbury's chief Justin King went with me to the Windward Islands, he was delighted by the farmers' sophisticated understanding of what the consumers wanted. He watched with fascination as Rennicks Doxilly chopped bananas from the tree with his sharp machete, weighing them up in his hands and deciding if the bananas were going to end up in the smaller 'Kids Packs' or as general loose bananas.

'I have never', said Justin with his characteristic enthusiasm, 'seen farmers so aware of their customers. That's the beauty of Fairtrade – it's connecting the only two people who matter – the producers and the customers. The rest of us are just intermediaries.'

The banana farmers knew the British public's interest in quality and environmental protection, but they were hungry for more information, cross-examining the Sainsbury's boss about what else he thought consumers were looking for. Keen to reduce their reliance on bananas, they also wanted to know what other Fairtrade products the British might buy. Justin advised them to start with other products they already knew how to grow. Limes were coming through as a hot favourite to try when the Chair of the islands' Small Ruminants' Association piped up.

'Justin, I hear you have many problems with mad cow disease and foot and mouth over there in England, so do you think people would be interested in Fairtrade goat meat?' Justin tactfully suggested the British public probably wasn't quite ready for that just yet.

Fostering this people-to-people connection is at the heart of our yearly promotional centrepiece, Fairtrade Fortnight, when local supporters organise over 10,000 local events across the UK and dozens of Fairtrade producers from across the globe travel to all corners of the country. The truth of this hit me on a trip to the West Country during 2007. At a packed town hall in Devizes in Wiltshire, I used a shopping bag as a prop. I could sense vividly the people behind each of the products I took out.

'These peanuts', I said, 'are from a smallholder group in Malawi whose manager was telling me yesterday that, at forty-two, he is in his bonus years. Because life expectancy in Malawi is now forty, thanks to poverty and Aids. This wine', I placed it on the table, 'comes from an economic empowerment farm in South Africa where Maria Malan, who was a domestic servant under apartheid, is now a manager of 200 people.'

Up shot a hand in the audience, 'How's Maria? She came to stay with me last year when she was speaking in Wiltshire.'

Up went another hand, asking about Denise Sutherland, a banana farmer who'd visited years before and who the GMTV breakfast programme had filmed in the Caribbean that week for a piece on Fairtrade Fortnight. We all felt an amazing sense of the global bonds built up by the Fairtrade movement. These links can throw up surprising insights about both sides.

Peter Gaynor is the Executive Director of Fairtrade Mark Ireland. He is an untiring advocate of the involvement of trade unions in Fairtrade, with a throaty smoker's laugh and an engaging dishevelled appearance. He recalls a visit by Renwick Rose from the Windward Islands during Fairtrade Fortnight 2006.

'I spent two weeks on a train with him visiting towns around the country. It was a brilliant visit and helped Fairtrade banana sales double the following year. A few weeks later I had the opportunity to visit him in St Vincent with an Irish TV company making a documentary about Fairtrade bananas.

'What struck me there, and I'd never realised it before, were all the historical links between Ireland and the Caribbean. One of the districts on St Vincent is called St Patrick's and there are loads of Irish names in the phone book. When the islands were being populated with slaves from West Africa, a huge number of Irish people were being sent there as indentured servants to work in the houses of slave owners. The Irish could get their freedom if they worked for five or six years. Of course, it took a lot longer for the slaves to get their freedom. There is a whole history of the Irish in the Caribbean we know little about – it seems to indicate we operated on both ends of the victim/perpetrator spectrum. It was amazing to hear, though, that the expression on St Vincent for someone's best friend is "me Paddy". So we can't have been that bad!'

In 2002, Guillermo Vargas Leiton of the Coocafe co-operative and I had a particularly punishing tour round Britain, as he tirelessly explained how 'Fairtrade is helping people build real democracy from below'. We arrived in a freezing cold Dundee and were hurrying, heads down, arms crossed, out of the station when Guillermo stopped dead in his tracks. On the corner a homeless man was selling the *Big Issue in Scotland*, and there on the front cover was a photo of Guillermo holding coffee beans in his hands. After chatting to the seller, and moved by this coming together of two schemes to tackle the economic roots of poverty, Guillermo bought a copy to show people back home.

'I am so inspired', he said, 'by what ordinary people are doing to build Fairtrade here – and especially the way they're working with your young people. I'm going back to Costa Rica with ideas of how to talk more with our children too.'

The grass-roots campaign is working. I remember when the Foundation was rethinking its strategies back in 2001, the forthright Director of Cafédirect, Penny Newman, challenged us to make the FAIRTRADE Mark as famous as the Woolmark. With a sinking heart, I searched the web and discovered that eight out of ten people knew the Woolmark (indicating pure wool clothing). At that time, only two out of ten recognised the FAIRTRADE Mark. With awareness inching up a few percentage points every year, it seemed we'd take decades to match Woolmark. I saw it as an aspirational goal – not one we'd achieve in a hurry.

Amazingly though, today, survey after survey seems to confirm that about eight out of ten people know about Fairtrade and recognise the Mark.[5] It's also a relief that not many people today think it stands for the government's Office of Fair Trading – whereas four out of every ten people thought this when we first started out! The range of people who know about and support Fairtrade is also growing. In the early days Fairtrade shoppers were typically middle-class, middle-aged women. But now they come from all age and income brackets – with twenty-five to thirty-four-year-olds the age group where recognition of the Mark is growing fastest.

And some recent research funded by the UK's Economic and Social Research Council seems to bear out our strategy too, finding that '... the most effective campaigns to encourage ethical consumption are those that take place at a collective level, such as the creation of Fairtrade cities, rather than those that target individual behaviour. The research suggests that ethical consumption is best understood as a political phenomenon rather than simply a market response to consumer demand.'[6]

All the hard slog of people manning stalls on freezing high streets, or speaking in church halls, was like the water gradually filling up behind a new dam. It took years to rise, but when it did, and the turbines of sales started to turn, the results were electric. Since 2001, sales of Fairtrade products in Britain have been roughly doubling every two years, topping almost £500 million a year by 2007. It's all the more amazing when you think a good portion of these soaring Fairtrade sales are in products like coffee, tea and bananas where overall sales are generally stagnant.

Seven out of every ten households buy Fairtrade products. Consumer research by the Dragon Brand Agency concluded that 'there are no barriers to the concept', while leading market research company Mintel called Fairtrade the 'king of the crop' in the ethical foods market.[7] The food trade's in-house journal the *Grocer* said that, '2006 will go down in history as a time when the importance of price waned and healthy and ethically sound food

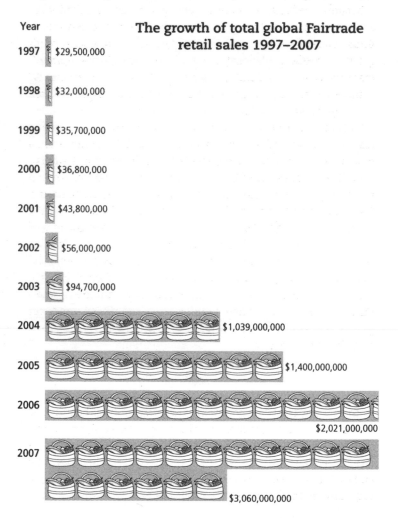

The growth of total global Fairtrade retail sales 1997–2007

Year	
1997	$29,500,000
1998	$32,000,000
1999	$35,700,000
2000	$36,800,000
2001	$43,800,000
2002	$56,000,000
2003	$94,700,000
2004	$1,039,000,000
2005	$1,400,000,000
2006	$2,021,000,000
2007	$3,060,000,000

became the battleground ... The rise of Fairtrade is also having a wider impact upon public expectations of how companies should trade with their partners in developing countries – it is no longer acceptable for companies to turn a blind eye to poor practice.'[8] While we can be under no illusions that price is still the big day-to-day battleground – there has been a major underlying shift in expectations about company behaviour.

In some products Fairtrade is starting to notch up a significant share of the market. For example, one in five tins of cocoa sold in British supermarkets are now Fairtrade. Maybe that's because it's got the backing of the real experts in this area – the Women's Institute! One sunny Sunday when I was addressing a regional WI conference in a hotel high on the clifftops in Eastbourne, I asked why they bought Fairtrade.

'I always buy Fairtrade cocoa because it makes much the best-tasting chocolate cakes!' replied a lady beautifully turned out in a blue tweed suit. You cannot get a better recommendation than that.

By 2006, global sales of Fairtrade goods stood at $2.2 billion.[9] In the early years Fairtrade sales were highest in the Netherlands, Switzerland and Germany but today Britain and the US top the Fairtrade sales charts. Some countries where Fairtrade got started a bit later are now speeding ahead at an incredible rate – Ireland saw sales rise by 77 per cent in 2006, Canada by 54 per cent, and Australia and New Zealand nearly threefold. All of which leads to the most important statistic of all: more than 7 million people – farmers, workers and their families – in some 3,000 producer groups across fifty-nine developing countries worldwide now benefit from Fairtrade.

With so many Fairtrade goods on sale today, in small health food shops to all the major supermarkets, and 400 companies now selling Fairtrade products in the UK, it's easy to forget what a struggle it was to get the very first product on the shelves. In the end that honour went to Maya Gold chocolate – and many people rallied round to help it take off. What few people know, though, is that the Foundation originally planned to launch the FAIRTRADE Mark on one of Britain's largest tea brands.

While failure has few fathers, success they say has many mothers. Certainly the story of the birth of Fairtrade could be told by so many different people in different parts of the world. It seems they were all arriving at the same idea at about the same time and then encouraged and inspired each other. It reminds me of when my son was born. Days went by and we had no name; my Geordie partner was warming to ancient Northumbrian names like Ethelred so the need to find an alternative was getting serious; then my daughter suggested Oscar, after our neighbours' cat. Delighted with such an unusual name, we agreed thinking he'd be the only Oscar in the country. And yet we found thousands of families had come to just the same decision at the same time.

The Fairtrade Foundation was set up in 1992 by a clutch of development organisations – CAFOD (the Catholic church's development wing), Christian Aid, the New Consumer, Oxfam, Traidcraft Exchange and World Development Movement, with the National Federation of Women's Institutes coming on board soon after. Fairly traded products had been around since as far back as the Second World War when groups like Oxfam sold handicrafts from war-ravaged communities in Europe. In the US the Mennonite Central Committee started selling embroidery from Puerto Rico by setting up Self Help Crafts of the World – later Ten Thousand Villages. But while the range of products you could buy had grown greatly since then – especially with the advent of alternative trade organisations like Traidcraft – you could still only really get them at the back of the church hall, in One World shops or by mail-order.

Now the organisations came together to put Fairtrade goods into mainstream shops and supermarkets where most people shopped, drawing on the model pioneered by the Max Havelaar organisation in the Netherlands in partnership with coffee growers in Mexico. They set up the Fairtrade Foundation to label products so consumers could buy with confidence knowing that, as it said on the tin, the producers had got a better deal.

Excitement levels rose in the Fairtrade Foundation's then tiny, attic-room office with the news that a big tea brand might be the first to sign up. Fairtrade was going to enter the mainstream with a bang, it seemed. The Foundation's then Director, Phil Wells, nurtured from the germ of a contact with a senior manager at the tea company who had been a local Traidcraft rep for years. In secret talks, he gradually persuaded the company that the organisations behind the FAIRTRADE Mark were serious about working constructively with companies – on condition they submitted to rigorous standards and inspections to ensure tea workers got a decent deal. The discussions were delicate – coming after years of campaigning by WDM and others about poor pay and conditions on the tea estates – but moving along nicely.

But the negotiations were blown apart at the last minute after Christian Aid (who were on the board of the Fairtrade Foundation) published double-page newspaper adverts comparing workers on tea estates with the treatment of battery hens, implying, 'You wouldn't accept this for your chickens. Why accept it for tea workers?'

While the adverts were not directed at that particular tea company, they took it as an aggressive broadside and called off the talks. The fallout sent the fledgling Fairtrade Foundation reeling. It was a disastrous false start. Furious rows erupted, re-igniting concerns for some about whether they could both set up Fairtrade labelling and still be able to criticise the bad practice of companies. Would they be muzzled? Would it ever work? Could they criticise and encourage?

At that time the vivacious Julia Powell was central to the team of three staff. An artist by training, she started at the new Fairtrade Foundation on a twelve week contract in 1993. She ended up staying nearly ten years, living through all this high drama. Wearing her trademark little black retro dress with a swingy shirt and arty jewellery, she told me the story over a white wine spritzer in the pub one evening soon after I joined: 'The tea debacle threw us into deep crisis. The staff really weren't sure whether the coalition behind the Foundation would hold together after this setback. And we didn't have another suitor waiting in the wings interested in getting the FAIRTRADE Mark on one of their products. The Foundation was also totally strapped for cash. We decided we would have to go ahead anyway and launch the idea of the Mark in April 1993 – but without any products carrying the Mark! The media and the public gave it a warm response. Encouraged, we invited businesses to apply, and waited for the calls to come in. And waited. But the phones never rang. Again it seemed the Fairtrade idea just wasn't going to fly.'

She laughed, flicking her blonde hair and doodling furiously over the table's supply of beer mats, 'It was clear the big companies were hoping Fairtrade would just fade away before it even got going.'

Cafédirect, a company that sells 100 per cent Fairtrade hot drinks, started in 1991; it had already got its coffee on sale in supermarkets by then. But they didn't want to carry the FAIRTRADE Mark unless other companies did.

'Eventually we decided to launch a campaign to press the supermarkets to start stocking FAIRTRADE Mark goods. We knew the supermarkets were the key. If they made it clear they wanted Fairtrade products, we thought the supplier companies would respond.'

Soon supporters of Oxfam, Christian Aid, student group People & Planet, Women's Institutes and others were handing in 'coupons' at tills across the country asking supermarkets to stock Fairtrade.

Meanwhile a tall, tanned, articulate American, Craig Sams, founder of a new company, Green & Black's (and Whole Earth Foods from which it grew), was in the foothills of the mountains of Belize trying to find a new source of organic cocoa for his chocolate. A coup in Togo in West Africa had blocked supplies for the organic chocolate he'd just started making.[10] Craig met up with Justino Peck, the leader of the Toledo Cacao Growers Association (TCGA). The farmers were staring ruin in the face after US chocolate giant Hershey had left them in the lurch.

The Maya Indian farmers had borrowed money and planted trees encouraged by a promise from Hershey to buy their cocoa at 1.75 Belize dollars per pound. The initiative was part of an aid-funded project to develop cocoa in this mountainous, remote part of southern Belize. But it takes five years for cocoa trees to produce pods you can harvest – and in the meantime international cocoa prices had dropped. Hershey said it was only prepared to offer 55 cents now – a far cry from the promised $1.75. Feeling betrayed by the company, the farmers faced destitution as the banks started to call in their loans. Craig put an offer on the table. If they converted to organic, he would buy their cocoa at over twice the current price and on a long-term contract.

One day, out with Justino visiting some farms, they stopped at a roadside café. Two men in a white jeep pulled up and took Justino aside. They were aid workers from the cocoa project who'd been training farmers to use chemicals and 'modern' methods. They urged him not to go organic – predicting disease and falling yields – and told him not to trust Craig. The pressure was huge. But with the backing of Belize's Agriculture Minister, the farmers decided to sign up. They set about getting the Soil Association organic stamp of approval. Craig and his partner, Jo Fairley, started experimenting with recipes in their kitchen for a dark chocolate flavoured with citrus and spices to reflect how the Maya had used cocoa in ceremonial drinks. They christened it 'Maya Gold'.

When the story reached the Fairtrade Foundation in London, they suggested to Craig the chocolate could become the first FAIRTRADE Mark product.

'We sent a delegation to Belize to meet the farmers in January 1994,' Julia recalls. 'I remember the excitement in the office as reports came back that the growers wanted to apply for a Fairtrade certificate.'

Farmers who had been on the verge of burning their cocoa trees and resorted to becoming migrant workers to pay off their debts set about clearing the weeds engulfing their farms in hope of a new start.

So far, so good. Now the chocolate needed a shop willing to sell it. Sainsbury's had shown interest but an internal debate was raging. They already stocked one dark chocolate. As dark chocolate wasn't a big seller back then, they needed a very good reason to stock another. But the campaign coupons were by now piling up.

'We were receiving more letters on Fairtrade than anything else,' one of its executives told Julia. 'Even more than the perennial issue of the length of the queues!' Stocking Maya Gold provided a way for Sainsbury's to show they were responding to their customers' calls for Fairtrade products, he said.

The launch date of 7 March 1994 was set for the first product carrying the FAIRTRADE Mark to go on sale in Britain. A rush of animation came to Julia's face as she recalls events.

'We knew this was our crucial break to show that Fairtrade was more than a noble idea – that it could actually work in the real world. We had to show the still sceptical supermarkets that people would put their money where their mouth was. But we had only about eight weeks from getting the OK until launch. We decided to launch it at the BBC Good Food Show to underline the message that Fairtrade was high quality as we had to overcome the prejudices left by the past. So we wanted people to come over and taste its excellent flavour. I managed to rope in celebrity chefs like Gary Rhodes, Anthony Worrall Thompson and Michael Barry to help us get media coverage. We also got showbiz celebrities Joanna Lumley and Angus Deayton on board.'

Julia's chutzpah and powers to excite celebrities about Fairtrade were legendary and secured the endorsement needed to help win public support. The public were also gearing up the campaign. Meanwhile there was frenzied activity to get the chocolate ready to go on the shelves. It was being made at a factory in France because all the British factories were tied in with the big multinationals. Someone from Green & Black's had to fly over to Bordeaux to collect the first batch personally. They then speeded up from Gatwick with the precious merchandise in their boot – arriving literally minutes before the launch.

The chocolate was a hit and the first Fairtrade-certified product got a good write-up from the foodies. Writer, broadcaster and campaigner for 'real food' Hugh Fearnley-Whittingstall tasted the chocolate and gave it an enthusiastic write-up and recipe for the *Telegraph*. He's been a strong champion of Fairtrade foods ever since. Maya Gold went on to be a big commercial success. In Belize more and more farmers were joining up to the TCGA and benefiting from the Fairtrade system. Sadly, despite repeated requests from the Foundation, Green & Black's still have not converted their whole range to Fairtrade. And, in an extraordinary turn, in 2005 Green & Black's was gobbled up by Cadbury's for an estimated £20 million. As we furiously exchanged worried emails, they pledged that Maya Gold would stay Fairtrade.

In 1994, with the crack in the door now open, the development charities got their campaigners to pile in to press more supermarkets to stock Fairtrade.

'Jo Fairley took Maya Gold to the buyer at Tesco,' says Julia. 'He'd given her short shrift.' He told her he wasn't going to 'list a product just because it's backed by a bunch of Christians'!

But it wasn't long before he changed his tune and was back on the phone saying, 'You'd better get over here, we're being bombarded by telephone calls. From vicars!'

Soon it was in all the major supermarkets, quickly followed by the next products carrying the Mark in Britain: Clipper tea and Cafédirect coffee.

Despite Maya Gold's success, it was still only one Fairtrade brand at the premium end of Britain's £4.6-billion chocolate market. Britons are the biggest chocolate eaters in Europe, munching through ten kilos of the stuff a year each. Four out of five bites of the chocolate we take in Britain are produced by just three huge players: Cadbury's, Masterfoods (Mars) and Nestlé. Consumer loyalty in chocolate has been built up literally over generations – and is not shifted easily. Nine of the top ten brands have been around since before the first half of the twentieth century. And even they struggle to make new chocolate bars fly off the shelves; when was the last time you saw a totally new bar? That's why they keep reformulating the old favourites – just how many different ways can you rehash a KitKat? Over twenty in the UK alone, it turns out; everything from chunky format tiramisu flavour to a low-carb KitKat. Though I think the Japanese KitKat Uji-Kintoki Milk with Azuki Bean, Green Tea and Cream is perhaps my personal favourite. It really does exist, I promise.

To break through in this incredibly tough market and win a better deal for cocoa farmers being squeezed by plummeting world prices we needed to open up on all the fronts. But back then the major firms were definitely opposed to Fairtrade.

Meanwhile, the winning team behind Cafédirect were getting together a grand coalition – Christian Aid, The Body Shop, Comic Relief and TWIN – to produce a dedicated Fairtrade chocolate brand. Even more ambitiously, this venture would be part-owned by Ghanian farmers themselves.

Comfort Kwaasibea is a formidable pillar of Kuapa Kokoo ('good cocoa farmers company' in the local Twi language), the co-operative in Ghana that the farmers formed in 1993 and that would supply the cocoa for the new Fairtrade chocolate venture. Beginning with just 200 farmers across 22 villages, Kuapa has now grown to 1,200 village societies covering 45,000 farmers, nearly a third of whom are women. Having first met Comfort when she was touring the UK to tell the story of the co-op, it was a real treat to catch up with her again in Ghana. Resplendent in a bold floral print kaftan-style dress, she was holding the fort in the storeroom owned by the co-op.

As I stand talking to her, a thin, wrinkled old man staggers in, bent double under the enormous sack of cocoa beans he is carrying on his back. He's walked 5 kilometres through the forest from his farm to this collection point. He throws it down on the magnificent iron weighing scales and wipes the sweat from his face. Comfort, elected by the farmers of the village co-operative as their recorder, officiously checks the weight and writes it down in the co-op's ledger, and then stamps the sack. The farmer puts his thumbprint beside the record. It's a proud symbol. Most cocoa farmers have no idea where their cocoa goes – and have never tasted chocolate in their lives. By contrast, the Kuapa Kokoo farmers own their own chocolate bar.

More farmers collect in the storeroom and, with a press of kids straining in around the door, start debating how they are going to invest the premium they will earn from this year's Fairtrade crop. One farmer wants to buy mosquito nets to prevent the malaria that still kills regularly here; another is pressing for further support for the local school. It's going to be a tough decision as funds are limited; the co-op is only able to sell some 3 per cent of its cocoa under Fairtrade terms as the market is still so small. The conversation moves on to the co-op's strategies – how they want to improve quality, who is going to attend the upcoming Annual General Meeting on behalf of the village, and hearing from Comfort about how their chocolate, Divine, is selling.

Back in the UK, Divine's Managing Director Sophi Tranchell, feisty campaigner and businesswoman, is a bit of a superwoman who seems to have more hours in the day than the rest of us. Sophi was, as you'd expect, an activist in the Anti-Apartheid Movement. When Nelson Mandela had been released from prison and with the end of apartheid imminent, she recalls going to one of the last protests in support of the London boycott of South African goods outside Sainsbury's.

'To our surprise, they called us up to have a chat: "So, what do you want us to do now then?" they asked. I just said: "I don't know!" I didn't. But I remember thinking how much potential there was for channelling the power of the consumer boycott into new ways of campaigning for change.'

Soon she was doing just that when in 1998, Sophi was charged with selling the new Divine Fairtrade chocolate bar in the hugely competitive market, with practically no capital behind the company.

'We'd got a great-tasting chocolate. It had some excellent reviews from the experts. But it was still a huge gamble launching Divine chocolate. A lot of people thought "It's a nice idea but it'll never work."' The key hurdle was making it available for the public to buy easily. 'And it still is.'

She says one of the hardest parts was getting her foot in the door to talk to the supermarket confectionery buyers. When they did get in, though, the buyers were often hooked by the Divine story.

'It was amazing. A lot of these guys had little idea what a cocoa pod looked like or that it came from Africa or what kind of people grew it. They didn't forget meeting us.'

It was tough enough getting the supermarkets to stock Fairtrade products – but we only buy half our chocolate bars in supermarkets. The rest we get in newsagents, corner-shops, kiosks. Mars have 1,500 people who go round these places every day checking their products are on sale and displayed properly, points out Sophi. Divine didn't have the resources to match that.

Only a phenomenal response by supporters to Christian Aid's 'Stock the Choc' campaign succeeded in getting Divine bars into Sainsbury's stores across the country. Campaigning remains vital for Divine's success, including with children, says Sophi, 'When we launched our Dubble bar for kids, we teamed up with Comic Relief to get across the serious issues behind Fairtrade in a colourful, fun way.'

They've recruited 50,000 on-line 'Dubble Agents' who pledge to 'change the world chunk-by-chunk' – joining campaigns like signing a manifesto for a fairer deal for cocoa growers. Certainly, kids do seem to get Fairtrade. I'm not sure if it's their strong instinct for justice – or for chocolate.

It was a long hard fight but the Divine gamble did pay off. With a turnover of £9 million a year by 2007, the company paid its first dividends of over £47,000 to the members of Kuapa Kokoo as shareholders in the company. In the same year the company launched Divine chocolate – 'Heavenly Chocolate with a Heart' – on Valentine's Day in the United States.

There was a further twist to the tale when The Body Shop was bought by L'Oréal, part-owned by Nestlé, makers of KitKat among other things. It appeared that Nestlé was to be the part-owner of a Fairtrade chocolate company. But this was averted when The Body Shop donated all its shares back to Kuapa Kokoo – so further increasing the farmers' stake in the company. The company's original investment in Divine was one of Gordon and Anita Roddick's initiatives to support fledgling social enterprises with similar aims to theirs. Now that Divine and Kuapa Kokoo had made a success of their business, The Body Shop decided it was time to stand back and hand over their investment to the farmers.

Sophi says that the Divine business model, part-owned by producers, represents 'the next stage' in the history of the chocolate industry. 'We'd like to be the Cadbury's of the future …

But we'd like to shift the way that business is done.'

Fairtrade has taken little bites into the huge British chocolate market, pushing overall sales from £1 million in 1998 to £35 million in 2007, an extraordinary achievement that many said couldn't be done in such a fiercely competitive market. The next pioneering step along the way was when in 2000 the Co-op unveiled an own-label Fairtrade milk chocolate bar, made from chocolate sourced from Divine. Britain's first supermarket own-brand Fairtrade product was born.

Behind the move was Brad Hill, a Salford man born and bred. He's been at the Co-op twenty-eight years, ever since leaving school, working his way up while studying part-time. By 1997, he was in the so-called 'impulse' section: 'We had all the big brands knocking on the doors, pushing for more shelf space and we had one Fairtrade chocolate languishing on the bottom shelves, taking up valuable space. We knew it was part of the Co-op's values but every year we'd debate how to get that product off the shelf! It was ironic because then I got recruited into the team pushing the responsible retailing agenda and the next day I was back telling the impulse team we needed more Fairtrade products!

'It wasn't easy getting Fairtrade through the business then as the products were unproven and seen as niche products for the beard and sandals brigade. We launched bananas in 2000 and it had taken a long time to get to shelf. But the principles fitted with the whole values of the Co-op and the FAIRTRADE Mark gave us the communications tool to talk to consumers about it. And once you understand what Fairtrade actually means, it carries an infectious passion – and then you want to do whatever you can to make it work.'

Brad certainly got the bug, 'I was working on converting all our own-label chocolate bars to Fairtrade. I was very nervous. We just didn't know if the consumer would come with us on this one so all the work was around how much this would cost the business in the worst case scenario – if everyone switched to buying big branded products instead of Co-op chocolate. We were convinced the quality was right and the pricing was only a slight increase, and still less than the big branded bars. But I was nervous. We launched the product and held our breath. We were tracking sales on a daily and weekly basis. And within just a few weeks, we realised we needn't have worried at all. In fact, sales of Co-op's own-label chocolate rose by a staggering 50 per cent in the following year – at a time that the brands' sales were static. So people were clearly switching across to the Co-op's Fairtrade chocolate.'

Brad puts the runaway success down to communicating with customers about the injustice in the cocoa trade, and giving stories of the Fairtrade farmers on the wrappers. At that time, the Co-op sold £3 million a year of own-label chocolate; that figure is now, says Brad, £7 million – and it emboldened them to switch all their own-label coffee, as well as launching other lines.

'Fairtrade does hook you and reel you in,' says Brad who is now Fairtrade Strategic Development Manager. 'For me, it was when I went to Ghana for the first time after working on Fairtrade for three years. We were driving along and pulled up to chat to two guys we saw by the side of the road splashing in water they were pumping out of a shiny new tube well. Before, they said, they had to collect water contaminated with disease in buckets from the river. Then they asked what we did and we discovered that they sold the cocoa that we bought as Fairtrade – it was a fantastic connection, a real Fairtrade moment.'

The Co-op move doubled the Fairtrade chocolate market in Britain at a stroke – and boosted Kuapa Kokoo's Fairtrade sales by a third.[12] The switches to Fairtrade have 'fundamentally reshaped supply lines' at the Co-op – cutting a supply chain in cocoa of something like fifteen middlemen down to just six steps from grower to consumer – while 'offering much improved returns for smallholder growers' according to David Croft who led the move at the Co-op.[13]

Then David left the Co-op for, yes, Cadbury's. The big companies are, it seems, circling us; we keep bumping into them; I can feel their breath warm on my neck and it leaves me cold with fear. Only 1 per cent of the chocolate we buy in our supermarkets is Fairtrade, and aside from Cadbury's takeover of Maya Gold, none of the big three chocolate companies have launched their own

Fairtrade bar. Yet. Will the multinational companies try to steal our clothes, claim to be awfully nice, offer a little charity here, the odd check that there's no child labour there – but change little for the farmers? Will they attack and undermine us outright? Or will we be able to persuade them to follow Fairtrade standards and put their huge commercial muscle behind really delivering for farmers and transforming the industry?

The Co-op challenged chocolate manufacturers 'to make at least one product in their range carry the FAIRTRADE Mark' and other retailers to 'follow our lead with their own-label chocolate'.[13] But Brad Hill is disappointed that after five years, 'We sell more Fairtrade chocolate than all the retailers put together and actually we don't want to be in that position. There are too few brands out there embracing Fairtrade. It's the right way to do business – actually, it's the only way to do business and they should be questioning themselves about why they aren't doing Fairtrade. It's commercially viable, it can even be commercially advantageous, it's driven by the public, and it is right on the social side too. Business should listen.'

While we battled to increase sales of existing Fairtrade products like chocolate, we were also under pressure to certify a greater range of Fairtrade products. When I'd been in Bonn at the head office of the international Fairtrade network FLO, letters and emails used to pile up from farmers all over the world queuing up to sell via Fairtrade. Gaston from Bolivia kept insisting on visiting me with his Brazil nuts; fresh fruit growers argued that if we could label bananas, then what about a whole fruit basket?; growers of small red bananas in Ecuador suggested we label their fruit, which was famed for being better than Viagra – which certainly would have been a good new marketing ploy for Fairtrade.

We were all totally overstretched. Many within the Fairtrade movement argued our energy should go into pushing up sales of the products we already had before jumping into new products. We shouldn't spread ourselves too thinly, was the view. But what kind of answer was it to say our system wasn't ready to cope with more products yet and so we couldn't help the farmers that grew them? Fairtrade Foundation Deputy Director Ian Bretman was convinced that a wider range would work for growers and shoppers too.

As he put it, 'When people have their Fairtrade coffee or tea – what do they want with it? Their Fairtrade chocolate biscuit, of course.'

He was adamant that if we were serious about bringing Fairtrade into the mainstream then we couldn't just focus on getting a few products into more and more shops – we also needed to expand the presence of Fairtrade. So in 2001 we made a decision to aim for a Fairtrade lifestyle and expand the range of Fairtrade products on the market. It was a turning point for Fairtrade in Britain. In 2001 there were about 50 products certified by the Foundation – by 2008 this had grown to over 4,500.

Remember going to the supermarket back then? In most cases, yes, Fairtrade products were there. But you'd have had to hunt around to find one or two Fairtrade coffees and teas, perhaps a couple of chocolate bars or bananas in bags hidden away at the bottom of the shelves, and often out of stock. You'd rarely see Fairtrade in any other aisles. If you didn't need coffee or tea you'd probably forget about Fairtrade altogether that week. And then, maybe, in future weeks too. By contrast, if you go into a supermarket today you not only have multiple chances to buy Fairtrade – from South African lemons to Kenyan Roses, Malawian peanuts to Brazil nuts gathered sustainably in the Amazon rainforest in Bolivia. And seeing that Fairtrade pineapple from Ghana may remind you to seek out the Fairtrade honey or juice you need too. The result? All groups of Fairtrade farmers gain.

Important too for increasing sales has been extending the range of shops where you can buy them – even to the discount stores many assumed would refuse to engage with Fairtrade.

'Lidl is one of Germany's cult brands,' says Dieter Overath, Director of the Fairtrade group TransFair Germany, about this leading discount supermarket in a country with the lowest food prices in the industrialised world. Discount supermarkets account for over 40 per cent of food sales and 90 per cent of the population visit such stores every week in Germany. 'A few years ago, we had got about as far as we could go with the mainstream supermarkets. They said that they were having to concentrate on price and that the difference with Fairtrade prices was too great. Then Lidl came to see us.'

TransFair was changing its strategy and the discount chains were changing theirs, looking to upgrade, moving into new sectors like organic. 'We spent six months negotiating with their senior management. With their reputation, we thought it would be more difficult, they would be tougher at driving a deal. They launched their Fairglobe brand with ten products in June 2006. We got roundly criticised by people, NGOs and retailers, for working with a discount chain but none of their fears has come true.' Dieter says the figures prove that there has been no race to the bottom for retail prices in Fairtrade, nor has it ruined the market for others. The result was growth in the market for everyone – and thus for Fairtrade producers.

Instead, it has enabled TransFair Germany to communicate about Fairtrade with the majority of the population who had hardly ever heard of Fairtrade before and convinced many other companies that they needed to join up. 'We've gained 200,000 new weekly customers, plus the fact that Lidl paid for the first-ever adverts on Fairtrade in the popular newspaper Bild-Zeitung. What's more, the retailers who had not made a move before are now doing so: other discounters are testing specific products, the biggest conventional retailer has brought out a Fairtrade coffee and another has upped its Fairtrade line to sixty products.' Even Tchibo, Germany's largest roaster and one of the world's largest green coffee buyers, has recognized the value of sustainable development and have modified the company's approach to corporate responsibility. Having introduced 'Vista' in the out of home market in Germany during the previous year, Tchibo then introduced their first consumer-facing product (Hausröstung/ Home roast) in the 1,100 Tchibo shops in autumn 2008. During the coming years they are planning on sourcing a major part of their coffee from sustainably developed sources.

Until recently, if you turned off London's Oxford Street, and wandered along Baker Street, you'd soon see a huge frontage belonging to that revered British institution, Marks & Spencer. Through the old revolving doors you would pass into a splendid reception area with a perfectly polished floor and stunning Art Deco pillars rising up above you. This was a company that prided itself on its social responsibility record, and yet a decade after the launch of Fairtrade in 2004, it still didn't carry a single Fairtrade product. In fact, it was the last major supermarket holding out.

Ian and I were escorted up to a meeting room and served tea in a silver teapot and beautiful china cups, with little chocolate biscuits wrapped in gold paper. The people we met were equally charming. They spent the meeting telling us what a caring company they were, how much effort they put into their relationships with their suppliers, how M&S customers had always had fierce trust and loyalty in their brand – and how they just couldn't put another label, such as our Mark, on their products. As I stirred my tea, the conversation went round and round.

But despite the – terribly polite – rebuffs we didn't give up talking to them. The potential was so huge. Ian felt the key hurdle was their policy against carrying other trademarks because they only stock own-brand products.

'We need to find a way of meeting them halfway,' he muttered. 'Once we've got a foot in the door, we'll be able to go on from there.'

'But you can't be a labelling organisation without a label on the packet,' I said. 'That's how we work. We can't compromise on that or every company will be wanting to break the rules and how will the public know what is or isn't Fairtrade?' I couldn't see a way round the problem.

But five years of patient work by Ian building relationships at the company bore fruit with the idea of trying out Fairtrade coffee and tea in their in-store coffee shops – the third largest in the UK, we discovered. That way they could just list them as Fairtrade in the menu but didn't need to cross their red line and put the FAIRTRADE Mark on a product in the store. Bingo!

By this time no one could ignore the growing commercial

problems at Marks & Spencer. Even its famously loyal shareholders were starting to get jittery – culminating in one of the highest profile and most acrimonious takeover bids in recent British corporate history. In spring 2004 flamboyant retail billionaire Philip Green revealed his plans to buy the company – amassing an estimated £9-billion war chest, then the largest sum ever raised in Europe by a private individual.[14] In the boardroom bloodbath that followed, the company lost both its Chairman and Chief Executive. Stuart Rose was brought in as the new boss to fight off no fewer than three attempts to take over M&S before Green finally threw in the towel. Rose and Green even reportedly got embroiled in a bizarre incident of fisticuffs outside the Baker Street offices. The crisis over, Rose then had to start turning round the company's slumping sales and deserting customers.

In our discussions with M&S you could feel the impact of the change at the top immediately. Among the sweeping changes Rose introduced – symbolised in the move to a new glass high-rise office building in Paddington – was a wholly different attitude to Fairtrade. All the work to raise consumer awareness paid off as the new boss drove the company to listen to what customers wanted – suddenly Fairtrade fitted.

Ian led the work to turn his idea of the coffee shops into action – culminating in an iconic photo of Stuart Rose holding a mug of coffee with the FAIRTRADE Mark as he launched the total switch to Fairtrade in their chain of Café Revives in September 2004. In contrast with their fears, the M&S sky didn't fall in – in fact quite the reverse. Sales grew and customer feedback was enthusiastic. Ian was keen to capitalise further on the breakthrough, with the new M&S now keen to explore some bigger shifts to Fairtrade.

So amid high secrecy, the Foundation and M&S set up 'Project Rooney' – the Bond-style code to keep the project secret from the competition, this time influenced by Football World Cup fever. It was then the boldest Fairtrade undertaking to date: to switch all M&S's coffee and tea to Fairtrade; not a bean or leaf was to be left unturned. In classic retailer fashion, this major switch had to be done tomorrow or ideally yesterday. We had just six months to go until launch to help all their existing suppliers meet the Fairtrade standards (or find new suppliers if needed), ensure all this was verified and properly signed off, packed and in the shops in time.

Virtually weekly a task force from M&S and the Foundation would update on progress on all the logistics of switching M&S's thirty-five different varieties – or SKUs, 'Stock-Keeping Units' as they're known in the trade – of tea and coffee over to Fairtrade, remembers Richard Anstead the Foundation's tea and coffee man. Formerly at giant multinational company Unilever, Richard decided he wanted to work in Fairtrade after travelling in Africa and seeing the problems of poverty first-hand.

'There were twenty-plus people from their side dealing with all the different aspects of the switch – the buyers, food technologists dealing with safety and taste, packaging designers, logistics experts, their corporate social responsibility people. There were just one or two from our side juggling it all,' he remembers with a chuckle. 'The path of every product and all the issues we had to sort out on each one were plotted on the mother of all spreadsheets through to the big bang of launch in Fairtrade Fortnight.

'Coffee from Kenya was a tricky one. The government there had only just changed the rules to allow direct purchases from coffee farms. But this was the first time they'd been used by anyone – and the first Fairtrade coffee from Kenya. It was uncharted territory for everyone and it all took more time – which we didn't have. We really went to the wire.'

On tea, a late problem emerged. The question was how workers on one estate were paid when they were at work but not actually processing the tea as they waited for the fresh tea leaves to arrive from the fields. It was just one issue on one tea estate, but because the tea from this garden was needed in a key blend it was holding everything up.

'M&S's tea buyer was tearing his hair out,' says Richard. 'It was a detail in some ways. But that was the whole point. There could be no compromise on all suppliers meeting all the FLO standards in full – no matter what could have been argued as the "greater good". From all sides we just worked flat-out to make sure the rules were met. And now those tea factory workers up in the highlands of Kenya get a better deal because of Fairtrade.'

In Fairtrade Fortnight 2006 M&S announced its coffee and tea switch – over £20 million of retail sales and leading to a jump of 18 per cent in national Fairtrade sales of coffee and 30 per cent in tea.[15] The move was set to benefit 70,000 tea and coffee farmers. And the company were doing this without raising prices – taking a hit on their margins but picking up extra overall sales of 6 per cent since the switch.[16] M&S had become the first major retailer offering only Fairtrade coffee and tea, and – bless their Fairtrade-certified cotton socks – the first high street clothes shop to start using cotton from fledgling groups of Fairtrade cotton farmers. It had taken many years of persistent effort from us, and pushing and support from the public, but M&S had moved from a Fairtrade laggard to a Fairtrade leader.

The shift was part of a wider trend by supermarkets to position themselves as greener or more ethical than their rivals – rather than just cheaper. In January 2007 I was invited to the much-awaited launch of M&S's big new push on sustainability – a £200-million-pound initiative dubbed 'Plan A'. It was already running in the morning bulletins before I went to the press conference – they seemed to have rushed out the news because they had heard rumours that Tesco was about to steal their thunder with its new green plan! We had been in confidential talks with M&S about the Fairtrade aspects of the plan for months. It was clear they were serious about pushing the boundaries.

The launch was at the grand Royal Society of Arts building just off the Strand in the centre of London. There was a genuine buzz among the audience of NGOs' representatives and journalists. It was an impressive plan and Fairtrade was a core part of the commitments, including a pledge to convert key high-volume ranges of clothes to 100 per cent Fairtrade cotton, amounting to 20 million garments over the following year – the largest order of Fairtrade cotton ever. They were also pledging to convert all the sugar they sold in bags and used in their jams and marmalades to Fairtrade.

And yet as the commitments on other areas rolled off the Powerpoint presentation – including an incredible pledge that

M&S would become carbon neutral within five years – I felt a rising sense of failure. Compared to the scale of commitments on carbon emissions, why hadn't we achieved something equally big and bold, like all M&S's products from Africa being Fairtrade? Had we failed to capture the opportunity of this moment for the farmers we worked with? Was our system too complicated and slow for M&S to be confident of making bold public commitments for the future? I should have been celebrating at the announcements but I felt impatient, angry, even depressed. Maybe Fairtrade would never truly come out of the niche.

Negative thoughts were still swirling round my head as I called in at my local M&S in Brixton to buy some bananas for the children on the way home. My eyes scanned along the lines of Fairtrade coffee and tea. I saw the Fairtrade cotton clothing, chocolate, fruit. We may still be very far from our aim of Fairtrade being the normal way people do business; but Fairtrade is no longer a drop in the ocean – thanks to the determined efforts of the public and producers. They had believed that a fairer way of doing things was possible and had worked together across the globe to build that vision from the local level up. The scale of the changes we'd seen in a business like M&S would have seemed a pipedream just a few years ago.

My earlier sense of failure now ramped up my determination to increase the scope and impact of Fairtrade on a much larger scale. I walked out so absorbed in my grand visions that I left my credit card in the machine at the till! When I came back to earth and rushed back to the shop, I found it safely handed in. I knew we were right to stake our money on the best side of human nature.

3

To Hell and Back

'We just received this – so we thought we could unwrap it with you. We've bought it with the money from our first Fairtrade premium,' says Ganga, in a nylon sari of vibrant lilac and blue swirls, as she bends over a brown cardboard box.

She has a focused face under her neatly parted and plaited hair with its few strands of grey. Everything she does has a sense of purpose and controlled energy. Her turquoise bangles jangle as she squats to cut through the plastic bindings holding the parcel together. I join the expectant circle of a dozen farmers – men and women, young and old – and a growing band of shy, but curious, children.

We are standing in a courtyard outside the small white building that serves as the office, storeroom and general hub for ETC Chetna Organics, an organic Fairtrade cotton farmers' group in the Indian state of Andhra Pradesh – found slightly to the right of the centre on the V-shaped map of India. Although a vast palm tree in the courtyard throws a welcome shade over us, the late afternoon air is still fiercely hot and dry. I can taste the sandy dust being blown in from the surrounding fields. Fresh from a grey, wintry Britain I was revelling in the tangible feeling of the sun on my skin. I love the dusty, dry heat, which for me is so full of associations.

As a child, I was lucky enough to have lived three years in India, in Pune where my father worked for Formica, which – this being the 1960s – was sweeping the world and whose tabletops are still a staple of all good Indian cafés. I have never been able to stop going back since, the most precious time being two formative years volunteering with farmer and workers' groups in the 1980s. I was privileged to stumble first into a former freedom fighter in Maharashtra, Mr Deval. Dedicated after independence to fighting poverty, he discovered that a community of very poor, lower caste people – the so-called Untouchables renamed by Gandhi as the Harijans or children of god – in fact owned tiny parcels of land that had been mortgaged away to the moneylenders decades before. With his backing, the bank was ready to give a loan so they could buy their land back. But the plots were unsustainable and would soon have been lost again. So the people pooled their land, formed an association and were now able to farm very effectively, even putting in precious irrigation. With Mr Deval's leadership they started selling grapes of such good quality that they were exported to Kuwait for a good price. They all had more in their pockets, but a percentage was set aside every year for community projects – gradually building proper houses as most of them still lived in straw huts; teaching new skills like sewing; investing in the farm. It was a triumph. Here were people at the bottom of the caste pile, so recently relegated to collecting human and cattle waste, who were now the proud owners of the village's first and only tractor. Their inspirational achievements soon spread, being replicated across nearby villages.

As a fresh-faced New Internationalist-reading politics student, my notions that cash crops were a problem diverting people from growing badly needed food, were challenged by all that this group of Harijans had achieved. I learned from them the power of not just cursing the darkness but also, as the Chinese proverb has it, lighting a candle. And many years later, when I first heard about

Fairtrade, I kept thinking back to that amazing community and today I wonder if perhaps they would like to sell their grapes to the UK under the Fairtrade label.

So I was in my element meeting the cotton farmers. First we'd met the wiry strong women working flat out harvesting the cotton. Old women with lined dry skin and big silver anklets were bent over double, or squatting as they carefully gathered each fluffy white ball spilling out from the split-open seed pods, or cotton bolls. They moved between the lines of low shrubs leaving aside those with still maturing delicate white – and then pink – flowers. They filled first the plain white cotton sling bags – used to ensure no dyes or alien fibres contaminate the precious organic crop – and, then, the large sacks at the edge of the field brimming with cotton.

Now Ganga pulls open the parcel to reveal a polished, stainless-steel box about three feet square and six inches thick. From another parcel emerges a digital display box with buttons. The group claps softly and smiles.

'It's a weighing scale,' Ganga says proudly.

I grinned back – her enthusiasm was infectious. Why, I asked, had they chosen to spend the premium on a set of scales?

'One of our biggest problems before we joined the Fairtrade system was the moneylenders,' she explains. 'We had to borrow at the beginning of the season to buy seeds and equipment – and to pay extra workers to help us harvest the crop quickly when it's in peak condition. They used to charge us huge rates of interest. Just months later we'd have to pay back a third as much again as we'd borrowed. What's more we *had* to sell them the cotton. Often they'd cheat us when it came to weighing the cotton – fixing the scales so they didn't have to pay us for the full amount.' An old, thin, toothless man with a white turban and grey stubble nods angrily at the memory.

As she rubs the shiny metallic surface of the slick modern equipment in front of her, Ganga concludes: 'By working together we can now get proper bank loans at a fraction of the interest rates of the moneylenders. And we can't be cheated by anyone when we sell our cotton – because we know how much it weighs.'

It made perfect sense. This group of farmers had acquired more than a fine weighing machine. They had also made a stride towards taking control of their lives. By buying the scales, they were saying they were no longer going to be victims of the powerful. They were investing in a brighter future and they were tipping the scales of power.

Cotton has a bloody history. The early British Empire ruthlessly stopped Indian peasants weaving traditional hand-spun cloth, cutting off weavers' hands. India was forced to become no more than a supplier of raw cotton for the Lancashire mills. Even this was sidelined as Britain found a source of cheaper cotton – grown by African slaves transported to the US plantations and treated with unparalleled brutality. That's why when Mahatma Gandhi launched his non-violent opposition to British rule in India, he called for a boycott of British cloth and took up making handspun cloth or khadi. Indeed, the spinning wheel in the centre of the Indian flag was Gandhi's idea to put his vision for rural livelihoods centre stage.

But hope for the future has been in short supply among Indian cotton farmers recently. Between 1998 and 2005, 4,500 cotton farmers committed suicide in just this one state alone, part of a wider epidemic across India's cotton-growing regions.[1] Many of these took their own lives overcome by debt. They had been squeezed into despair between, on the one hand, the rising costs of fertilisers, seeds (increasingly genetically modified) and of having to use more and more chemicals to keep down pests and, on the other, falling prices for raw cotton.

Back at my hotel, flicking through the newspapers, I stumbled on an article picturing the grieving, destitute widow of a cotton farmer with her five children. Her husband, it reported, had got up one night, gone out into his fields and drunk a bottle of the pesticides most cotton farmers use. His distraught family had found him dead among his cotton plants early next morning. Such farmer suicides have prompted anguished debates in the Indian media and parliament about whether the rural poor are being overwhelmed as previously government-regulated markets are opened up to the rest of the world.

As ever in the streets of India's giant, animated democracy, everyone is ready to share their strongly held opinions. The 'new India' had forgotten about the poor majority of Indians who still live in the countryside, one tea-seller lectured as he handed me a steaming cup of my favourite sweet *chai* – years ago always served in a glass or a clay cup, now in a plastic cup. No, argued a motor-rickshaw driver to me as, hand on hooter, as he swerved through the busy streets of Hyderabad around cows, pedestrians and cars with terrifying speed. He had moved to the city a few years back, he shouted as the gold decoration suspended from his mirror danced in the morning sunlight. His son was working in the Gulf. India needed to build up modern industries, so that more people could quit struggling against the odds on the land and get jobs in the city, he insisted as he turned round to address me rather more intently than he was watching the road.

As we'd driven the three hours from the cotton-growing fields to the booming confident high-tech metropolis of Hyderabad – nicknamed 'Cyberabad' – the stark contrast between the two Indias had reeled past the car window. I could certainly see the force of the rickshaw driver's view. It's easy for us in the West to throw up our hands in horror at the dirty factories, crowded cities and the call centres of the new India which are creating jobs and incomes for millions. We live, for the most part, comfortable lives with all the benefits of modern urban societies – societies forged out of the fiery crucible of Industrial Revolution that marked the shift away from farm-based economies. And it's easy for all of us passers-by to romanticise a rural idyll with pretty mud and straw-thatched huts, small villages and slowly wandering cows.

Free-marketeer critics of the Fairtrade movement, such as the Adam Smith Institute, say that by advocating support for small farmers – whether growing cotton in India or bananas in the Caribbean – we are driven by such a romantic view of jolly peasants living off the land that is out of touch with the future.

Farm commodities, they say, no longer matter. Fairtrade, they argue, is a well-meaning, but misguided, attempt to stem the tide of the modern, globalised economy and interfere with the march of the market.[2]

Mulling over these thoughts, I glimpsed a group of labourers squatting to eat their chapattis in the parched fields, a bullock cart piled high with straw ahead of us, a woman with a huge copper pitcher of water on her head returning from the well. The farmers in the fields passing my windows weren't some kind of minor economic relic to be quietly consigned to the dustbin of history. They were the two-thirds of India's people who still live in the countryside, and who, for the most part, want to go on living there – but want to live in dignity.[3] It's almost the same on a global scale with half the world's people living in rural areas.

It's not an either-or: India needs Cyberabad and cotton, factories and farming. But I remain convinced that if the world is serious about changing the obscene fact that 2 billion people still live on less than $2 per day, then helping small farmers grow more food and earn more cash from their land has to be a top priority. And that's why Fairtrade matters as a living model of how farmers in developing countries can stay and thrive on their land *and* be part of the modern global economy. But it seeks to do that by tackling the roots of what keeps poor farmers poor.

My journey into the glaring injustice and double standards of the global cotton trade began several years before my visit to Chetna – with the dreaded 'tea towel challenge'. Soon after starting at the Fairtrade Foundation in 2001, I was doing the rounds of the NGOs who set up and own the Foundation to find out how they saw things. Ian Bretman and I were up in the warren of offices of the old Oxfam House in North Oxford, meeting David Bright, who sourced goods for their shops and catalogues worldwide.

He wasn't hiding his impatience about the state of progress on Fairtrade. Oxfam had been part of this project from the beginning, had helped fund the development of the Fairtrade Foundation's work, and their supporters were vital in steadily building support for Fairtrade. But now they wanted to see it go mainstream.

'To be honest, Harriet, we want to see more change and faster,' David declared. 'You're going too slowly in Fairtrade. We have to see more products with the FAIRTRADE Mark, and sales shifting up a gear.'

As I nodded my assent I was caught up short as he tossed a tea towel on the table.

'A supermarket wants a Fairtrade tea towel in their shops by Christmas. Can you do it?'

I knew straightaway it wasn't possible. In those days, the Fairtrade label was only on to a small handful of products, and cotton wasn't one of them. Colleagues in France and Switzerland were researching the options and in touch with farmer groups in West Africa, India and Peru. Yet it was very, very early days. Each commodity has its own characteristics that we have to take into account when we set the Fairtrade price and other standards. We would have to wrestle with how to make trade fairer within a complex chain from field to high street: growing the cotton; ginning it (separating the fluffy 'lint' from the seeds it grows around); spinning it into yarn; weaving or knitting this thread into cloth; dying it; and, finally, cutting and stitching the cloth into finished items like clothes, sourced from factories in locations across the world that change with every new fashion season's supply. It was a minefield.

And while there had been lots of publicity about the 'sweatshop' conditions suffered by workers making clothes for our high street, people knew little about the plight of the farmers growing the cotton. Achieving a Fairtrade cotton product – even as mundane as a tea-towel – would be a huge challenge.

But I could see that an exploration of the intricacies of the world textile and garment trade was not really what David was after at that point. To say no would just entrench his view the Foundation couldn't deliver the goods. I knew from my first weeks in the job that we were strapped for funds, people and support to make the very shift he wanted to see. We had to keep Oxfam on board. But to say yes, and not deliver, would be worse. The silence was growing longer, stretching out before me, as David waited for an answer.

'We can't manage it by Christmas,' I stumbled. 'We need to do it properly. It will take time. But we will do it,' I heard myself say. Only on our way back on the train to Paddington station did the scale of the commitment hit me bang between the eyes.

I was in no doubt about the pressing need to develop Fairtrade cotton. A staggering 100 million households around the world depend in some way on the growing, processing or selling of cotton.[4] And a catastrophe was unfurling for poor cotton farmers with prices for their crop crashing – due in large measure, as I was to discover, to the government handouts of some of the wealthiest nations to their cotton farmers. When we were in Oxfam House in 2001, prices had slumped to 42 cents for a pound of cotton – the worst prices in thirty years and, in real buying power, the lowest ever on record.[5]

Farmers in African nations like Burkina Faso, Benin, Chad, Mali, Togo – several of them among the very poorest nations on earth – were devastated by the price crash. But in contrast to when drought and famine hit the same countries, no TV cameras had arrived to report the news of this man-made disaster, it wasn't on the front pages of our newspapers, and most people have probably never heard it mentioned. And yet the privation it caused was killing people just as surely as drought.

Cotton supports an estimated 10 million people in this dry arc of countries to the south and west of the Sahara. Families in Benin rely on cotton for half their family income – to buy everything from clothes to schoolbooks, from food to medicines.[6] Out of every $10 the country earns from exports, $4 comes from selling cotton – paying for services such as hospitals and schools and vital imports like fuel.[7]

Most of the cotton here is grown on small family farms of about a half to two hectares, alongside food crops like millet. Farmers usually use animals for ploughing, but all the planting, weeding and harvesting is done by hand. It's hard work. But it makes good use of one of the few assets these families have – their labour. It also creates jobs for the poorest of all – the landless – in work like harvesting. Furthermore, much of the income small farmers earn from cotton is spent on basics in the local market – so spilling over into extra jobs and income in the local community. In short, when prices were at a decent level in the early 1990s, cotton growing in West Africa had been helping farmers win their long battle against poverty.

Some people worry that if farmers grow cash crops they grow less food for their families. But here small farmers who took up cotton actually grew more corn too as they rotated their fields between the two crops and started to add fertilisers bought with cotton earnings. During this period, the UN's World Health Organisation found that among families growing cotton, poverty levels were falling, while income, intake of food and health were rising – at a time when other rural communities in the same region were growing poorer.[8] But, as colleagues from the French Fairtrade group returning from the region told me, crashing prices were reversing all these hard-won gains.

A cotton farmer from Burkina Faso, Seydou Ouedraogo, explained: 'We have a saying, if the head of a fish rots, of course the rest of the fish also rots. In my country, the head of the fish is cotton. When cotton is sick, everything is sick, because it's cotton that allows us to get what we need – our food and our nourishment.'[9]

Malian farmer Seydou Coulibaly looking back in 2007 said, 'For about six years now I have struggled to make enough money to feed and clothe my family because of the price of cotton on the world market. In my village we have difficulties paying for the costs of basic education, health care, and even drinkable water. We never had a doctor in the village but we used to have a nurse and a midwife. We could only afford to pay one, so we had to let the nurse go. There are five water pumps, but three of them are broken and we do not have the means to fix them. So we are left to share two in the whole village, among people and animals.'[10]

It was an unknown crisis. In the UK just a tiny handful of companies were seeking to put Fairtrade into the fashion industry. These were the committed pioneers – old-timers like Gossypium whose owners lived with the Indian farmers for years, Traidcraft and Bishopston Trading, as well as newcomers such as People Tree, founded in Japan but spreading its wings to the UK, and start-ups like Epona and Hug. We knew at the Foundation that we would want to develop and launch Fairtrade-certified cotton with these dedicated companies. But we would also need to get the big companies on board if we were going to have significant impact for the farmers.

Out of the blue in 2003, we got a call from right within the fashion world. Veteran fashion designer and campaigner Katharine Hamnett wanted to give out Fairtrade goodie bags during her high-profile return to London Fashion Week, after nearly a decade's absence. She wanted to make her point loud and clear about the grotesque contrast between the glitz and profits of the fashion industry and the desperate plight of the farmers growing the cotton in the garments dripping off the models.

No one does loud and clear as well as Katharine Hamnett. She'd inspired and amused a generation when at the height of the peace movement's opposition to new US nuclear missiles in Britain, she'd gone to a Downing Street reception hosted by Prime Minister Margaret Thatcher wearing a T-shirt declaring '58 % Don't Want Pershing'.

As soon as the Fashion Week was over, patron George Alagiah and I went to talk to her about taking Fairtrade into the clothing market. We were welcomed into her beautiful, rambling North London house. Lounging in a sofa, trendy shirt unbuttoned revealing his large chunk-chain necklace was her friend, Greg Valerio. He was chatting with a leading woman social activist from Ethiopia about the possibility of importing jewellery. Working with small-scale miners, Greg had set up a fair trade jewellery company in response to the appalling conditions facing miners. He was working with Katharine on an engagement ring collection. The miners and the public he said would be interested in Fairtrade-certified gold; the Foundation just didn't have the resources to follow it up then, though we agreed to keep in touch.

Katharine was preparing for a trip to Mali with Oxfam to highlight the cotton farmers' problems. In a long flow, without pausing for breath, she gushed out her concerns about the cotton trade skipping from its greedy use of water to the dangers of GM seed taking over. Passionate and determined to shift the industry's indifference, she ran through her long personal campaign to get the fashion world to be greener and more aware about the source of its clothes – in the teeth of apathy and cynicism. Back then, most fashionistas assumed Fairtrade meant dreary sack dresses and worthy sandals. Katharine wanted to do Fairtrade – but she wanted to go mainstream, working with big companies. She clearly had someone lined up, but wasn't letting on who was in her sights.

I tried to steer a course between responding warmly to Katharine's commitment and evident ability to get things done – and being up-front about the many hurdles we still had to overcome on Fairtrade cotton. She was impatient for action. Our complex rules were a bureaucratic annoyance to her. I was just hoping we could keep her with us for the long haul still ahead on Fairtrade cotton.

The more I read and heard about the scandal behind falling cotton prices, the greater my outrage and compulsion to meet both the tea-towel – and now, fashion – challenges. The long-term decline in cotton prices was, in part, down to stiff competition from man-made fibres like polyester – but only in part.

Cotton is very significant – 40 per cent of the fibres we use today come from cotton, and there is a huge appetite for cotton for products as diverse as bedsheets and cosmetics, banknotes and cotton wool.[11] But African and Asian cotton farmers face markets that are loaded against them.

Rich nations, pre-eminently the US, give vast handouts to their farmers to grow and export cotton – so undercutting other producers and pushing down world prices. The brazen scale of these government subsidies still makes my mind boggle. The US Government lavished $4.7 billion on just 25,000 American cotton farms in 2005. That's more than all US aid to Africa.[12] It's more than the total national wealth of cotton-reliant Burkina Faso.

Small farmers there are among the most efficient in the world – they can grow cotton for less than a third of the cost of their high-tech, large-scale counterparts in the US. But the US government handouts to their farmers mean they can knock this cost advantage aside and outsell the Burkinan farmer any day. It would be bad enough if the US only used its subsidised cotton at home – meaning West African farmers couldn't sell their cotton into the US market. But it's worse. The US sells 70 per cent of its cotton crop to the rest of the world. It's the world's biggest exporter by a long chalk. And when US-grown cotton is bankrolled by its government that means lower prices for farmers in places like Burkina Faso. Research shows a direct causal link between low prices hitting West African cotton farmers and US subsidies to a handful of farmers who dump their surpluses on world markets.[13]

As India's outspoken Minister for Commerce and Industry Kamal Nath has argued, 'Indian cotton farmers aren't competing against US cotton farmers. Our farmers are competing against the US Treasury.'

The US rhetoric around their subsidy programme is couched in the language of support for 'family farms' and the traditional American rural way of life. In reality, the largest 10 per cent of cotton farms hoover up three-quarters of all the handouts. Just ten cotton 'farms' (better known as vast agribusinesses to you and me) received subsidies of $17 million.[14]

US President George Bush famously complained that, 'More and more of our imports are from overseas.' Armed with this insight on international trade, he promised to be a 'strong advocate of free trade' and to 'work tirelessly to open up markets for agricultural products all over the world'.[15] And indeed he has when it comes to pushing nations to open up their borders to US exports; but when it comes to cutting the US's own trade-distorting subsidies it's a different story.

The cotton price collapse of 2001 saw the climax of this madness. Contrary to the laws of supply and demand, the scale of the US cotton subsidies rocketed as world prices fell from the mid-1990s. With more cash on offer, US farmers responded by planting even more cotton.[16] The US doubled its cotton exports between 1998 and 2001. As this subsidised cotton was shovelled on to the global market, world prices plummeted. While not on the US scale, the EU was also handing out even bigger per field subsidies to Spanish and Greek cotton farmers – further pulling down world prices. The International Monetary Fund (IMF) – the official body charged with keeping global finances stable – estimates that the subsidies pushed down what cotton producers got for their crop by more than a third. Another study says African cotton producers are losing over $200 million a year because of the subsidies.[17]

As a joint petition of cotton farmer groups from Mali, Burkina Faso and Benin to world trade ministers declared: 'Cotton producers of West Africa have clearly understood that to get out of poverty they need to work hard, which they have done. Having managed to produce a record harvest of cotton, they are now faced with the collapse of world cotton prices. Frankly, we are starting to doubt whether rich countries really want to reduce poverty in developing countries... By subsidising cotton producers, the US is threatening the survival of the cotton sector in Africa.'[18]

Little wonder cotton became a flashpoint in the stalled world trade talks that were launched in 2001 with a pledge to focus on trade rules to help poor countries. If the talks were to live up to their 'development' promise, there could hardly be a clearer case for action than cotton. But as the talks have dragged on without result, frustration in poor countries has grown.

When trade ministers met in Hong Kong in December 2005, the Trade Minister of Chad, Ngarmbatina Odjimbeyee Soukate, wearing a traditional dress made of local cotton, stood before her fellow ministers from around the world, couching her presentation not in the normal dry language of economics and diplomacy but as 'an appeal to the human conscience'. Speaking of the plight of poor farmers across her nation she said, 'Simply remember that we too are human beings.'[19]

At one point, another cotton exporter, Brazil, won a ruling from the World Trade Organisation, which regulates world trade, that US cotton subsidies broke the rules. But the US has done all it can to dodge the ruling. First they appealed; that lost, they dragged their feet on implementing any changes.[20] And still the wrangling continues.

The US Farm Bill in February 2007 set farm subsidies for the following five years amid talk of switching support away from products like cotton towards incentives for environmental protection instead. But as one Washington trade analyst wryly commented: 'There is less to this than meets the eye.'[21] Most subsidies are continuing pretty much as before. Farmers in West Africa face little prospect of a rise in low prices any time soon.

In light of all this, I nearly crashed my bike when I was cycling round the mega-junction at Elephant and Castle in London, and saw a huge billboard featuring a Heidi-like pouting model in a cotton meadow. The ad declared cotton to be 'soft, sensual and sustainable', and bid me to 'look for the mark'. I wondered if this was some big ad campaign for Fairtrade cotton I'd somehow managed to miss in a planning meeting. But as my eye traced down I saw it wasn't for Fairtrade cotton at all – but for the COTTON USA Mark promoted by the National Cotton Council of America!

With the subsidy scandal persisting, we had to move quicker to get Fairtrade cotton into the shops – to provide a lifeline to small cotton farmers, to put the spotlight on the unfair subsidies and to give the public a way to show their support for change. But getting that Fairtrade cotton on to the hangers was proving hard. The international Fairtrade body FLO had agreed the detailed standards for Fairtrade cotton by 2004 – including measures to help farmers shift away from the usual pesticide- and water-hungry ways of growing cotton, and later banning genetically modified (GM) cotton seed.[22] There were now cotton farmers' groups lining up to sell Fairtrade.

But the brainteaser was what to do about unfair practices in the rest of the supply chain which turns that cotton into clothes. Arguments raged with groups campaigning against exploitation in factories as well as with the alternative trading companies who sourced clothes from artisans – including some such as Bishopston Trading for whom the whole process from the spinning and dying to the sewing is hand-made by co-operatives in one south Indian village.

The ideal would be to offer, say, a Fairtrade shirt that was certified with the FAIRTRADE Mark for all stages of its journey –

from the farmer's field to the factory. But could we set the price and monitor against full Fairtrade standards at so many different levels? What would standards look like for the ginning or spinning mills? If they were only spinning Fairtrade cotton one day in the year (because quantities are still so low) should they get a share of the benefits? And could we persuade them to meet costly higher standards for their workers? One farmers' group trying to ensure decent wages in the ginning factory told me they were threatened by all the local ginners who said they could not afford higher wages all year round just to process a tiny amount of Fairtrade cotton.

Developing and monitoring such standards would take a long time. The cotton farmers didn't have time – they kept pushing us to launch. But would the public think everyone involved in each step of the manufacture was gaining Fairtrade benefits? Would problems in the factories risk the public's trust in the Mark? The arguments went round and round.

Finally international agreement was reached: we would start by ensuring the benefits of Fairtrade went to the cotton farmers' organisations. As with other products, each player in the manufacturing chain would have to register with FLO so we could trace the Fairtrade cotton all the way through its complex journey – so the consumer could be sure the T-shirt they were buying was made from Fairtrade cotton. More than that, all parties would have to provide evidence of how they are meeting core International Labour Organisation (ILO) standards on working conditions. It was a big step forward. For almost every company who signed up to use Fairtrade-certified cotton, it was the very first time that they had been required to trace the thread of cotton all the way through the whole process back to the farmers.

To make sure no one overclaims, companies have to make it very clear that the full standards of the FAIRTRADE Mark apply to the cotton, not all stages of the process. They can say that a shirt, is 'made with Fairtrade certified cotton' not that it is a 'Fairtrade shirt'. Meanwhile, at the international level, research continues into if and how we could apply full Fairtrade standards right through the process.

It was a difficult deal to secure. But finally everyone agreed and soon sales were taking off in France and Switzerland. In November 2005 we launched in the UK with ten pioneer Fairtrade companies, followed in March by Marks & Spencer, the UK's largest clothing retailer, launching a range of clothes.

Sales were explosive. Three months after launch the entire world supply of Fairtrade cotton had run out! We'd never experienced such a runaway success. We had a queue of independents and high street brands, from Monsoon to Next, wanting to join in and some 80 per cent of Fairtrade cotton globally was now being sold in the UK. Across West Africa and India we were involved in furious activity to enable more cotton farmers to sell on Fairtrade terms.

And Katharine Hamnett? In March 2007, Katharine unveiled her new range of stylish tops for Tesco made from Fairtrade- and organic-certified cotton, using her hallmark sloganeering: 'Choose Love' for women's slouch T-shirts or 'Save the Future for Me' for kids' T-shirts.

She shared with the *Observer* her early feelings about working with Tesco: 'When I went to see them I thought I was going into the jaws of hell, but they said they were interested in doing ethical clothing so, good. I don't care if people do the right thing even if it's for the wrong reasons, but actually I think they're really trying.'[23]

However, in September 2007 she pulled out of the deal telling the press she was 'incredibly disappointed' and that Tesco had broken promises to roll out her range and promote it in-store. Tesco, for their part, also said they were 'disappointed' but that 'she is wrong to question our commitment', pointing to their 'many organic and Fairtrade lines from socks to school uniform with lots more to come next season'.[24] The incident showed once again just how fragile Fairtrade advances can be – though we remain confident that Fairtrade cotton sales will soar in coming years, and Tesco has indeed significantly scaled up the amount of Fairtrade cotton they are using.

In 2007 alone, sales of Fairtrade-certified cotton in the UK have grown seven-fold, with companies such as Debenhams, Next, Monsoon, Topshop, TK Maxx and Sainsbury's all selling clothes made with Fairtrade cotton. And continuing rising sales will enable thousands more cotton farmers to participate in Fairtrade.

But just as important has been the wider impact the launch of Fairtrade cotton has had on the market: a mere five years ago, literally only a handful of companies in the UK knew where their cotton came from. Today, while very few companies are yet buying significant volumes of Fairtrade cotton, for the first time ever it has become an issue on the high street agenda; the companies are all having to consider how and where they buy their cotton and a few have transformed the way their business operates across the long supply chain. That is the larger sort of shift that Fairtrade can help bring about when it throws open the window on a whole new sector and lets the winds of change blow in.

And we didn't forget the tea-towel challenge either. I'm glad to say that you can now buy several types of tea towel made from Fairtrade-certified cotton – and I hope they're put to good use in Oxfam's kitchens. And an even more glamorous product has hit the shops – a Fairtrade cotton dishcloth from a company called Minky. Our vision of a Fairtrade lifestyle is becoming real.

The cotton in this cloth comes from a co-operative of small farmers in Mali – a country where fewer than two in five kids go to primary school. So first they decided to use their Fairtrade premium to build a school – as the nearest one was seven kilometres away and many local children just couldn't attend.

Comments Bamakan Souko of her involvement with a Fairtrade co-operative in Dougorakoroni, 'Women now join in the decision making. The women are now involved in the harvest and decisions about production. We were part of the decision to build a new school.'

The co-operative secured a deal that if they built the school, the government would supply the teachers. As soon as the first two classrooms were up, they were flooded with eager children. So the next year, they built more and persuaded the government to build two classrooms. So now they have a proper school. Meanwhile a neighbouring co-op has built a concrete grain store so less of the precious harvest is lost to pests. They can buy food after harvest, releasing it gradually over the year and so protecting local people from large swings in food prices.

More widely, Mali is taking the first steps to gain more of the value of its cotton, including Fairtrade cotton, by improving quality and by setting up ginning factories and textile mills. It's an uphill battle – but in villages like Dougorakoroni the difference decent and stable prices make to farmers is tangible. It shows that once people have this break, then they can go on to achieve much wider changes to their lives.

And Fairtrade cotton sales have been taking off across Europe. In Switzerland, Migros, the country's leading supermarket chain, stocked Fairtrade and organic cotton products from mid-2005, as did a major department store and one of the largest – and most ethically oriented – chains of stores, Switcher, whose CEO has won various awards for social entrepreneurship.

In France, La Redoute, the second largest seller of womenswear in the country and one of Europe's largest mail-order firms, started with a line of Fairtrade cotton products from March the same year. Ultra-trendy fashion label Blue Bretzel also signed up and was at London Fashion Week with T-shirts and sweaters that blend Fairtrade cotton with cashmere and bamboo fibres, with a promise to create a range for the menswear chain Celio with shops in France, Spain and Belgium. The leading Danish clothing company, Bestseller, is launching a range of organic and Fairtrade cotton T-shirts, jeans and sweatshirts through their own Jack & Jones shops and other retailers, in thirty countries. Fairtrade cotton products are now available in twelve countries, after more recent launches in Germany, Canada, Australia and New Zealand. The US is engaged in a process of consultation to determine when and how to launch Fairtrade cotton or clothing more generally.

However, one of the biggest actual – and potential – markets for Fairtrade cotton is workwear. The French post office, the French railways, Paris airports and even one of the largest waste disposal companies all dress some of their staff in garments made using Fairtrade cotton. Hopefully it's just the start of companies and local authorities finding a way to support farmers in poor countries.

Another coup for Fairtrade came from a bank wanting to make money from cotton . . . literally. The Dutch NGO Solidaridad rallied enough public support to persuade the finance minister and the President of the national bank to agree to add 31 tonnes of Fairtrade cotton to banknotes for strength and quality, in the Dutch version of the €10 note. Launched in The Hague in July 2007, other European banks are being asked to follow the Dutch example.

The focus is now on enabling more farmers to meet both Fairtrade and quality standards to be able to export their cotton. And that takes money. The initial work to develop standards for cotton had been possible in part because of a grant from the UK Government's Department for International Development led by then Secretary of State, Hilary Benn. Benn was a Fairtrade enthusiast, recognising the public support and revelling in its practicality, but among his officials there were sceptical voices, inclined to dismiss Fairtrade as marginal to the 'real world' of trade policy. A couple of years before we'd been reviewing progress on cotton.

'So, when am I going to be able to buy my Fairtrade boxers then?' he'd joked as he fingered the pile of raw cotton I'd brought in as a prop.

Recalling his remark, I bought a pair of the new M&S Y-fronts with Fairtrade certified cotton and sent them off to him with a little note attached. Knowing the strict requirements on ministers to declare gifts, and not wanting to embarrass him into inscribing in the solemn record that he'd received a pair of kecks, I scribbled that I'd quite understand if he couldn't accept them. Far from it, came the reply. The minister was most pleased with his new apparel and had packed them for an upcoming official visit to Malawi. And, anyway, they could be declared as 'clothing'.

One evening I pedalled home from work, my bike bags bulging with fruit and veg from Brixton market, and opened the front door to a barrage of needs from the children. Like Pavlovian dogs, it seems they only have to see me to feel hungry. The next step in unpicking the Fairtrade cotton problem was pushed out of my head by mashing potatoes, washing muddy PE kit and helping with homework.

My fourteen-year-old daughter Neena was struggling with her history homework. She had to find out about the Great Depression. I'd never studied it at school so I wasn't much help – but, as we scoured the BBC Education website, grim black and white pictures of lines of unemployed farmers in the dustbowl came into view. It struck me as strange that she now knows all about the Great Depression and what lies behind this by-word for the collapse of economic order. And yet few people know that millions of farmers and miners in poor countries have suffered even worse price collapses very recently.

The story of cotton could be told on product after product grown and sold by poor farmers in poor countries. Statistics from the United Nations' Food and Agriculture Organisation (FAO) track what has happened to the real prices paid for commodities vital to developing countries for the forty years from the 1960s to the 1990s. And nearly every single graph falls down the page. For cotton, bananas, rice, sugar, coffee, tea, cocoa, jute, the prices paid to farmers have fallen down, down, down to rock-bottom levels. The prices of cocoa and coffee, for example, halved over the 1980s and 1990s.[25] Behind every falling line lie wrecked lives.

Take tea: the real prices paid for tea fell by a shocking 54 per cent between the 1980s and 2005.[26] Today the price of tea means we can get bags for 0.023p – the milk and sugar probably cost more. Research conducted by Martin Isark, the author of *The Supermarket Own Brand Guide*, found that the price of a cup of tea has plummeted to the lowest levels ever for us drinkers. While the average UK weekly wage would have bought 6,870 tea bags in 1977, today it can buy 29,800. Isark told the *Scotsman* that: 'The low prices are bad for everybody in the sense that people just get conditioned to paying the same amount of money for tea and do not treat it with any respect . . . The tea industry, the brands and the promotional bodies require a good shake-up; they have for the last thirty years failed miserably in the promotion of an excellent product.'[27]

The impact has been disastrous. In India, as many as 136 tea estates in three states alone closed recently, leaving thousands of former workers and their families without jobs, income, or the drinking water, electricity and medical treatment they received on the plantations. Reports from West Bengal in early 2007, where these wider global problems have been compounded by the loss of preferential export contracts to the former Soviet Union, described over 15,000 unemployed tea workers suffering from severe malnutrition as they were left to survive on rats, wild plants and flowers. At least 150 people had died of hunger as a result.[28]

Addressing African leaders in 2003, French President Jacques Chirac said there is a 'conspiracy of silence' about the commodity crisis.[29] It would be naive to believe this silence was an accident. The uncomfortable fact is that we in the rich countries are doing rather well out of this flow of cheap raw materials: we pay less for food and clothes and inflation is kept down. Our purses are fuller because poor farmers in poor countries are paid less. This is the harsh reality of the so-called global village. It is a deeply, uncomfortably, feudal village.

In contrast, Britain's wealth has more than tripled in real terms in the last twenty years.[30] Of course, not everyone has benefited to the same degree; of course, too many people in this country have to watch every penny they spend. But the majority of the population are richer than ever and are in a position to pay fair prices for goods coming from poor nations.

Instead, as figures from the Office for National Statistics reveal, we are spending less and less on our food and non-alcoholic drinks. In the 1950s, the average household spent a third of income on food. That has fallen to one sixth. In fact, we're only spending marginally more on food and drink than on leisure.[31]

So why is this happening? For each product, there's a long and particular story. Changing tastes are one issue – people drinking fizzy drinks or bottled water instead of tea and coffee, for example. New technology is another – jute sacks and rope being pushed out by plastic bags, steel containers and nylon ropes. But there are overarching trends too. There is oversupply of many products and when too much coffee or cocoa is on the world market, prices fall.

But poor farmers in rural Ghana or the mountains of Ethiopia cannot just uproot their trees, plant something else for a bit, then plant more coffee bushes again a few months later when prices in London or New York bounce back. They have few choices or flexibility; that's what being poor means.

Another factor is that, at least in some commodities like coffee and tin, producer and consumer governments used to agree to act to moderate the boom and bust cycles. But now international markets have been left to run riot. It's like a funnel: often millions of producers are selling ultimately to a handful of vast global companies, with turnovers bigger than that of many African nations. So it's a buyers' market all the way – and prices just keep getting pushed down. In coffee the market has rattled through unpredictable and violent peaks and troughs. As one farmer told me, prices 'go to hell and back'. There are 25 million coffee smallholders growing coffee – many are isolated poor farmers at the mercy, first, of unscrupulous local traders and, then, just four gargantuan companies controlling over 60 per cent of world sales.

But even beyond the multinational companies, it is the giant supermarkets that increasingly have greater power in the global food market. Indeed the world's biggest supermarket chain, the US giant Wal-Mart, is now the world's biggest company[32.] In the UK the top five supermarkets now account for more than £7 out of every £10 we spend on groceries. To take one stark example, in 1989 supermarkets sold us about a third of our fresh fruit and vegetables, by 2003 it was 80 per cent. And as supermarkets source nearly all of this directly from importers and not through wholesale markets, increasingly farmers in developing countries are selling their crops straight to supermarkets – even locally as supermarkets expand in developing countries too. The rise of the supermarkets has had three main effects.

First, their buying power gives them huge influence over the prices farmers get. Suppliers have few options – sell on the terms of supermarkets or don't sell at all. The job of the buyers who lead the day-to-day business of sourcing goods for the supermarkets is to increase sales and profits, usually by squeezing costs;

inevitably the cuts get passed down the line to the weakest link of all, the farmers.

Second, supermarkets can impose demands on suppliers – from super-stringent hygiene demands to insisting on the farm company paying for special promotions such as 'buy one, get one free'. I remember some banana farmers commenting how the supermarket they were supplying stipulated they install a supply of drinking water; not for the workers to drink – even though they had none – but to wash the bananas in; a fruit which nature supplied with a thick skin to protect the part you actually eat. Of course, some of these demands are not bad in themselves, but it is the suppliers who carry the cost of implementing them. It is true that the Fairtrade rules also make demands on the farmer too, but the difference is that they get a direct financial benefit in return; it is a partnership.

I often meet farmers who show me the huge files of endless rules and regulations they must meet to supply Western markets. Increasingly it is not governments that impose what business would normally dismiss as 'red tape', but business itself; a process that analyst of supermarket supply chains Bill Vorley calls the 'privatisation of regulation'. Often it is only the large players who have the resources to cope with meeting these rules. One study found this was one of the main reasons why the proportion of small farms compared with large farms supplying fresh vegetables for export in Kenya had fallen from 75 per cent in 1997 to under 20 per cent now.[33]

Third, the power of supermarkets is particularly strong in the fastest growing and potentially most lucrative markets – the new products farmers have changed to as earnings from traditional exports like tea and coffee have dropped. Fresh vegetables now make up 20 per cent of Kenya's exports, compared with 3 per cent at independence. The influence of supermarkets over poor farmers in poor countries is likely to increase in the coming years, which underlines why Fairtrade is going to be more and more important. Fairtrade protects the farmers from price cuts, encourages long-term trading relationships and by ensuring farmers are organised into groups helps strengthen their position.

Unstable and uncertain income from selling commodities makes it hard for countries, communities and farmers to invest and plan for the future. It also undermines their ability to get greater value out of what they produce – for example by improving quality or processing the crop more to retain a greater amount of its final value inside the country of origin. Business always hates uncertainty – and it is one of the reasons it is so hard to attract investment in commodity-based industries in developing countries. Moreover, rich countries have a barrage of trade rules, such as higher taxes for more processed products, which make it harder for developing countries to move into manufacturing.

Nevertheless, in the roller-coaster ride of commodity prices, the extreme dip of 2001 has been followed by an upward swing in the last few years for some products such as coffee and cocoa. The voracious appetite of China's booming factories for raw materials has helped lift prices for metals – giving some important respite to copper exporters such as Zambia. China has been expanding its investment in raw materials in Africa – from oil in Angola to platinum in Zimbabwe, and in 2005 alone trade between the continent and China tripled.[34] And as cheap Chinese exports have cut the prices of many manufactured goods, there are even signs that the long-term fall of commodity prices as against manufactured goods may have been arrested.[35]

So, some people say, doesn't this spell the end of the commodity problem? Unfortunately, I don't think so. Crucially, while the prices of farm commodities have generally gone up from their real low point of 2001, they have seen nothing like the recovery of metals. Some, such as cotton or tea, have enjoyed none of this recovery. In others, the price increases all too often benefit speculators but never filter down to the farmers.

Moreover, even with these recent rises, commodity producers are still getting meagre returns compared with the past. Even in metals real prices are still only half what they were in the mid-nineteenth century.[36] Rises have also been fuelled by short-term speculation as commodities became a place short-term investors moved their money for a time. While the experts are not all agreed, few predict the rises of recent years continuing. One detailed study by the IMF showed metal prices staying strong for the next few years – but with major falls after that as new reserves are opened up and extra supplies start to kick in.[37]

Undoubtedly higher prices for some commodities have given some producers some respite after many years of disastrously tumbling prices. However, this does not mean the pressure is off tackling the commodity price problem and that we can start soft peddling on Fairtrade. Just the opposite, in fact. We may want to fine tune the Fairtrade model in the future if price patterns do adjust. But we should see this period as a precious chance for the whole international community to learn from the past and ensure we do not run into the same cycle again. We should be grasping the opportunity to lock in long-term commitments to guarantee producers a better deal for the future.

The subsidies rich nations give their farmers also drag prices down and price farmers out in poor countries. It's not just cotton – rice, beef, maize, milk, fruit, and vegetable oils all feature. Rich countries spend just over $1 billion a year on agricultural aid in poor nations. But they spend nearly that *every day* subsidising their own agriculture, costing poor countries $24 billion a year in lost earnings.[38]

Sugar illustrates this, par excellence. Early on we'd started certifying Fairtrade sugar. But for years, we've been frustrated by limited progress in expanding sales. It did not help that the EU has been bankrolling European farmers to grow sugar beet at the expense of poor sugar-cane producers. Such subsidies were part of the wider Common Agricultural Policy (CAP), which reflected a founding political deal of the EU after the Second World War. The goals of economic ties to overcome old enmities, stable farm prices and a Europe self-sufficient in food may have been laudable, but the CAP soon grew into a costly Frankenstein, often with damaging side-effects on farmers in developing nations. Its long overdue reform has moved at a snail's pace, leaving it as a kind of time-warp policy stuck in post-Second World War Europe, rather than the twenty-first century. It was really only the entry of the countries of the former Eastern bloc that started a process of serious reform, as extending its support to farmers in these nations would have seen the CAP budget mushroom completely out of control. Nevertheless the CAP is far from dead.

Until 2005, the EU was paying its farmers three times the world price to grow sugar; so they were growing 4 million tonnes more sugar a year than Europeans could get through. The EU then paid a handful of European sugar manufacturers, to the tune of more than $1 billion a year, to flog this surplus on the world market – so pushing international prices down by about a third.[39]

It was a triple whammy for sugar growers in poor nations: they could not sell freely into the vast European market; they were pushed out of selling in other parts of the world by subsidised European sugar; and they got less for what they grew.

The EU did used to buy set amounts of sugar at high prices from the African, Caribbean and Pacific (ACP) countries with which it has traditional ties. But for a very poor country like Mozambique this quota amounts to less than four hours' worth of EU sugar consumption. Without the subsidies (not only in the EU, but the US, Japan and other countries), Mozambique could have developed a thriving industry selling sugar at very competitive prices.

In November 2005, after years of haggling, EU farm ministers finally agreed to cut the price paid to European farmers to grow sugar because of concerns over whether the payments would pass WTO rules and some member states' reluctance to continue subsidising such an expensive regime.[40] The change will also mean, though, that ACP sugar producers will lose the high price paid for their sugar quotas – and for some higher-cost producers like Jamaica it will be tough to adapt. The EU was also slated for cranking up a huge compensation package for those sugar producers within the EU following the deal, while offering limited help to poor ACP countries losing their quotas.

Nevertheless, with subsidies to EU farmers falling, European overproduction and dumping on world markets should also fall – enabling those developing countries that can produce competitively priced sugar to sell more. Big business has been quick to adapt to the move. Associated British Foods – the company behind the Silver Sugar brand – took over Southern Africa's biggest sugar producer Illovo in July 2006 in a £317-million deal.[41]

The company plans to double its output from sugar-cane farms across Malawi, Zambia, Swaziland, Tanzania and Mozambique to import sugar to Britain – under the duty-free terms the EU has offered the poorest nations from 2009.

So, with this sugar shake-up, we need to redouble our efforts to ensure that the potential benefits do reach the poorest producers. The Fairtrade Foundation is also keen to ensure that smallholders in ACP countries losing their protection, like Mauritius or Belize, survive; and Fairtrade appears to offer their last hope, just as it has been a lifeline for Windward Island banana farmers.

More Fairtrade sales could make all the difference to someone like Jameson Mabviko who farms three hectares as part of the Kasinthula Cane Growers (KCG) scheme in Southern Malawi, near the border with Mozambique. A builder, carpenter and trained – but unpaid – church pastor, he lives with his wife, Dorothy, and five of their nine children in a house he built himself. He even made the bricks from clay soil, firing them on an open fire. The house is in Laughi One village, back from the main road that connects Chikwawa town with the Nchalo Sugar Factory.

The house is a little bigger than some of the others dotted around. Made from orange brick and corrugated metal roofing, it is a grade above the more common mud and thatch. Inside, to afford some privacy, a piece of yellow material drapes loosely over the doorway of Jameson and Dorothy's bedroom where they have the only bed. A blue knotted mosquito net is suspended over it and clothes are draped over lines hanging from the walls. The children sleep on mats. A dinner table, which fills one room, is covered with a cheerful, brightly coloured cloth. The living room, where the family says their prayers in the morning, is dark, though light filters in through the brick-size gaps in the wall. The room is empty but for a calendar hanging on a wall, a shallow metal bucket filled with coloured plastic containers, and a bag of cement.

Around the outside are foundations where Jameson was planning to extend his house to provide a washroom and a bigger living room. Just the cement and metal roofing will cost him almost a year's income, so he will build gradually as expenses allow.

Behind the house is a small thatched mud hut where Dorothy prepares lunch over an open fire in a corner. Here they store water in big plastic buckets and drums. Dorothy collects it from a communal pump half a kilometre away, carrying the water in a plastic bucket balanced on her head.

Jameson explains, 'Some neighbouring villages don't yet have a water supply and so women have to collect water from the river. This is very dangerous – people have been dragged away by crocodiles.'

Before converting to Fairtrade, Jameson and other association members were making just £20 a month from their cane, partly because they were paying off debts they had unknowingly accumulated when the government had originally set up the scheme.

'How can I survive on this and feed all my children?' he says. 'I work very hard. I work in sugar cane and then on my food crops. I take out weeds to improve production. Cane needs good care. That's why I wake up early and work hard.'

When someone in the family gets malaria it costs nearly £5 – a week's income – to treat. New strains of malaria are very common in this part of the world and Dorothy and Jameson each get it about once a year. To send one child to college for a year would account for eight months of his current income. Education is seen as one of the few possible ways of escaping the crushing poverty which so many in Malawi endure – and families will make huge sacrifices to give their children the chance of more schooling.

In spite of their poverty, Jameson and Dorothy are very generous. When they can, they organise a party for the 200 children from a neighbouring village orphanage. Most of the children's parents have died from Aids and they had no other relatives to take them in. Other pastors help out and arrive with their congregations, bringing the number of guests up to 500. They build shade huts to shield people from the scorching sun. Dorothy cooks huge quantities of porridge that is served with sugar and water. There is music, singing and dancing and a pastor preaches.

When the farmers got the news of their first Fairtrade orders since becoming Fairtrade certified, it was a great moment.

Jameson's family started to plan the modest – but life-changing – things they could do with the extra income.

'I want many things for my life,' he says. 'I want to finish building my house – I want a good house. I want seats to sit on. I want to make a good future for my family. My son Onesema wants to learn how to drive so he can get a job, but this costs too much. My daughter Hannah wants to learn how to use a computer.'

Jameson's wife, Dorothy, feels keenly the hardship her children have endured, 'I want my family to be able to eat good things. I don't want my family to be hungry and poor and I want to end the suffering of my children.'

Their first 750 tonnes of sugar ordered in 2004 on Fairtrade terms from three UK companies generated an extra £40,000 for the group. Jameson is on the committee of farmers deciding how to spend the Fairtrade premium. First they set up a supply of clean water to villages that didn't yet have it. They also planned to restore a clinic to treat the debilitating tropical diseases including cholera, diarrhoea and bilharzia that regularly strike. The group will negotiate with the government to supply a qualified nursing sister and medicines when the clinic is ready. They also aimed to build a primary school for the furthest village and a secondary school near to the office. They only need the building materials as the community will supply the labour. Without these schools children have to walk eight kilometres or they simply don't go.

But all this depends on two things. Being able to compete fairly in Europe without their sugar being undercut by heavily subsidised EU sugar. And people buying Fairtrade sugar. In Britain Kasinthula's sugar can be found in products such as packs of Co-op and Billington's Fairtrade sugar and Traidcraft's best-selling Geobars.

Kasinthula Operations Manager Brian Namata, famous for wowing hundreds of Co-op supermarket staff at their annual conference, says, 'You know the proverb "Give a man a fish and he will eat for a day, teach a man to fish and he will eat for ever"? At the moment we know how to fish, but UK shoppers should maintain us by buying our fish. If they do that then we won't have to hold our hands out for their assistance.

'Buying Fairtrade sugar is a sacrifice for consumers because there are cheaper brands available. But they gain more from buying Fairtrade sugar – more satisfaction. I hope they have the social responsibility to assist others who are willing to assist themselves. I hope they will because we are struggling farmers who will have to go back to the EU for a donation. We don't want to resort to begging.'

In 2008, in a market shifting move, the iconic brand Tate and Lyle switched all their retail sugar to Fairtrade, securing the future for 7,000 sugar farmers in Belize.

When I had sat with my daughter and her homework I had learned how the Depression, and then the war, spurred the world to set up international organisations to manage the economy and prevent it ever happening again. The mastermind behind this plan, the great economist John Maynard Keynes, argued for the International Monetary Fund and the World Bank – both established as the Second World War was ending. However, people often forget Keynes also wanted a mechanism to stabilise volatile commodity prices. He had insisted it was critical to ensure 'proper economic prices should be fixed not at the lowest possible level, but a level sufficient to provide producers with proper nutritional and other standards in the conditions in which they live . . . and it is in the interests of all producers alike that the price of a commodity should not be depressed below this level, and consumers are not entitled to expect that it should'.[42]

Wise words tragically ignored. Developing countries kept up the call for better ways to manage commodity prices – to prevent their extreme troughs and peaks, and their long-term decline compared with the prices of industrial goods – to no effect.

Some faltering international steps were taken towards setting up or strengthening commodity agreements between producer and consumer countries in the ten core products most critical to developing countries – like tin, cotton, coffee, sugar. But rich nations weren't prepared for measures with real teeth. By the 1980s the commodity agreements that did exist were collapsing or had been left impotent, as desperate nations scrabbled to earn whatever they could from their exports as prices plummeted. The free market fundamentalism by then sweeping the world wanted nothing to do with such ideas of managing world trade. While often practising protectionism themselves, with breathtaking hypocrisy rich countries were preaching a new gospel at poor countries: radically open your economy and cut government intervention as the path to development.

In 1989, the International Coffee Agreement – originally negotiated between the US as the world's largest consumer and the key producers Brazil and Colombia – collapsed after the US pulled out. As the market became awash with coffee, prices went into freefall and, with some ups and downs, fell further still until the low point of 2001.

Fairtrade has been the people's response to a blindingly obvious need to moderate unrestrained markets. When producers and consumers join together through Fairtrade to set a stable minimum price and to channel trade specifically to help people overcome poverty, they are, in effect, setting up 'people's commodity agreements'. And governments should be shamed by the fact that ordinary people across the globe are showing the way.

For some, even Fairtrade is meddling too much in the laws of the market. Our free market opponents argue that markets in products like coffee will come back into balance 'naturally'; that smallholders cannot compete with large, mechanised coffee plantations and so should diversify into other crops – or just leave farming altogether. Debating with such critics, I've struggled to stay calm while explaining that their world of theoretical 'perfect' markets is divorced from the realities of the powerless and ignores the human and environmental costs. Perfect markets in textbook economics depend on access to perfect information, finance and a range of resources all in short supply among disadvantaged farmers.

Nor does the tiny amount of Fairtrade encourage farmers to overproduce as critics suppose. Quite the reverse: if farmers are earning less and less, they have to grow more crops just to keep food on the table. By contrast farmers in the Fairtrade system have the breathing space, the access to information and credit, to move out of their dependence on one crop or to add value to it. Which is exactly what many groups are doing just as soon as the Fairtrade income gives them that chance.

Moreover, farmers' groups can only enter, and then sell, in the Fairtrade system if they have a buyer. There's no Fairtrade equivalent of the EU's Common Agricultural Policy or the US Department of Agriculture prepared to pay for crops no one actually wants to buy.

After one heated radio phone-in on this issue, I emerged from a dingy meeting room in our rabbit warren of a central London office, and I bumped into Gerardo Arias Camacho, founder member of Fairtrade coffee co-operative Co-operativa Llano Bonito in Costa Rica. I shared the argument.

'Diversify into what?' he exclaimed in exasperation with those economists who 'sit in their offices and give us advice but have no idea of the realities'. Most coffee farms are up mountains on slopes not well suited to other crops; the farmers have known for generations how to grow coffee but may not have the knowledge to grow or market other crops – and it is not so easy to find markets for other products; which ones?

People's only option, says Gerardo, is to migrate. He knows what he's talking about: after his father's coffee farm earnings slumped, at eighteen Gerardo set out with a group of other young men on a terrifying journey to Mexico to jump the border into the US. He spent eight days without food or drink getting across the desert into the US. He was fleeced by men posing as policemen who threatened to turn them in. When you come from a small village to a huge city and on such a long journey, 'you feel as terrified as a chicken in a wolf's lair' he says. His aim was to earn enough money to 'help my family buy a truck' as a way for them to make a living back in Costa Rica. For years he managed to earn money – and learn perfect English. His brothers have stayed, but Gerardo wanted to go home and set up a co-operative so other coffee farmers could stay on their land.

His group have put considerable effort into improving the quality of their coffee, upgrading their skills, undertaking more of the processing of the coffee, finding new markets – and, yes, exploring other options. Not to replace coffee, but to supplement their income and reduce their dependence on one crop. In Gerardo's co-operative, for example, they have developed Macadamia nuts, and even 'Latino Chips' – packets of crisps made from plantain bananas and cassava available in different flavours: paprika, garlic, salt, natural, bacon, chilli and lime, black pepper – which they export to Belgium apparently!

When *Financial Times* Trade Editor Alan Beattie visited Fairtrade cotton farmers in Mali, he kept asking the question raised by the free market critics: Are you growing more cotton since you got involved with Fairtrade? In each village, farmers explained patiently the system of crop rotation they operate to maintain soil fertility, which meant that cotton was usually planted on no more than one-third of their land. Other farmers talked about improving the quality of their cotton production, to get the best possible price, and were keen to understand if they could find a market for other products, such as peanuts or shea nuts (now popular as shea butter in cosmetics). He concluded: 'Worries about inducing oversupply also look somewhat over the top, given that any co-operative growing any product anywhere in the world can sell only as much at Fairtrade prices as has been ordered from that co-operative by buyers. Cotton is an annual crop, so farmers know their demand before planting . . . In theory, Fairtrade prices could encourage non-cotton-growing villages to enter the market, but as yet there is little evidence. In Batimakana, just as before, only 20 per cent of the land is used for cotton, though farmers say quality has improved. Mamadou Toungara, head of Batimakana village, says: "We will keep growing cotton as long as people keep buying it. We will change if the next cash crop is more profitable. But we haven't found it yet."' [43]

Of course, economists raise a panoply of further questions about Fairtrade. Certainly, as Fairtrade grows, its model will need adapting constantly, and perhaps changing dramatically. And no one deludes themselves the Fairtrade system could be applied to all trade tomorrow. But it is a start; it is making a difference now; and it does show that you can manage markets in a way that

The Arabica Coffee Market 1989-2008: Comparison of Fairtrade and New York Prices

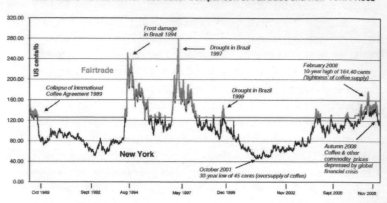

NB Fairtrade price = Fairtrade minimum price* of 125 cents/lb + 10 cents/lb Fairtrade premium**
When the New York price is 125 cents or above, the Fairtrade price = New York price + 10 cents
*Minimum price was increased from 121 cents/lb on 1 June 2008 **Premium was increased from 5 cents/lb on 1 June 2007
The NY price is the daily closing price of the second position Coffee 'C' futures contract at ICE Futures US (New York Board of Trade)
© Fairtrade Foundation

Falling World Cotton Prices

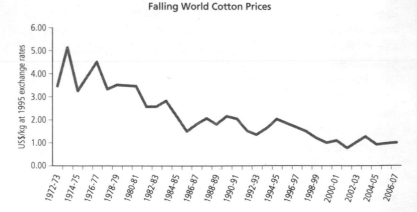

This chart adjusts world cotton prices to reflect the constant value of the dollar at 1995 exchange rates
It shows that in real terms growers recieved five times more for a kilo of cotton in 1973 than in 2007

Data source: Cotlook A Index

is commercially, socially and environmentally successful. And that is the message for governments.

The Vicar of Dibley, the classic Dawn French BBC TV comedy series, is always good for a laugh. On the eve of 2005, the Christmas Day special edition was good for more than that. It was the unofficial kick-start for the momentous Make Poverty History campaign that built up towards the G8 summit in Gleneagles. The weekend before, the call for serious action on aid, debt and, most of all, trade brought thousands on to the streets of Edinburgh.

I was there with Raymond Kimaro, the Tanzanian elder statesman of the Fairtrade movement and board member of Britain's leading 100 per cent Fairtrade coffee brand, Cafédirect, whose coffee the leaders were drinking. Marching around Edinburgh's historic streets, Raymond was enjoying the crowd with the fluttering rainbow of banners and balloons.

Later, he climbed on to the platform at the rally and soon had the vast crowd going in an African chant. Into the booming microphone he tells them, 'By strengthening their organisation and marketing skills, by improving health, water and education facilities, by diversifying into new economic activity, and by improving environmental protection programmes, farmers and farm workers in Africa who supply the Fairtrade market are already working towards making poverty history for themselves. Being able to make a living from the sweat of one's labour should be a basic human right, safeguarded by governments, for all people in Africa and elsewhere.'

I hear later how wine writer Oz Clarke is inspired by Raymond's straight-talking appeal for farmers to get an honest day's pay for a honest day's work – and he speaks out on the issue on the evening Daily Politics television show, a symbol of how the debate on fairer trade has penetrated from the margins to the centre of political debate. Soon the Foundation's feisty Head of Communications Barbara Crowther whisks Raymond off for a radio interview. Raymond tells the presenter how the success of Fairtrade shows you can run trade in a way that tackles poverty and injustice. Barbara leads our campaign work and represents us in the Trade Justice Movement (TJM), a coalition of more than eighty groups working on development, human rights, the environment and consumer issues, together with trade unions and faith groups. Through TJM we are part of the wider campaign for fairer trade rules for poor countries, an end to the farm subsidies in rich countries – like those in cotton – that prevent poor farmers selling their products, allowing developing countries to protect their fragile economies and laws to stop big business profiting at the expense of people and the environment.

One achievement of the coalition was a new law requiring companies quoted on the UK stock market to report on environmental matters, workers, social and community issues, and to show how directors are performing on these issues, so bringing responsibility to boardroom level.[44] The move came despite vehement opposition from business about the costs this 'red tape' would burden them with. I was reminded of the same kind of arguments I'd heard when I'd been campaigning many years ago at the Low Pay Unit for a national minimum wage in Britain – now a reality but in those days dismissed as potentially disastrous economic interference in the free market. We always pointed to Winston Churchill's arguments for an earlier measure on minimum wages, that without it 'the good employers are undercut by the bad, and the bad are undercut by the worst'. So too, I believe that we need global rules to set minimum social and environmental standards to prevent those companies increasingly committed to fairer trading practices being undermined by the unscrupulous traders. And, through TJM, we are pressing for these.

Trade can help stimulate badly needed economic growth in poor countries. But it won't *necessarily* lead to growth or reduce poverty, which is why trade must be managed in ways to deliver the best results. In Fairtrade we are quite clear there will need to be big changes to world trade rules and better controls on the way companies do business across the globe if farmers in developing countries are really to work themselves out of poverty. After the protests in Edinburgh, Barbara was off to Gleneagles to get our message to the journalists from around the world – as well as getting to meet Bono in the process! But despite the groundswell of support for trade justice, the G8 meeting did little to make progress on trade – even if it did commit to some further action on aid and debt.

Fairtrade adds to the campaign for trade justice by providing evidence that trade can be fairer and contribute to development, and still be commercially successful. It shows in practice that there is another way to run trade. It's not an abstract policy position – it's a reality being proven every day by thousands of producers and businesses worldwide. It builds a model of trade that benefits people and the planet itself, which we would still need even if all the trade barriers and farm subsidies were done away with. Fairtrade also plays a more practical role in building a broad-based movement for change. Most of us, faced with the intricacies of world trade rules go cross-eyed – or fall asleep, or both. But we all go shopping. So, Fairtrade is an easy way in. People start to think about trade, hear about the problems and some potential solutions. So when David Joyce took on a new education project at the Irish Confederation of Trade Unions (ICTU) to engage unions north and south of the border on international development issues, he found that, 'Fairtrade was one of the more practical expressions of the issues, so I set about promoting it to our members. It just seemed like a good initiative for the unions to get involved in.' From a very different standpoint, Newsweek magazine argued Fairtrade threw a new light on the orthodox trade system, declaring, 'Free marketeer, stand warned. There is another way to trade.'45

What's more: the worldwide groundswell of public support for Fairtrade, shown above all else in the rising sales every year, sends a strong message to governments that the public want trade to be fairer. It helps give our governments a mandate to take the big, bold steps needed to change world trade rules. It is summed up in one of our most popular leaflets, to which the public were asked to attach the FAIRTRADE Mark from a product they've recently bought, under a message to the Prime Minister saying: 'I believe in trade justice and have put my money where my mouth is. Time you followed suit.'

4
Swimming with Sharks

'When you drink your coffee, remember that behind every cup there are faces, there are people,' says Merling Preza Ramos. Merling's energy and utter commitment to Fairtrade tumble out of her as she speaks. She's talking nineteen-to-the-dozen – my rudimentary Spanish only just keeping up. Merling is the General Manager of the PRODECOOP Fairtrade coffee co-operative in Nicaragua. She has a warm, open face – remarkably young looking given that she's not only the mother of four children, but also has two grandchildren. But she is also a tough business negotiator and a forceful political player in the Fairtrade movement. Developing and running their 'super-co-operative' of forty local coffee co-ops is a remarkable achievement for this woman in a macho society. It now has 2,300 farmers as members, nearly a quarter of them women, spread across the region of Segovia in northern Nicaragua – one of the poorest countries in Latin America. I was thrilled when Merling put her name forward and was accepted on to the Fairtrade Foundation Board as the representative of the Latin American and Caribbean groups.

PRODECOOP has been going for just over fifteen years. And yet through Fairtrade it has boosted its members' income, provided school scholarships, books and equipment to coffee farmers' children, and set up a revolving social fund to help farmers with big outlays like medical bills or improving their housing. It has helped the farmers change nearly half their output to organic methods and has built facilities so they can process and store their own coffee. Two of its young people have learned the highly skilled profession of 'cupping' coffee for its taste and qualities. And PRODECOOP's coffee has won top awards for its flavour. But none of this has been easy. Merling has been through war, hurricanes and the savage battering of the international coffee markets, so I ask her what is the secret of her success.

'I'm the manager of the co-operative – and, of course, I always want to be able to report good sales and good profits at the end of the year,' says Merling. 'But I am also responsible to an elected committee of farmers who always remind me: "Who is the profit for? Who are we selling for?" That makes sure I keep the right balance.'

It's a role Merling has brought to our board. Whenever plans are being hotly debated, she interjects with a smile: 'One small question: why is this good for the farmers?' As we walk the tightrope balancing the interests of producers, consumers and companies, Merling's little question helps keep us as focused as she is.

She says, 'The most constant challenge I face in Fairtrade is combining being a professional, commercial manager with staying true to the spirit of solidarity, to helping the weakest. We have made big strides in improving quality and income. We are all proud of winning our awards. If you came to our offices you might think we were a private company, we are so professional. But all this is motivated by our desire to improve the lives of our people. Trading coffee is a tool to change people's lives – not an end in itself.'

Merling is speaking to me as we take some time out in a couple of comfy chairs in the lobby, while around us conference delegates rush to their next workshop sessions. Fairtrade producers from right across Latin America compare notes in animated groups in the corridors – brazil nut farmers from

Bolivia, honey gatherers from Mexico, indigenous people exploring solidarity tourism schemes. We're at an international convention on Fairtrade in the southern Mexican state of Chiapas in 2006. Hosted by the local state government, it's been opened by no less than Vicente Fox, the Mexican President. It's hard to believe it is less than twenty years since coffee growers in the neighbouring mountainous state of Oaxaca exported the first ever, tiny consignment of Fairtrade-labelled produce to the Netherlands in 1988.

Our vibrant, growing movement is going from strength to strength. But debates about the underlying tension in Fairtrade, between bringing about radical social change and real world business success, are just as live today as when those Mexican farmers sent their first coffee. For we are, as former Director of Fairtrade pioneer group TWIN, Albert Tucker, always said of our engagement with the world of business, 'swimming with sharks'.

Critics fire at us for failing on one count or the other. On the one side they say Fairtrade is fatally compromised by working with big businesses and the supermarkets. We allow Fairtrade to be their ethical fig-leaf while their day-to-day way of doing business remains as based as ever on squeezing the lowest price out of suppliers to extract maximum profits, say these critics. Fairtrade cannot hope to do anything in the face of the ravages of the commodity crisis and global trade rules fixed against the poorest.

Another group of detractors say Fairtrade isn't 'real' business at all. It may give guilt-ridden Westerners a way of feeling good, but it distorts the market with subsidies and a host of bureaucratic rules. Fairtrade just encourages farmers to live in a charitable bubble protected from the disciplines of the market – which will do them no favours in the long run, they say. Others, still, worry whether Fairtrade reaches the poor farmers it is meant to, whether it really makes a difference.

But Merling is unequivocal: Fairtrade has changed the lives of the farmers in her co-operative. It's not only that Fairtrade brings them a better, more stable income. It's not only that they grow coffee in a better way – under improved environmental and social conditions. It's that they, the producers, have a new, more equal relationship with the consumer. At the heart of Fairtrade is a new form of exchange, a new way of doing business, says Merling. As for the standards, certification checks, the Mark – they may appear bureaucratic to some from outside, but it is only the machinery of the FAIRTRADE Mark that allows us to use mainstream channels and reach consumers in order to put this new relationship into practical action.

None of this means Merling is uncritical. Far from it. She is passionately outspoken in fierce internal debates about the future direction of Fairtrade. While here in Chiapas I know that I will face some hard grilling from her and others in the CLAC, the network of Latin American Fairtrade producers over why, for example, the international Fairtrade body FLO has not yet shifted ownership of the organisation over to the producers, as had been promised. They were right on this, we had not moved fast enough – though the pledge has now been met. But she also passionately defends Fairtrade from its external detractors because, for her, it is not a theoretical economic debate or a glib consumer gimmick. It's a way of life that has been wrestled from the teeth of hostile economic forces and powerful vested interests – part of a lifetime spent fighting for a fairer, more equal society.

'I come from a family of six children. Latino men are very macho so as the first child I was a disappointment because I wasn't a boy,' she laughs. 'But I became very close to my father.'

'When I was a child, we had a small coffee farm up in the mountains. During the civil war it became very hard for my family. All the time we feared being kidnapped or killed by the Contra guerrillas. We were in a war zone. In the end we had to leave our land and move to the town where my father started a transport business.'

After the Sandinista revolution in 1979, a fifteen-year-old Merling volunteered in the new government's nationwide literacy drive. Living with a poor farming family, she taught adults to read – people who had been denied a chance to go to school during the Somoza dynasty's thirty-three years of brutal dictatorship.

'The experience has stayed with me all my life,' she declares.

Merling also went on the yearly brigades to help bring in the coffee harvest.

'That reconnected me with the realities of the countryside and the coffee farmers,' she says.

So after doing a degree in business studies, getting married and starting a family when still young herself, she returned, training farmers to manage the coffee co-operatives as businesses. The Sandinista government set up co-operatives sharing out the land among peasant farmers from the huge estates of the Somoza clan and the handful of powerful landowners who had controlled more than half the country's farmland. The co-ops were organised to raise the income of the farmers, increase national wealth and defend against the attacks of the US-backed Contra rebels trying to reverse the revolution.

Like many young people of my generation, I was inspired by Nicaragua's struggle to build a new, fairer society and supported the Nicaragua Solidarity Campaign in Britain. I bought Campaign Coffee sourced from the co-operatives. In the US, Equal Exchange was also importing Nicaraguan coffee in defiance of the US trade embargo; the coffee was roasted in the Netherlands and so was considered to be from that country. The Reagan government threatened to close the loophole – provoking a big campaign to stop them. While this 'solidarity trade' was very small scale, it was one practical way to support Nicaraguans assailed by both the Contras and the US economic blockade.

At this time, academic and activist Robin Murray, was in charge of an economic unit at the Greater London Council (GLC). They were to try to find new solutions to tackle severe unemployment in London. As word spread about their innovative interventions in the economy, they received requests to set up trade deals from some of the new radical movements and governments, like that of Nicaragua, who were cut out of the mainstream trading system. A bewildering array of proposals whirred through the GLC fax machine – from Land Rovers for the Polisario Front in Moroccan-occupied Western Sahara to equipping a canning factory for pineapples in Vietnam. This was turned down as on closer investigation it transpired to be motivated by local political rivalries and there was a perfectly good factory already in the area! It was trade as solidarity – dubbed 'buycotts' in contrast to the highly effective boycott of South African goods organised by the Anti-Apartheid Movement. At that time, says Robin, they saw themselves as working in solidarity with governments, newly independent nation states or political movements who were would-be governments rather than with the farmers or workers directly.

With literally days to go before the GLC was abolished by the then Prime Minister Margaret Thatcher, the work was spun off into an independent group, called the Third World Information Network (TWIN). For the funds to be transferred to a new organisation in time, a 'committed young Welsh lawyer worked day and night over one weekend to find a legal framework to let us do it under the complex laws on local government,' recalls Robin.

'TWIN started sourcing gold from Nicaragua – the perfect match if you were boycotting South Africa's apartheid gold at that time,' says Robin. 'It helped that the Board of TWIN included a former metal dealer and an exiled ANC activist versed in the gold trade.'

On one occasion a consignment of gold was on its way from the mines in hills riddled by fighting, when the Contras attacked the house where the gold was being stored. They turned the place upside down, but found nothing. The next morning the gold was recovered from its hiding place – in a 'fully charged chamber pot', as Robin delicately puts it.

'Some of our other efforts were less successful – such as the hairbrushes made of cactus needles from Mexico,' laughs Robin; though they did later find a market for the cactus fibres with The Body Shop who used them in body scrubs. 'We used to hold our committee meetings in a room in London's Islington, before it was trendy, accompanied by an insistent knocking coming through the floorboards. In the storeroom below, an Eritrean political exile and carpenter employed by TWIN reassembled rocking chairs which had been shipped from Nicaragua in sections that did not quite fit together properly. It took him a year to knock them all into shape. By then, home furnishing shop Habitat had brought out a beautiful and very similar rocking chair for half the price. We couldn't compete. Another hard lesson learnt.' And, indeed, being able to produce to export quality is now embedded in the Fairtrade standards.

Back in Nicaragua, Merling had bumped into Paul Rice, a young American then working in Nicaragua, who introduced her to early ventures into Fairtrade. Paul Rice was later to become the highly entrepreneurial Chief Executive at TransFair USA, the sister organisation to the Fairtrade Foundation. Good looking in a Tom Cruise kind of way, he's also good talking; indeed our French colleagues always break into Sister Sledge's 'We Are Family' song at the mention of his name after one of his rousing speeches to the Fairtrade 'family'. Now he regularly clashes with Merling on Fairtrade policies as he wrestles with the challenges of the vast American market. 'But I still love Pablo Arroz,' laughs Merling affectionately.

'I went to Nicaragua', says Paul, 'and spent a summer working on some farms. This was in 1982, Nicaragua was in the middle of a revolution in which they were giving land to the poor, and helping poor people organise co-operatives as a way of building a community framework for development and for sustainability. I found that very exciting, so I went back after I finished college thinking I would stay in Nicaragua and work with farmers for a year, get my field experience. Instead, I stayed for eleven years and lived in Nicaragua through the Contra war and lost a lot of friends in the war. I worked with farmers and with co-ops.[1]

'It was a very exciting, but also a very difficult, time because of the war, and that led me to Nicaragua's first coffee export co-op, which I led for four years, and we started selling to Fairtrade buyers in Europe. Fairtrade had been around in Europe for a long time, and there were a few pioneering companies here in the US that had been doing Fairtrade on their own for the last twenty years, but there was no over-arching labelling initiative or certification initiative that could take that effort to scale.

'I realised that markets didn't have to be the enemy. That, in fact, markets could be an incredibly powerful force for liberating the poor and that Fairtrade was a really interesting, innovative, powerful model for approaching that. And that if I stayed in Nicaragua I could continue to impact the lives of 10,000 families, but if I came back to the States and tried to replicate what the Europeans had done with Fairtrade, and put Fairtrade on the map in a much bigger way in the United States, that maybe I could impact the lives of 10 million farmers.

'So I moved back and went to business school and got some tools and then launched TransFair a few years later.'

Meanwhile Merling helped set up PRODECOOP's first Fairtrade exports to the US, in partnership with American Fairtrade pioneer Global Exchange.

'When we started we hardly knew anything about the international coffee markets and what customers were looking for. Listen – we didn't even know how to make a good cup of coffee. Honestly – we used to drink really horrible coffee!' she laughs.

Merling goes on, 'Also we had no money.' But the Fairtrade rules say coffee importers should be prepared to pay up to 60 per cent of the contract up front. This made all the difference, she explains. They could pay their farmers the Fairtrade price as they delivered their coffee through the picking season. It would have been too expensive – impossible even – for them to borrow enough to do this. So this crucial provision in the standards really helped them get started.

'In those early days Fairtrade seemed like a light showing us a way out of our troubles,' she says.

Its mettle was tested to the full when disaster struck in 1990 as world coffee prices tumbled. Merling recounts bitterly, 'The farmers faced disaster . . . It was only where we had set up Fairtrade that we could sell our coffee for a decent income, and that is what saved our farmers.' PRODECOOP rose from this time of crisis and Merling's fierce loyalty to Fairtrade is born of all it gave her community. It also underlies why the guarantee of a fair and stable price is at the very heart of the Fairtrade system.

When a second, even deeper, slump in coffee prices hit ten years later, it was again only Fairtrade that prevented members of her co-op suffering the desperate fate of many other coffee farmers. High quality coffee that sold for $1.60 per pound in 1999 was fetching just 48 cents by February 2002 – well below what it cost the farmers to grow it, estimated at the time to be 75 cents per pound.[2] By comparison the guaranteed minimum price via Fairtrade was $1.26.

With no money coming in for their own coffee and no jobs picking it on the big plantations, three out of five families in the coffee-growing region of Matagalpa were forced to emigrate to other parts of Nicaragua or to neighbouring countries like Costa Rica to find work.[3] Nearly half the children in the Nicaraguan countryside were suffering from malnutrition, the UN's World Food Programme found at the time.[4]

In 2002 and 2003 hundreds of farmers set out on a nearly one hundred mile walk to the capital Managua, in a 'March of the Hungry'. They decamped outside the President's palace and petitioned the government for help. Nine hungry children and seven adults died on the way.[5] Bertha Salinas, two of whose children died, said: 'We have been coffee workers all our lives, and have reached a great crisis now. We are ashamed at having reached this situation. It is the first time I have been at such a low level.'

Thousands of hungry farmers flooded into makeshift roadside camps in the region in desperation and protest. The Fairtrade Foundation's tenacious press manager Eileen Maybin accompanied the BBC to Nicaragua to cover the tragedy and returned with searing stories of the human misery she witnessed.

She always remembers the family she met who were surviving just on plantains and salt while the BBC filmed moving pictures of the malnourished children – children of coffee farmers. And this at a time when the coffee multinational companies were posting record profits.

The National Assembly passed a law authorising a package of help for destitute farmers, but it was vetoed under strong external pressure from the International Monetary Fund. One of Merling's fellow managers from another Fairtrade co-op petitioned the government – and some landless workers were given land as a result and some are now proud Fairtrade farmers.

So for the farmers of PRODECOOP, Fairtrade's guarantee of a stable, decent price meant the difference between farmers being able to stay on their land, rather than having to abandon it to find work or face the poverty and degradation of unemployed migrants in roadside camps. It meant that their children could have a better life and go on to higher education. It is little wonder that people like Merling feel so deeply about Fairtrade.

The same intensity of feeling is in the air back in a packed conference hall, where Merling and I join those gathering to hear some of the founding heroes of the Fairtrade movement. Victor Perezgrovas, manager of a Mexican coffee co-operative and elected leader of the Latin American Fairtrade farmers, stands up to speak.

The hub-hub in the room dies down to an expectant hush as Victor, who is also on the FLO international Board, positions himself in front of the microphone. As is the tradition here, he starts with a courteous list of acknowledgements to hosts and guests. He celebrates the role of Latin America's peasant farmers in pioneering Fairtrade. He speaks of how Fairtrade was born here in Mexico from their yearning for justice, for a fair return from their land, a real say in their community.

Of course, Fairtrade has not been a magic wand to solve all their many problems. But today farmers from some of the poorest, most forgotten communities from Tierra del Fuego to the Rio Grande are realising their hopes for a better future through Fairtrade. What's more, they can now say they run their own businesses exporting millions of dollars worth of quality products to markets across the world. Among the farmers in the room there is immense solemn pride at what they have achieved against all the odds. I am blinking back the tears. All around me, other women do the same, while men look sombre.

By now the meeting has an air of almost religious intensity. So it's no surprise, perhaps, when Frans van der Hoff, a Dutch worker-priest from the liberation theology tradition who has lived with coffee farmers in the hills of Oaxaca for twenty-five years, takes the floor. An image of a modern St Francis of Assisi, this tall, grandfatherly figure exudes a kind, but intense, air. In fact, he's also great fun, with a wicked sense of humour. Though he's been feted for his work all over the world, including being awarded France's top medal, the Légion d'Honneur, he still lives side by side with the farmers.

One of the original architects of Fairtrade, he always tells how its rootstock is among these *campesinos* tending their coffee bushes beneath remote cloud-clad mountains.

'In the academy of the fields and with the coffee growers as teachers, I have learned a lot, more than in the different universities where I happened to have studied and taught,' he often says.[6]

He had heard the painful story of the raw deal the farmers had always had trading their coffee. For years they'd had to sell it at rock-bottom prices to the *coyotes* – the nickname used by farmers across Latin America for the sharp-dealing middlemen who prey on them like their wild dog namesakes – who'd ride up into the hills where they lived. Since they had no other buyers, no way of transporting the coffee themselves to the city of Ixtepec and little information about prices in the market, they had no choice but to sell their coffee to the *coyotes* at whatever price they offered. When better roads opened, the farmers did try selling their coffee directly to a factory in Mexico City. But they wasted many days taking their coffee to the capital, sometimes on public transport, and the farmers weren't paid until the factory had sold on their batch of coffee, often months later.

Then a group of farmers told Frans they'd had enough. They wanted to work together to try to find a better living from their coffee. In 1983 they set up a co-operative, the Union of Indigenous Communities of the Isthmus Region (UCIRI). By collecting their members' coffee together, building a processing centre and warehouse, and then selling it as a group they cut out the *coyotes* and did improve the return they got for their coffee. Also, since the farmers still largely used the methods passed down through the generations and could afford to use few chemicals anyway, they discovered they could with few adjustments become certified as organic and gain a price premium – which they also did. But the farmers' hard-won gains were being wiped out by the plummeting price of coffee on the international market. Families just didn't have enough to live on. Their children's schooling suffered as poorly paid teachers went absent for weeks. Many villages still lacked drinking water and electricity, while housing was cramped and inadequate.

So it was that, on a trip to the Netherlands in 1987 to drum up sales for their organic coffee, Frans and a group from UCIRI first discussed the idea of setting up what he calls a 'Different Market' for their coffee with Nico Roozen, the brilliant, intense, bespectacled Director of the Dutch church-based development organisation Solidaridad. Frans's vision was of a new way of trading where 'the power of the strongest does not determine the rules of the game'. Instead, 'the weakest, those who are producers and the consumers along the continuum of the market chain are essential in setting the rules'.[7] Their aim was to rewrite the normal rules of trade – and to do this by using the channels of mainstream business.

Fairtrade does not 'disrupt the normal mechanisms of the dominant market,' says Frans. 'It doesn't create artificial commercial conditions, but rather, new ones based on justice. To pay the producer the real price for producing a product is not only economically rational but is grounded in the most elementary of ethical principles.'[8]

Frans's address – sermon even – refocused my thoughts on the compelling vision at the heart of Fairtrade: consumers and producers reaching out across the world to create a better, more humane form of exchange instead of the law of the jungle that characterises much international commerce. But, as he stresses, the whole point about Fairtrade is that it's not about dreamy visions or chanting slogans about what's wrong with globalisation; it's about making practical change. It is the living alternative.

So the question facing Frans and Nico was how, or whether, they could build on the diverse ventures that had gone before – from the solidarity traders to the church stalls of fairly traded handicrafts – and turn this next vision into action. Despite the fact that some alternative shops, development charities and churches had been importing and selling coffee from groups like UCIRI to committed supporters since as far back as the 1960s, this kind of fairly traded coffee had only 0.2 per cent of the Dutch market. Over the next two years, Nico and Frans, together with church organisations, NGOs and trade unions, explored various models to overcome the main obstacle in Fairtrade coffee: that consumers needed to be able to find it easily on the high street.

To crack this problem they came up with three options: launching a totally new Fairtrade coffee brand in the mainstream market; persuading a big coffee company to buy a proportion of its blend from small farmers at a fair price; or set up an independent labelling system to guarantee the shopper in the supermarket that the producers had got a fair deal.

They looked into all the avenues. They feared that breaking through the deeply entrenched patterns of the Dutch ground-coffee market with a whole new Fairtrade coffee brand would be very risky and swallow millions in marketing. They also worried that it would make the other coffee roasters into competitors rather than potential allies. But they held on to this as a fall-back. In fact, they went as far as having packaging made, as even just a couple of months before the planned launch of the Fairtrade label, they still hadn't got commercial coffee roasters signed up.

A coalition of NGOs and churches had been campaigning since 1986 to persuade Douwe Egberts, which controls some 65 per cent of the Dutch coffee market, to source from groups like UCIRI in Mexico, as well as in Tanzania and Congo. The company and the NGOs did hold talks. But in the end, the deal foundered because the company was not prepared to source as much of its coffee on fairer terms as the groups were demanding. Douwe Egberts didn't seem to believe the Fairtrade label would persuade significant numbers of Dutch coffee drinkers to switch brands; a big miscalculation, as it turned out.

Meanwhile three medium-sized roasting companies had welcomed the principles of Fairtrade labelling, no doubt also seeing it as a chance to obtain some share of a market so dominated by Douwe Egberts. In 1988 the Max Havelaar Foundation,[9] the Dutch inspiration for the Fairtrade Foundation, launched its new Fairtrade label on three Dutch coffee brands with UCIRI's Mexican coffee.

Douwe Egberts dropped out of talks at this point, although the company did pledge to move 5 per cent of its coffee to fairer sources. Eventually, the company opted to work with two ethical assurance schemes, both of which fail to stipulate anything on the central issue of a fair price to farmers. The company still does not have any Fairtrade-certified coffee.

To the joy of Frans, Nico and the Mexican farmers the Fairtrade label was a huge hit. By the end of 1988, an astonishing 65 per cent of Dutch consumers had heard of the Max Havelaar Fairtrade label, the coffee was being stocked in major supermarkets and sales had grown to an amazing 1.7 per cent of the Dutch market within a year. Meanwhile, spurred on by the success in Holland, development agencies helped set up further Max Havelaar organisations in Belgium, France and Switzerland, which soon led the way in developing new products and showing how successful Fairtrade could be. Indeed the people of Switzerland, where the market is dominated by two powerful supermarket rivals both committed to Fairtrade, still buy far more Fairtrade products per head than any other country worldwide.

Initially, different markets had their own marks. Britain prided itself on a 1980s-style thick double F; the Danes loved their elephant; the Americans still stand by their figure with scales in front of a globe. It was Ian Bretman's vision and perseverance that steered everyone to agree on one international Mark. But only after long anguished negotiations, with tears and slammed doors as each country fought for their preferred new design or struggled to defend their old one. The Danes, in particular, were convinced that consumers wouldn't buy Fairtrade without the elephant symbol. All countries, bar the United States, have now adopted the new blue and green Mark designed for us by leading communications agency Interbrand.

The single FAIRTRADE Mark shows that a minimum set of rules have been met. And within twenty years from its launch a Fairtrade coffee system would unite over half a million coffee producers, several hundred coffee companies and many millions of consumers worldwide.

Coffee remains the single most important Fairtrade product. There are now certified farmer co-operatives in some thirty countries, with sales topping over 62,000 tonnes in 2007.[10] Fairtrade brings coffee farmers in the scheme an estimated $56 million extra a year. In fact, global Fairtrade coffee sales increased by

71 per cent in 2007.[11] In fact, global Fairtrade coffee sales increased by 53 per cent in 2006. Powering this, and key to the future, has been the runaway growth of US sales especially in the so-called 'speciality coffee' market. It's not been easy for Paul and his team, given the sheer scale of the the vast US market. So he has sought different strategies, perhaps dependent less on the grass-roots support and more on engagement with major companies like Dunkin' Donuts or Starbucks as well as the committed brands like Green Mountain Coffee.

Frans finishes his speech by saying how far we have come on Fairtrade. But, he says, it has been a long, hard journey. And he warns, too, about the threats posed by success.

'We must be wary about moving on to the main road. It may seem straight and fast – but we need to watch it does not take us away from our real destination. I will continue to take the windy, mountain road.'

His words elegantly prefigure much more hotly argued debates we are to have over the following days about the direction of Fairtrade. After the speeches the rapid passing round of a celebratory glass of tequila soon cracks the heavy mood. Everyone's laughing now and snapping their cameras. Frans van der Hoff strolls up to me, grinning. Soon we're locked in hot debate about whether or not multinationals – and especially Nestlé – should be allowed to seek Fairtrade certificates for their products, and about when the Fairtrade coffee price will be raised. As evening closes in, the debates are far from resolved but at least we understand each other better.

John Kanjagaile is a lively and young-looking fifty-three, a shrewd business brain, a quick wit and a democrat through and through. His wide cheeks are always breaking into a big smile as he plays on the meaning of words, slapping people on the back, laughing readily. But he's deeply serious about the business of change.

John is the perfect guide to how Fairtrade coffee actually moves from crop to cup. As well as working closely with the coffee farmers he farms himself. He also rubs shoulders with the traders who buy every week in Tanzania's national coffee auction – and deals directly with importers and roasters all over the world. As a member of the FLO Certification Committee, he checks through applications and inspection reports from farmers' groups wanting to join or remain on the register of Fairtrade producers. He's also used to persuading consumers and businesses to go Fairtrade.

So he knows each of the three pillars which support the Fairtrade system: the farmers' organisations and the regional organisations that represent them like the African Fairtrade Network; the international Fairtrade body FLO which sets the standards and issues certificates to producers that meet them – also providing regular checks to ensure producers and companies are abiding by the rules; and the organisations, like the Fairtrade Foundation in Britain, that issue licences to companies to use the FAIRTRADE Mark and promote the Fairtrade habit amongst the buying public.

But when I meet him he's doing his day job. He's the Export Manager for the Kagera Cooperative Union (KCU), with its 60,000 farmers in 125 local village co-operatives scattered across hilly countryside on the western shores of Lake Victoria in north-west Tanzania. John is based, not in Kagera, but in the main trading centre for the Tanzanian coffee business in Moshi near Mount Kilimanjaro.

'I am a child of the co-operative. My family are coffee farmers and KCU paid for my schooling. It's in my blood,' he tells me. John did well at school. He went on to study to be an accountant and then worked as a taxman. But he always felt the call of his community and wanted to put something back.

'I have about sixty trees. Prices fell so low, coffee became like a hobby. But I couldn't abandon my trees. I inherited them from my father and grandfather. I came to look on my trees as you go swimming or play football. One man considered cutting down his trees but his friend said, "What will you talk about with the other men?" Low prices are good for the international corporations that sell coffee, but not for us. When I sell Fairtrade I get three times as much as I would normally – so I can send three children to school instead of one.'

In 1986 he resigned from his government job and joined the co-operative because 'it's doing the right thing for the people of Kagera region'. He's worked his way up to become the Export Manager – employed by the farmers through the co-operative to find buyers for their coffee abroad and a better income from their coffee.

Many of the farmers in Kagera are very poor – with just an acre or two of dry land to provide the food and income for a whole family. When they first talked to farmers about Fairtrade, they met some sceptical responses.

'Why would anyone want to pay *more* than they have to for our coffee?' they would ask him, convinced there must be a catch.

Once KCU members decided to apply for a Fairtrade certificate by signing up to the international Fairtrade standards, there was lots of work to do with farmers and the village co-ops to help them understand and implement the standards.

Farmers are ready to change the way they do things when they see that it brings benefits for them in the long run, John tells me. It's vital everyone in the system keeps to the standards, and that we can track every bean of Fairtrade coffee from the farmers through traders to the pack of coffee on the shelf or cup of coffee in the café. It's this tough system of clear standards, audits, certificates and tracking through the whole supply chain which means consumers can trust what it says on the tin – that the producers are guaranteed a better deal. Or so they can, as John puts it, 'tell a lion from a leopard', conjuring up an image of the consumer stalking the aisles of the supermarket jungle to pounce on the FAIRTRADE Mark.

The Fairtrade system is demanding and independently monitored, 'It's hard, long-term work to achieve those shared goals of raising social and environmental conditions. But we also have to go at a pace that's realistic for poor farmers.'

He says that people in consuming countries need to understand that farmers, who may be struggling to provide food and income for a family off a couple of acres, need support and information to understand and implement the Fairtrade standards. Sometimes a producer group does need to be 'decertified', which means they can no longer sell as Fairtrade, but he feels this means the FLO system has failed in its job to help support that group meet the standards.

'When we first started, we went round all the village-level co-operatives to see how they were collecting their coffee. We found some were collecting coffee from farmers who were not members. Farmers said they didn't know they had to be registered. We explained everyone had to be properly registered so that we could know all our coffee was grown meeting the standards, and so everyone who actually grew the coffee gets the benefits. So people started to understand.'

John explains how KCU works at a regional level so that each co-operative has the systems in place to meet Fairtrade standards and to ensure that farmers get all the benefits they should. The key point, he stresses, is that all this happens within the democratic, accountable structures of the co-operative. So the main mechanisms for running Fairtrade day-to-day are controlled by the farmers themselves. The audits and annual inspections from FLO act as external checks, and they ensure the system is implemented consistently across all the countries, he says. It's a rigorous system and at KCU they make sure they can account for everything when the inspector calls.

FLO works with a network of around 100 local inspectors across the world who visit producer groups once a year to check that standards are being met. For example, they check that the group have indeed decided democratically how to spend the premium of 10 cents per pound of coffee.

The system aims to tackle the poverty and social injustice at the core of international trade. People sometimes confuse Fairtrade labelling with the various schemes that ensure the goods you buy are made in a way that is 'exploitation-free' with no forced labour, or doesn't damage the environment. Fairtrade does do these things, but it is much more ambitious too. It aims to tackle the causes of the poverty and powerlessness that often lie behind why people and the environment are being exploited in the first place. People, for example, cut down forests because they are desperate for land to grow food; or take badly paid, dangerous jobs because they need to earn money. The core of the Fairtrade labelling system is about ensuring that traders give producers a fair deal, and that the farmers and workers are democratically organised so they can improve their position as the increased resources flow in. So if a group is Fairtrade certified, it doesn't mean everything is perfect. But it does mean that the foundations on which to build are in place.

Fairtrade takes the rules of the marketplace and turns them on their head:

- Where the market has a bias towards big-scale farmers, Fairtrade explicitly favours the smallholder. Indeed, in most products such as coffee, rice, sugar, cocoa, cotton, spices, honey – only smallholders can sell as Fairtrade.
- Where the market looks always for the cheapest price, Fairtrade sets a minimum price plus premium, to enable farmers to cover their costs sustainably and invest in a better future.
- Where the market puts profits first and ignores the social and environmental costs of trade, Fairtrade rules put social and environmental progress first and foremost.
- While the market takes power away from consumers and producers because power is with global companies and their shareholders, Fairtrade puts the public and growers centre-stage and empowers them, ensuring they gain more knowledge and information.

And yet, despite turning the market upside down, Fairtrade works in the market. It has to. There is no other option to hand today. So it's no wonder that it's a difficult balancing act.

This is how it works in practice. The international network of Fairtrade groups from consumer countries and producer organisations, FLO, sets standards for producers and traders through a process of research combined with consultation with each party such as producers, importers and civil society. Some of these apply to trade in all products while others apply to particular products.

The Fairtrade guaranteed price for bananas is, of course, different from that for coffee. (And the detailed standards for all the products are there for anyone to read on the FLO website.)

Some of the standards are known as 'minimum requirements', which everyone must meet to join the system. But, because the aim of Fairtrade is to help disadvantaged producers improve their lives over time, there are also 'progress requirements', which set out a plan of action for producers to reach goals in the future.

There are standards for smallholder groups, who dominate Fairtrade. But there are specially designed standards for workers on plantations in products, like tea or fresh fruit, ensuring they are free to join a trade union and organised to decide on the use of the premium.

Both smallholders and plantations have to meet environmental standards. About one-third of groups are also certified organic, and Fairtrade standards encourage them to work towards that. But for others, the standards outlaw the use of the internationally recognised most harmful pesticides, and say safeguards must be in place to prevent soil erosion, manage waste and protect natural ecosystems, while setting out joint plans to move to the use of organic fertilisers and natural pest management.

FLO then inspects producer groups that want to join the scheme to see whether they meet the standards and issues them a certificate if they do. Every year, FLO checks they are still keeping to the standards.

At the heart of the system is the pledge to pay producers a decent price for what they grow – uniquely among the growing plethora of ethical labels and claims we see on packets in our supermarkets. The prices are calculated to cover the costs of growing the product sustainably and earning a basic livelihood, which is worked out for each product and sometimes for each region. And FLO checks traders really are paying the set prices.

Farmers often tell me that the predictability the minimum price gives them to plan and invest in the future is one of the features they most value. But because Fairtrade is also about giving people the opportunity to better themselves and their communities, the standards also stipulate a premium that importers must pay on top. If the market price goes higher than the minimum price, the farmers get the market price plus the premium. So they always get more income with Fairtrade.

It's a complex and rigorous system. The Mark is like a simple clock face that tells us the time at a glance; but behind it are detailed workings that we can rely on to make it accurate. But you can be sure the watchmakers are in constant dialogue to get the balance right: are the environmental standards too high for poor farmers or too low for rising consumer expectations? Are we too much like policemen or not strict enough? Should we insist workers are members of a union to empower them or is that forcing what should be a free decision? Should we push standards higher or will companies all abandon Fairtrade if we do? The debates are hard fought but, critically, with the farmers' representatives part of the final decisions.

I first met John in Moshi in 2002 for a meeting of representatives from Fairtrade farmer groups to set up a network of producers 'to wake each other up more to expand Fairtrade in Africa', as John puts it. I was invited to explain our role in promoting Fairtrade in Britain, and I was to report back to the Department for International Development who were funding the initiative.

Once the talking was over, the group were going to visit the farmers who are members of a Fairtrade coffee co-operative, led by Raymond Kimaro. Our packed white minibus bounces along sending another covering of red dust over the intense greenness on each side. Sweet potato and yam vines rambling across the ground, cassava leaves waving like stick-puppet hands above their long woody stems, people-high blocks of maize topped with drooping feathery flowers – all are tinged with the red covering.

A small boy in a ragged, grubby T-shirt and shorts with holes tending goats on the verge waves energetically, grins and calls out to the group with the ubiquitous Swahili term used for white travellers, 'Mzungu! Mzungu! How are you? I'm fine!'

The driver veers suddenly, but skilfully, to the side to avoid a vast water-filled pothole which seems like it could almost swallow us up whole. I smile back and wave. The boy dissolves into giggles.

Mount Kilimanjaro looms over – as if keeping an occasional, but watchful, eye on our approach into its foothills. It's stunningly beautiful. No wonder a recent new venture of this co-op has been into ecotourism – giving visitors the chance of staying up in the hills and seeing how Fairtrade works first-hand, while also visiting the local sites and perhaps going to the top of the mountain itself.

Sitting next to me is the bespectacled Tadesse Meskela, from the Oromia Coffee Farmers Co-operative Union in Ethiopia. He is keen to compare notes with Tanzanian farmers here in KNCU, the Kilimanjaro Native Co-operative Union. It is not only Africa's oldest coffee co-op founded in 1924 (hence its colonial-era name), but also one of the first to export Fairtrade coffee from the continent. There is a hint of friendly rivalry too. The rich volcanic soils here produce coffees ranked among Africa's finest – including the rich and mellow Peaberry, legendary with coffee buffs. As Tadesse explains, his co-op also produces some highly prized coffee. He talks in the luxurious language of the professional coffee taster – 'our silky Harar with its strong blueberry finish'. His poetic descriptions and his passion for the farmers' craftsmanship and care summon up intoxicating tastes.

The minibus pulls up a steep track before it comes to a stop in a small group of houses. A delegation of local farmers is waiting to meet us. We unbundle ourselves into the warm steamy mountain air. Soon we're exchanging greetings and shaking hands with the farmers who are proud to show their fellow East African farmers what they are achieving and keen to share problems. They lead us to some school benches arranged under the trees.

The chairman explains how he and his fellow committee members are elected by the other farmers who are members in the village. Such farmer groups show that by coming together, they have strength in numbers and can pool resources for everything from processing to transporting their crop. The group doesn't have to be a co-operative (though often is) and can take a range of forms to be part of Fairtrade – but it must be democratically controlled by its farmer members.

A representative from the Gumutindo Fairtrade coffee group, on the slopes of another great peak, Mount Elgon, across the border in Uganda, bluntly expresses his shock that most of the farmers here are old.

'Where are the young people? Who will be your future?' he demands.

One man responds through a toothless mouth, shaking his head with concern, 'Ach, those fellows. They have all left this place. They say to us: "Who can live off coffee now? It is finished." They've gone to Dar es Salaam. They do whatever work they can.

'Two of my sons have gone. I say to them: "But you are coffee farmers. Who is going to tend my trees when I have gone?"'

That's why everyone is so determined to increase sales of Fairtrade goods. As John Kanjagaile says: 'Now the question the farmers ask me most is why can't we sell more of our coffee at the Fairtrade price? It's hard for them to understand that it all depends on people in faraway countries buying more Fairtrade coffee. I try to explain about all the work the Fairtrade organisations there do to persuade more people to buy Fairtrade. But all they see is that still only 15 per cent of what they grow can be sold at the Fairtrade price – even if it's up from 5 per cent a few years back.'

But John also worries about future threats to Fairtrade. 'Now that Fairtrade is growing, the big roasters want to start getting back part of the pie we've taken, by trying to get in on the Fairtrade market,' John warns. 'That's why you're seeing all these other labels growing and the big companies coming in to adopt them – Utz Kapeh, Rainforest Alliance, the Common Code for the Coffee Community and what have you. No doubt there will be others in future. But none of them offer the guaranteed price to the farmer, none of them give democratic control to the farmer, as the FAIRTRADE Mark does. If they really want to trade fairly with the farmers, why don't they adopt the Mark?

'These other labels may cause confusion in the market,' he worries, passing his hand over his head. 'The customer could get overwhelmed by them all and not know which really delivers fair, sustainable coffee. I worry the public could just end up giving up. That's why it's so important that we have one open and rigorous system. If people really want to help, then they should buy Fairtrade.'

After the discussion under the trees the farmers show us some of their *shambas* – the Swahili word used all over East Africa for the smallholdings that are still the livelihood for the majority of the people. I see one or two acres, spreading up and down the hillside around their home. Nearer the house, on flatter ground, they grow a range of food crops for the family – beans, maize, yams, cooking bananas, vegetables. As we thread our way along a winding path down the hill, there are coffee bushes shaded by banana trees, and sometimes lower-growing crops like beans underneath.

The farmer tells us, 'You pick only when the cherries have reached the best flavour. We come back to pick each bush throughout the season.'

These little red coffee cherries glistening in bunches up the stem in the dappled, powerful sun below Africa's highest mountain will trace an incredible journey passing through different hands until they reach the pack of Fairtrade coffee I buy in my local shop in South London. It is via this chain, with all its boring paperwork and checks along the way, through which the original vision of consumers and producers uniting for a better kind of trade is made real. I am reminded of what Sanou Alhassane, from a Fairtrade mango growers co-operative in Burkina Faso, said: 'That our mangoes make the journey to Europe, in competition with fruit from huge plantations in economically stronger countries, is a triumph of organisation and humanity.'

This extraordinary journey starts when these farmers pick their coffee cherries and bring them into the room used by the village co-operative for weighing, registering and storing. Here their membership is checked to be sure the coffee they are delivering is theirs and that they are part of the wider co-operative union. They remove the skin and pulp of the coffee cherries to get at the beans we'd start to recognise as coffee. It's an involved process. They soak the coffee cherries in water for several days until they start to ferment, dropping to the bottom of the tank as the husk softens. They then wind the cherries through the village de-pulping machine – which looks a bit like a large old-fashioned meat mincer – with the red blood of cherry husks and water spilling out as the hard beans covered in a mucus-like layer are collected in a battered tin underneath.

Eventually the farmers spread the beans out on long table-like racks to dry in the sun, turning them regularly to prevent them going mouldy or fermenting and so ruining the taste. Once dry, the coffee is put into bags, each one numbered and marked to ensure traceability, and taken to the central co-operative warehouse in Moshi. We followed the same bumpy route down from the hills as the coffee at the end of our visit.

First thing the next morning I make my way through the already busy centre of Moshi. I pass a group of noisy touts for some *dala-dalas*, shared taxis, with slogans painted across the back like, 'such is life'. A man passes me on a bicycle with five enormous stalks of bananas secured precariously with strips of old tyre inner tubes. On a bench under a tin roof veranda, a man is eating an impressively large plate of ugali for so early in the morning – the staple stiff maize porridge, with a soupy-looking sauce to dip it in. A woman wrapped in a colourfully printed kanga cloth on another table has a plate of enticing sugary mandazi doughnuts and a cup of tea.

John meets me in his office on the fifth floor of the nondescript 1960s concrete block in which most of Tanzania's coffee is bought and sold. It is no exaggeration to say that the fate of this nation hangs on these sales. Coffee is Tanzania's biggest export on which depend the livelihood of over 2 million farmers and their families. John's room is modest, but it's immensely significant that coffee farmers' have their own representatives where the traders do business.

'In fact, we call it the "Fairtrade Office" – we wouldn't have been here without Fairtrade,' he laughs, before paying tribute to the support he has received over the years from TWIN and Cafédirect.

'Back then we were not exporting ourselves. Then exporting coffee was like a dream. How can a farmer export coffee? He only sells to the auction. It was very difficult at first. When we first started exporting our own coffee directly with Fairtrade in 1990, the other big traders thought it was a joke. They thought we were crazy. They predicted the whole Fairtrade thing would be dead within a year or two. But as we started exporting – first, one container, then two, then five, then ten – they had to change their tune.'

Shaking his head, John remembers the excitement when they sent off their first container of coffee in a ship from Dar es Salaam in 1990. It arrived in Rotterdam and the shipper sent the shipment documents back to KCU's head office in Bukoba to confirm shipment. But the people there had no experience of dealing with shipping, and didn't know they needed to dispatch the documents to the importer so that he could collect coffee from the port.

'They put the papers in a drawer! None of us knew where they had got to for about a month,' John says with an embarrassed laugh. 'With a normal commercial importer we would have incurred penalties, but our Fairtrade importer understood and helped us to sort out the problem. Bit by bit we learned how exporting works, so that now we can confidently do business with conventional companies as well as Fairtrade.'

They're still only selling 15 per cent of their crop as Fairtrade. The rest is sold at whatever the prevailing market price is at the coffee auction destined for all that non-Fairtrade coffee in our shops.

'Of course, we'd like to sell more. But even that small proportion makes a big, big difference, and we share out the benefits equally among our members. It even helps us get a good price for the rest of our coffee,' he says.

The auction takes place every Thursday in a wood-panelled auction room with the auctioneer on a podium in front of chairs in rows where traders come in to bid for the different lots. They have expertly assessed the look and smell of this week's samples of green unroasted coffee lined up on tables at the edge of the room. They know what they are looking for, often taking orders from the big importers for different types of coffee to make up different blends.

Although you can nowadays export direct, John opts to put all their coffee through the auction, even when he has pre-agreed contracts with Fairtrade importers. It's confusing but John is reluctant to explain.

'I'm not sure I should reveal my business secrets ...' he chortles.

By putting all their coffee into the auction and buying back the containers needed for their Fairtrade clients, he can raise the going price in the auction and so the overall price commercial traders will pay for their coffee. It's a neat turning of the tables.

'When we start buying like that in the auction, other traders start to worry that maybe the whole consignment of twenty containers will be bought up, so they bid for them. That way we can push up the price a bit for our non-Fairtrade containers. As a result the rest of our coffee gets a better price – I reckon on average about $3 per 50-kilogram bag, which makes quite a difference to the farmers.'

He can only do this because of the certainty of the prices and orders KCU gets for its Fairtrade coffee. Also if prices are very low for a few weeks, he can hold back from selling in the auction as he has the steady stream of the Fairtrade sales to keep income coming in until prices pick up a bit.

As John says, 'We sell a small percentage of our coffee as Fairtrade but the benefits are much, much wider. Now we know how to export. We know people in Europe who give us information on the markets and I can meet importers in Europe and find new places to sell our coffee. Before we didn't know the language of futures or markets – now that is also our language and we can impart a bit of that to the farmers.

'The farmers simply used to sell their coffee to passing middlemen. They had no idea what happened to the beans or that a price set in London affected what they got paid here. Now when I go out around Kagera, they call out to me: "John, John, what's the price of coffee in London today?"'

The KCU farmers are exploring other ways of earning more, for example the co-operative is helping some farmers meet official organic standards – so earning a further price premium. Fourteen local societies have made the switch and others are planned.

'I couldn't believe it when we started selling Fairtrade organic coffee to New Zealand; I didn't even know where it was on the map!' John beams.

The farmers have also used a portion of its Fairtrade premium each year to buy a growing stake in an instant coffee factory, built back in 1960s in Kagera's main town, Bukoba. After fourteen years of buying into it, in 2004 KCU became the majority shareholder.

They're now able to process some of the farmers' coffee into instant coffee – so further increasing the income they can earn from their coffee.

Sales are not huge and more needs to be done to refurbish the factory's equipment. But, says John, they are selling instant Fairtrade coffee to countries like Belgium, New Zealand and Switzerland, with most of it going into African markets – especially over the border in Kenya. He also has a vision of expanding local sales of instant coffee.

'Even the tiniest village shop in the rural areas of Tanzania sells small packets of Tanzanian tea – along with other basics like soap, washing powder, lamp oil and cooking oil. So, why not our instant coffee too? We believe there's a sleeping market there. We want to be the ones to wake it up!'

The aim is to widen the co-operatives' sources of income and cut their dependence on exports. But it's always difficult for the groups to decide how to spend the premium with many competing demands, some urgent, some long-term.

In 2004 the co-op's General Assembly decided to allocate $2,000 of the Fairtrade premium to each local village society to spend on local projects. The money was spent on everything from fixing a broken bridge to setting up a village store so people didn't have to walk miles to buy soap or sugar. But, as is so often the case, many villages decided to spend the money on giving their children the best start in life they could: down-at-heel classrooms were renovated, new blackboards, schoolbooks and equipment were bought.

From Moshi and the auction the KCU coffee is loaded on to lorries and driven across Tanzania to the ports at Dar es Salaam or Tanga. There is another quality check before it is loaded on to the boat. As the co-ops have learned, that way if it is damaged in transit then it is the shipper, not the producers, who must pay. Then in great containers, the coffee makes its way to destinations across the world.

In this case the containers are destined for Britain. They make their way up the coast of East Africa through the Red Sea and Suez Canal and into the Mediterranean. After entering the Atlantic

Ocean and finally the English Channel, they arrive at the docks at Tilbury, on the Thames estuary.

Back in London, over recent months, the Fairtrade Foundation's man in charge of hot drinks, Richard Anstead, has been working with Greggs who run a chain of over 1,000 bakery shops across Britain serving 4 million customers a week. Following a successful move into Fairtrade juices, they have decided to switch all their coffee and tea to Fairtrade too. They have been seeking a company to supply the kind of coffee they want. In the end they decide to work in partnership with a UK roasting company, Gala, to select a blend of Fairtrade beans, roast and pack them for distribution to the bakeries. KCU's robusta beans have been chosen to go into the blend, along with a range of Fairtrade beans from other countries.

Gala then liaised with Richard about getting a licence to use the Mark on the coffee. Gala have to map out for him the whole chain: working back from their own roaster detailing who imports the green beans, who has exported them and confirming the producers' details. They do this for each origin of bean in the blend. In this case KCU arranges its own exports, but other Fairtrade producers may export through another company. Every company that takes legal ownership of the coffee must register with FLO and agree to meet the set Fairtrade standards. These focus on buying as directly as possible from certified Fairtrade producer groups; paying the Fairtrade price; offering pre-financing; keeping Fairtrade products separate from other ones in their factories or warehouses, and opening their books to audits so we can check that no company is cheating the producers or the consumers.

We are not claiming that all companies offering Fairtrade products are angels. In fact we assume none of them are – hence all our checking. Indeed, the Fairtrade Foundation never certifies or in any way judges the whole company, who may have thousands of other products in their range which are not Fairtrade (yet!). We do not monitor conditions on the boats or the factories and shops in the UK – those tasks best lie with the trade unions and government here. But we check that if a company has the

Mark on a product that they have met all the Fairtrade standards behind that product.

As Sophi Tranchell of Divine chocolate once remarked ruefully to me, 'I wish people knew how hard we have to work to have the Mark on our chocolate.'

Companies like hers, using many different ingredients like milk which can never be Fairtrade, also have to submit their recipes – all in total confidence of course. Multi-ingredient products such as biscuits, cakes or snack-bars have to contain Fairtrade ingredients whenever possible, so the sugar or cocoa or vanilla have to be Fairtrade but obviously the butter or eggs do not. There are rules about the percentage that must be Fairtrade for the Mark to appear on the wrapping. The aim as always is to maximise opportunities for producer sales, while maintaining public trust. But most products are straight-forward: if it's coffee or tea, it must be 100 per cent Fairtrade.

Richard explains: 'Whatever route it takes once it arrives here in Britain, it's our job to take over tracking the Fairtrade coffee. Once we are sure of the whole supply chain, we can give the company a licence to use the Mark on that product. The company, like Gala in this case, then has to report four times a year how much coffee they bought and sold.'

For example, coffee beans may lose up to a fifth of their weight as moisture is driven out during roasting. Some may be wasted in the factory. All this needs to be reported, so we can be sure that companies are not selling more to the public as Fairtrade than they have bought from the farmers.

To be doubly sure, the Foundation employ an independent auditor to check through the companies' books. It may not be the cutting edge of glamour and passion, but the rigour of our checks is vital to ensure that companies are holding true to the promise that the FAIRTRADE Mark makes to producers and consumers.

In fact the importer of KCU coffee is our old friend TWIN. From those early days of solidarity coffee, TWIN now provides a highly professional service transporting coffee for companies like Cafédirect or Gala. Once off the docks at Tilbury, our KCU coffee heads to Gala's coffee-roasting factory in Kent. It is here that after, yes, yet more checks, KCU's beans will be blended with other Fairtrade coffee and roasted in huge drums. Expert tasters sample the coffee in an elaborate dance akin to wine tasting with much sniffing and swirling, gargling and choosing, to get that perfect-tasting coffee for you and me to enjoy.

When Guillermo Vargas of the Coocafé coffee co-operative toured Britain in 2002, he said, 'When I think of Fairtrade, I think fair for the producer and fair for the consumer. To my mind, the two main players involved in trade are the producer and the consumer.' He's so right. The FAIRTRADE Mark, and the certification system behind it, are, in the end, just a tool through which the citizens' movement of growers and consumers can create change.

As Merling puts it, 'The Fairtrade guarantee is a commitment both ways. Consumers create a change to improve the lives of producers and their families, and producers commit to offering a responsible, sustainable product. The standards are our values; they show we're doing things correctly.

'But I cannot see Fairtrade just as this little grain of sand we each contribute; it's about the global context of smallholders being involved in an alternative model of trade. It cannot be the only model because we'd have to change completely the whole world to achieve that! But it is a working alternative.'

5
Many Raindrops Make Mighty Rivers

I'm an eternal optimist. But even as an idealistic young protestor standing beneath the imposing symbol of the apartheid regime in the heart of London, South Africa House in Trafalgar Square, I never, ever imagined being welcomed through its doors by a smiling, dignified, black woman High Commissioner.

As a student in the 1980s, I joined marches against the remorseless repression of black South Africans. While support for the Anti-Apartheid Movement was swelling our then Prime Minister branded Nelson Mandela a 'terrorist' and led a government adamantly opposed to applying pressure to end apartheid via sanctions. I remember shaking with rage as family friends argued that without the whites in charge, the country and the economy would collapse. Much of the international business community profited from propping up apartheid –

until international public pressure through consumer boycotts started to hit their profits.

Back then, when we watched on television as police tear-gassed and shot at crowds in the black townships, change seemed remote. Yet it was not. People often talk about the 'miracle' of the birth of the new South Africa – rightly in many ways. But this can slip into a sentimental notion that somehow change just 'happened'. In fact, it was only won through the long struggle and courageous sacrifice of the freedom movement's members, including Nelson Mandela's twenty-seven years in gaol. The ending of apartheid gave a generation hope. So our calls for an end to unfair trade, which may seem a distant dream, can be realised if we take action.

Here I was in 2003, cycling into the square in the early evening darkness of winter and seeing that same 1930s edifice, but with the flag of the new South Africa fluttering free in the floodlights; then entering under the statue of a golden-winged springbok and being guided into a grand wood-panelled room where the reception was taking place. I passed solemn, garish murals depicting the benevolent history of 'white civilisation' in this southernmost tip of Africa. One showed a grateful African offering up the fruits of the land to a group of early Cape colonists in wide-brimmed Dutch hats. How bizarre they seemed in a building now presided over by former ANC activist and academic Lindiwe Mabuza the High Commissioner. Or maybe they were an appropriate reminder of centuries of unfair control of the world's riches by its white minority.

We were celebrating one small reversal of this history: the arrival of the first products from Fairtrade-certified, black economic empowerment farms. In delicious irony, apples, oranges, grapes and wine, which once topped the boycotters' lists, were the first Fairtrade goods.

The High Commissioner welcomed the audience of farm workers from South Africa, huddled in their shiny new fleeces, importers, Oxfam campaigners and wine buffs. She was preparing to celebrate a decade since the birth of a free, non-racial South Africa in 1994. She talked proudly of the country's enormous achievements but stressed the huge way still to go, including the need for a fairer trade deal with Europe and measures to ensure trade benefited the poor, non-white majority. The challenges were now to develop the economy, provide jobs for the workless millions, generate the resources to pay for rebuilding, and redistribute economic power – the next steps in what Nelson Mandela calls the country's 'long walk to freedom' – including, as defined by him, freedom from poverty.

By coincidence, Fairtrade in Britain shares its year of birth with the new South Africa. And in a way we are grappling with similar issues: how to challenge, and then steer, the muscle of business towards empowering the economically weakest; how to build viable new ways of doing business to redress the huge inequalities in the globalised world economy; how to convert the power of consumers in rich countries into positive change for poor producers. In a very different context, we too are opening the way for new partnerships, between producers and companies, so that companies move from having a little bit of Fairtrade to making it part of the way they do business, ready to stick by growers when the going gets tough. And, interestingly, the development of Fairtrade in South Africa opens many windows on to how the landscape of Fairtrade may look in years to come.

If I were ever asked to put together a reading list for Fairtrade enthusiasts, at the top would be Steinbeck's 1939 classic *The Grapes of Wrath*. Although portraying the economic crisis that devastated US farmers, it could be a portrait of the crisis wrecking millions of farmers' lives in the developing world today. From his hawk-eye perspective, before swooping in on one family, Steinbeck depicts millions of smallholders driven off their land by the anonymous forces of 'The Bank', 'The Tractor', 'The Company' who turn farming into an industry with fewer and fewer owners, and workers left with 'a hunger in a stomach, a hunger in a single soul, multiplied a million times, muscles and mind aching to grow, to work, to create'. They are forced to travel far in the desperate hope of work picking cotton or grapes under any conditions and victimised for trying to organise into unions.

And yet, and yet, the resilience of the human spirit keeps breaking through. For man, Steinbeck writes: 'grows beyond his work, walks up the stairs of his concepts, emerges ahead of his accomplishments. This you may say of man – when theories change and crash, when schools, philosophies, when narrow dark alleys of thought, national, religious, economic, grow and disintegrate, man reaches, stumbles forward, painfully, mistakenly sometimes. Having stepped forward, he may slip back, but only half a step, never the full step back.'

I often think of those words as I agonise for the millionth time about whether we have got it right in Fairtrade. For surely we will slip back many times; as we stick our head higher above the parapet, companies will criticise and undermine Fairtrade subtly and openly, the press will slam us and problems will explode around us. But I am convinced that having, as Steinbeck puts it, walked up the stairs of the concept, we can never go back to a time when the public never thought about people who grew their fruit or rice, while companies and retailers played blind to the condition of producers in developing countries.

The Grapes of Wrath was playing in my head, as we entered the room to see a table overflowing with luscious green Fairtrade grapes and oranges – all bearing the FAIRTRADE Mark and the new brand, Thandi, meaning 'we bring love' in Xhosa. The fruits brought Fairtrade together with the South African government's programmes for black economic empowerment and land reform.

The grapes came from the 270 hectare Keboes farm on the banks of the Orange River in a remote area near South Africa's northern border with Namibia. Here the irrigated, bright green vineyards contrast with the rocky, desert-like land around them. It boasts one of the biggest, most modern packing sheds in the world, producing half a million cartons of high-quality seedless grapes during the early part of the European winter season and employing more than 1,000 people in the peak season.[1]

It's perhaps not everyone's image of Fairtrade. And indeed the bulk of Fairtrade produce is grown by small farmers who are the heart of the system. In most products such as nuts, coffee, cotton, cocoa, sugar, rice, spices, only organised smallholders can enter Fairtrade because there are millions of small farmers dependent on growing those products who need Fairtrade just to stay in the market and on their land. But in some products the most disadvantaged are landless people working on plantations – and they too need the benefits Fairtrade can bring. Furthermore, produce from such estates is needed to support smallholders' sales – for example to get the correct blends of tea. That's why, right from the early days, Fairtrade standards were developed for workers on plantations in some products such as fresh fruit, bananas, tea – and later wine and flowers.

These rules spring from the same core Fairtrade principles but are adapted to ensure the benefits of Fairtrade flow to the workers, rather than the owners, of the plantation. So, for example, the rules dictate that the Fairtrade premium is managed by an elected committee of workers. The standards incorporate the core International Labour Organisation (ILO) conventions on freedom of labour, freedom from discrimination and freedom of association and collective bargaining – and so insist workers' rights must be protected and that they are free to organise into independent trade unions.

So when estates convert to Fairtrade, they often have to take major steps to improve workers' conditions, such as offering better maternity pay. The workers also gain from the premium funds. The banana workers on the VREL plantation in Ghana, for example, bought a bicycle each out of the premium so they could get home quicker at the end of the day. But Fairtrade has also given workers a voice by strengthening the role of trade unions, sometimes on estates where no unions existed before. For example, the General Agricultural Workers Union (GAWU) in Ghana organised workers on a pineapple plantation applying for a Fairtrade certificate and negotiated a collective bargaining agreement – as also happened on flower farms in Kenya.

Interestingly that has spread back home too. Paul Kenny is General Secretary of the GMB trade union in Britain. He says, 'There are moral reasons why unions should support Fairtrade.

But there are also direct benefits to the movement here of standing beside people in developing countries. We first got involved in solidarity with banana workers in Costa Rica; now, thanks to that link, we've just recruited 150 union members at the ripening factory here in the UK so now both ends of the chain are organised. We have everything to gain from supporting Fairtrade and nothing to lose except poverty.'

Sivapackiam is a slight woman, but packs a punch on her tea plantation in Sri Lanka which sells Fairtrade tea to Clipper. When I first met her in 2001, she was at a meeting in a lovely Raj-style hotel in the hills where for the first time ever, workers, trade union officials, smallholders, estate managers and owners were all eating and staying together, debating how to build Fairtrade in Sri Lanka. Sivapackiam, together with shop stewards, sits on the joint body which has set up a revolving loan fund for the workers so they can borrow money at low interest. She still surprises herself: 'I used to be so afraid of the manager I would jump into the bushes when I saw him coming down the path. Now I am sitting round the table arguing with him.'

So for her Fairtrade was making a difference. But standards must adapt and improve in the light of experience. Certainly, no one in Fairtrade believes we have yet found the perfect answer to empowering workers on plantations. That is why we are constantly seeking to improve our work with trade unions and find new solutions.

For smallholder producers in South Africa, for example, of rooibos tea and raisins, the standards worked. But they believed that Fairtrade on large farms in South Africa should, and could, be pushed beyond the international standards.

Under apartheid, whites owned over 80 per cent of the land, generations of black and mixed-race 'coloured' workers have picked fruit for low wages and it is not changing fast. One 1994 study found that in Western Cape Province, the heartland of the wine industry, white people had living standards on a par with the five most developed nations in the world, while living conditions for black and coloured people in rural areas, many of them farm workers, were 'comparable to the worst in the world'.[2] In the vineyards, under the notorious 'dop' system, workers were given regular cheap wine instead of pay. Though officially banned in the 1920s, the system went on until the end of apartheid. Widespread alcoholism, and the highest levels of foetal alcohol syndrome in the world, leave children with stunted growth, facial deformities and impaired mental abilities.[3]

The question for the new South Africa was how to redress these legacies of apartheid – and for us, in Fairtrade, how we could best support change. The new government brought in laws to improve workers' rights, set a target that 30 per cent of white-held land should be transferred to black people and initiated programmes to promote the transfer of business control to the black majority. The idea was that black people should not just get better pay and conditions – important as that is – but should also get a fairer share of the country's economy. So the South African activists argued that Fairtrade had to support such initiatives and should only certify farms that are giving workers a significant stake (at least a quarter) in the ownership of the farm as a whole.

On the Keboes grape farm, the 300 permanent workers used government black economic empowerment and land reform grants to buy a quarter of the shares in the farm through a workers' trust, giving them a powerful stake in the running and profits of the enterprise – including setting workers' wages. The original company retains a 50 per cent share – and a contract to provide management services for the first eight years – and the remaining shares are owned by black empowerment bodies. A programme ensures the gradual transfer of skills, knowledge and responsibilities to the workers. Production manager Sammy Maasdorp, whose family have worked on Karsten Farms for years, is now responsible for sixteen hectares of vineyard.

He says, 'The fact that we are co-owners inspires us all and we know that everyone's contribution is important to be successful.'[4] In fact research on black empowerment farms shows the motivation of sharing in the decision making and profits has seen output per worker increasing by nearly a third.[5]

Undoubtedly the approach has its flaws and its critics, and the particular model depends on a government prepared to put resources and laws behind increasing workers' ownership. However, the concept of Fairtrade rules insisting on a gradual sharing of ownership and transfer of skills is a powerful one that I believe could be explored as one means to strengthen Fairtrade's engagement with plantation workers in other parts of the world.

Back at South Africa House, the High Commissioner reads out a message sent from Nelson Mandela appealing for shoppers to buy the new Fairtrade products from South Africa: 'Support for Thandi will help create a whole new generation of proud and committed fruit entrepreneurs, which will ensure that retailers and consumers have access to the finest fruit in the world.' Since then, Thandi sales have been growing and the Thandi Chardonnay 2003 won a Gold Medal at the London Wine Challenge.

No one's personal history can better tell the story of Fairtrade in South Africa than Maria Malan from the Stellar Organics vineyard, based on the Olifants River 275 kilometres north of Cape Town, where the workers now own a quarter of the business. A bundle of energy, she's been to Britain several times to promote their wine, sometimes teaming up with celebrity wine critic and Fairtrade enthusiast Oz Clark for some irresistible wine tastings where she tells how she rose to become Farm Manager, an unthinkable position for a coloured woman in the old days.

'I started as a domestic worker for the Rossouw family in 1976 and gradually began helping out in the farm lands with vegetables as a general labourer,' she recalls.[6] It took no time for the vineyard's owners to see her leadership qualities. She attended her first basic supervisors' course in 1982 and has never looked back. In 1990 she graduated to working with table grapes.

'It was hard work and a lot more serious. Table grapes are "vol fiemies" [meaning 'capricious' in her native Afrikaans]. This is where I really learned how to be disciplined and careful,' she says. She explains how scary it was to finish an eighteen-month course on growing them. 'There I was with my standard eight school qualification which I got in 1968, but in the end I was one of the first women to pass the course and one of the oldest too!'

Now she is responsible for 200 workers at Stellar, the country's largest organic winery. She goes on: 'Since we have joined the Fairtrade system, we receive on a periodical basis part of the profit of the farm. My life and those of my fellow workers has changed. After Stellar Organics became a Fairtrade-certified farm, the possibilities were there to improve our lifestyles and securities.'

South Africa gives some signposts to the way ahead for the Fairtrade movement. For South Africans quickly established a national fair trade platform, incorporating whole new areas for the future like tourism; proposed and shaped how the international Fairtrade standards could be raised for their country; opened a FLO office; and are now well on the way to starting Fairtrade labelling for their own market. For me, it's a motivating vision of how Fairtrade could, and I believe should, grow deeper roots within developing countries over the coming years.

In June 2007, I was ironing the kids' school uniforms while watching Tony Blair on the TV news make his emotional resignation speech. He called on us to: 'think – no *really* think' about how different Britain was ten years ago when he came to power.

On the BBC website, philosopher and author Julian Baggini reflected: 'A more permanent change of the last ten years could be the way in which issues of global justice and environmentalism have become mainstream. In 1997, Fairtrade coffee, campaigns such as Make Poverty History, and popular support for reducing our environmental impact were found only on the fringes of society. For instance, in 1997 Sainsbury's didn't sell any Fairtrade bananas. Soon all its bananas will be certified Fairtrade. The change is largely down to customer demand, which is ironic, because early advocates of such issues were generally of the view that consumerism was synonymous with selfish greed. . . Whether it is because of or despite his leadership, it seems indubitable that Britain has a greater sense of its global responsibility as Blair prepares to leave Downing Street than it did when he entered it.'[7]

The shifts in public concerns in the last ten years have indeed been remarkable. 'To judge the success of Fairtrade,' John Kanjagaile once told me, 'don't look only at sales volumes and market shares, look at the issues on the agenda, look at what the public are asking and what companies are debating. When we go into negotiating rooms with companies now, even if they're not yet doing Fairtrade, they all have to do something on social and environmental issues.'

As a 2007 Mintel report identified: 'Green is the new Black'. It found: 'People in Britain today are clearly moving towards more ethical lifestyles and are starting to realise that their actions have consequences. As British shoppers increasingly look to shop with a clear conscience, Mintel forecasts that the market will continue to grow for the foreseeable future.'[8]

People do not want to damage the planet or its people and as a result retailers that once competed only on price are now partly competing on who is the greenest and fairest of them all. But can this surge of interest be sustained? Can it be turned into real improvements for millions of producers? Will people make Fairtrade their daily, lifelong habit? How far can we take Fairtrade in the next five, ten, years?

Key to these evolving plans is Mike Gidney, the Chair of the Fairtrade Foundation, and Director of Traidcraft Exchange's Policy Unit. Usually en route to lobby ministers on world trade rules or supermarket dominance, Mike is always flying through our offices to ensure we stay on track with our core mission and remain accountable to our NGO owners despite the strong crosswinds constantly buffeting our little organisation.

Gesticulating wildly, and speaking nineteen to the dozen, he wastes no time outlining the vision: 'We've gone a long way – but Fairtrade needs to be ingrained into the fabric of our lives and the economy. To make this next step-change, we need to engage the public, businesses and governments so that they are ready to deepen their commitments. We need', he pauses, 'to start really transforming trade – so we can touch more lives more deeply.'

Top of our To Do list is keeping Fairtrade sales growing – so more producers of more products can have more benefits. There's much to celebrate about the take-off of Fairtrade. We've come a long, long way from the early get-togethers of banana and coffee producers, when their main call was for organisations such as the Fairtrade Foundation to invest more in growing the market. In fact, at one point, the coffee farmers even suggested investing some of their premium in marketing – an idea that was rejected in the end. But, far as we've come, we do not delude ourselves about the impact this is having on global poverty as a whole, and nor can businesses rest up, feeling they've 'done their bit'. Still only a tiny proportion of disadvantaged producers in developing countries can participate in Fairtrade – because it's still only a slither of the food we buy from overseas. So there is everything still to play for.

The good news is we have solid foundations to build on – a global system, a turn-key model that can be applied to new products, public appetite for more, many businesses ready to move from merely complying with Fairtrade rules to deeper commitment. Now we need to realise that potential to make a significant difference to poverty. In five years' time, Fairtrade in Britain could top sales of £2 billion, tipping the balance in favour of disadvantaged producers in developing countries. And perhaps global Fairtrade sales could reach $10 billion by 2012.

More importantly, we want to achieve that by embedding Fairtrade into the way companies trade and citizens shop. The first fifteen years of Fairtrade turned a seemingly wild idea into a living alternative with a foothold in the mainstream and thousands of companies involved worldwide. While having different strategies for each commodity, in the next few years we need to make Fairtrade the rule, not the exception, so it becomes what Mark Price, Waitrose's Chief Executive, calls 'the hygiene factor'. So, just as a company will always meet stringent hygiene rules for food products – they are the non-negotiables – so too Fairtrade could become part of the normal way of doing business with producers in developing countries, while enabling the more committed companies to go further still.

We can surely imagine the day when most bananas, and a good chunk of roast and ground coffee sold in British shops is Fairtrade. Other fresh fruit such as pineapples and grapes have also been making progress, with the supermarket chain Asda leading the way here along with the fresh fruit company Malet Azulet, who have worked with them and other retailers to achieve this. However, the potential for growth is still huge. And we will need clever strategies for those products that are stuck at the bottom of the Fairtrade sales league – like juices, rice, wine or nuts.

Britons are still a nation of tea-drinkers, enjoying more per person than anyone else bar the Irish. It was one of the first products to receive the FAIRTRADE Mark in Britain, with pioneer brands Clipper, Traidcraft and Teadirect leading the way and M&S later switching all its tea to Fairtrade. By 2007 still only 3 per cent of tea in the UK was Fairtrade, and not one of the big tea companies had converted a brand over to Fairtrade. But they look increasingly out of step and backward looking – and public pressure needs to call for change in this old-fashioned industry. Then, in October 2007, Sainsbury's made the dramatic announcement that they were converting all their own-label tea (to be followed by all their own-label roast and ground coffee) to Fairtrade – a move that would take Fairtrade to 10 per cent of the total UK tea market. It was good news for both producers amongst existing suppliers and for new ones in very poor countries such as Malawi. So, Mike Gidney challenges: could sales of Fairtrade tea come to where ground coffee is today? It starts to look possible, where even just a year ago it would have seemed very far-off. It wouldn't be a moment too soon for tea pickers, with Britons paying less than a penny a cup.[9]

As we consider future plans, Mike is turning to documents we've prepared showing Fairtrade sales. 'What about sugar?' he queries as his finger follows down the graph. It shows that, while sugar is vital to millions in some of the poorest countries, Fairtrade has to-date only notched up a sad one-percentage point of the UK market. As the trade is shaken up by changes in EU rules, we could set ourselves ambitious goals for sales both of sugar in bags and as an ingredient in the multi-ingredient products, like jams, biscuits or snack-bars.

Fresh fruit and vegetables are another area ripe for change. Matt North is the fresh-faced, straight-talking Londoner who's the banana and citrus buyer at Sainsbury's, where he's worked most of his life. Nothing in his conventional commercial CV would prepare you for his utter conviction that Fairtrade is the way to go in the future. And as the man who first envisaged their switch to 100 per cent Fairtrade bananas, his credentials are impeccable.

'I'd been visiting the growers in Central America and seen the difference small sums of money can make to the workers. Our customers clearly liked Fairtrade. So I thought if we went from 30 per cent Fairtrade in bananas to 100 per cent, we'd be ensuring the growers' premium went from one to four million pounds,' he explained to me one day, giving me some of the inside story on a process we'd seen from the outside. 'People were saying it couldn't be done but I'd had a few drinks at the summer ball so I collared Justin, our chief executive – for rather a long time, actually!

'Our bill for switching to Fairtrade is about £4 million a year in reduced margins because we're paying more to growers but kept prices to customers the same. But you can see it as a quality investment from our side. And we often invest much more than that in other moves to win over the public.

'Fairtrade is so great because it protects the grower – the grower bubble is sacrosanct from all our commercial pressures or drive for cheap prices. Everyone sees how much we're paying them, so we can be comfortable about it. It's just the fairness of it all.'

Matt has come to see us before he visits growers in South Africa and he's keen to discuss plans. 'I see Fairtrade as the gold standard for global sourcing from developing countries – our preferred option whenever possible. If in three years' time Sainsbury's hasn't switched other fresh products over to totally Fairtrade, personally I'd be absolutely gutted. Look at bananas – it has made such a difference, it's a great thing we've done and the model clearly works. So you've got to keep building on that success and move it forward.'

I am convinced that so long as the public keep on asking for Fairtrade, then we are barely out of the starting blocks with everything to run for. Take coffee, the most established product. While Fairtrade is very significant in roast and ground coffee, most people in Britain drink instant coffee where Fairtrade takes just 3 per cent of the market. Certainly Cafédirect Director Penny Newman believes that it should be possible to get sales of Fairtrade instant coffee up to the same level as ground coffee.

It also means going down all avenues: encouraging supermarket own brand, while ensuring the 100 per cent Fairtrade companies survive and prosper, enabling niche suppliers to do Fairtrade, but also bringing large companies on board. Whole swathes of business, in particular the big multinational brands, have yet to even look into Fairtrade, while in each sector the Fairtrade brands can lead the way.

In the world's largest coffee market, the United States, which accounts for a quarter of global imports, the impact of getting large companies to take up Fairtrade has been impressive. From 1998 onwards, TransFair USA developed an area-by-area strategy to promote Fairtrade firstly centred on San Francisco and the Bay Area, followed by the north-east. And they worked closely with the so-called 'speciality coffee' companies, who sell high quality roast and ground, and nearly always organic, coffee. The break that Fairtrade needed to go coast to coast came after the 1999 WTO summit in Seattle and well-publicised criticism of Starbucks' purchasing policies by Global Exchange. Starbucks signed up to buy Fairtrade-certified coffee for the US in April 2000, then in the UK in 2002, with their purchases in the US rising year on year. Since then US sales have been rocketing.

But the biggest test of our collective nerve came when Nestlé, having listened to all the calls for Fairtrade, agreed to develop a new brand of Fairtrade instant coffee. Whilst many people have drunk Nestlé coffee all their lives, there are others for whom Nestlé can spark some emotion, particularly on debates around the sale of infant formula milk to poor countries and coffee pricing. Oxfam initiated a campaign about coffee, their report highlighting companies' healthy profits at the very time farmers were getting paid less than it cost them to grow the beans. Resulting from their report findings came the call to multinationals, including Nestlé, to – among other things – start purchasing Fairtrade coffee; and now it seemed Nestlé had responded.

The phones went red-hot and the debate went up to the Board of the Fairtrade Foundation several times. The Fairtrade labelling system is open to any company willing to commit to the rigorous standards behind each product. It makes no comment or judgement on the company itself; only that the particular product carrying the Mark meets the rules. So decisions about awarding products the right to carry the Mark are made against objective criteria. But clearly this decision had wider ramifications that needed careful thought. It was a fierce debate and one of the most testing times for the Foundation as we consulted with our NGO partners and producers. Everywhere, opinion was divided. Some argued Fairtrade should not work with big companies at all, let alone multinationals that some could accuse of wanting greenish credentials, and should focus on the 100 per cent Fairtrade pioneers alone.

Others hailed this as a victory for public pressure in the UK – surely this was good news as a big company was responding to the concerns and changing priorities of its customers. People could also see the potential for much bigger Fairtrade sales. Everyone could understand the benefits for the smallholders in El Salvador and Ethiopia from whom Nestlé was buying. The rigorous assessment of the certification team showed the product met all the Fairtrade criteria – and that the smallholders were going to get the benefits as they should.

The Board voted in favour of Nestlé's Partners Blend carrying the Mark. The day the announcement was made, student group People & Planet launched a campaign welcoming the move and pressing Nestlé to do far more, which was, I thought, just the right response. Here was a major multinational, able to affect millions of lives, listening to people and starting to give them the Fairtrade coffee they wanted – but it was not enough and they could do so much more; indeed Nestlé had also recognised the need to consider incremental progress and to do more.

Tadesse Meskela from the Oromia Coffee Farmers Co-operative

Union is a fierce critic of the giant coffee roasters and the impact that prices have had on poor coffee farmers in Ethiopia.

He's only able to sell about a fifth of the co-op's coffee as Fairtrade and he needs to sell more. He told me how with the premium, the communities are gradually building schools for the children who were simply not getting an education. It's been a huge success.

'But we've just discovered that these new schools are suddenly empty.'

'Why?' I asked.

'Because at this time of year, their families have simply run out of money and the children are too hungry to go to school. Really the prices are killing us. People need more income.'

Facing those stark realities, Tadesse saw selling his coffee on Fairtrade terms to Nestlé as a real step forward – while always, always pushing them to do more.

Nestlé have taken the all important first step. But other big firms, such as Kraft, have yet to offer a single Fairtrade coffee in the UK. Instead, they have opted for a range of the other 'ethical labels' that carry no obligation to pay farmers a better price or buy from organised smallholder groups.

Part of the success of Fairtrade has been to put social and environmental issues and the plight of farmers on to global agendas, encouraging companies to see that consumers are not only concerned with price – that instead of always competing to offer the cheapest commodities, they can put real value back into our food and drinks. So any and all improvements that benefit producers are welcome. But there's a flipside.

We have to ensure that the gains the Fairtrade movement has fought for and won over the past two decades are not chipped away by companies opting for a proliferation of bewildering labels that confuse the public, and do not carry the same guarantees as Fairtrade.

There's no doubt that some alternative schemes have a lot of attraction: many are addressing issues such as the environment that are fundamentally important and are sometimes doing a good job in many ways. But it is the case that the companies, not the producers, are in the driving seat; the schemes make fewer demands on companies; usually even the largest plantations can enter and – most importantly – such schemes do not cost companies much because there is no minimum price to pay. But they are not, and have never claimed to be, Fairtrade programmes. By contrast, Fairtrade must seem hard work and expensive. For it is the only scheme that seeks to address the root causes of farmers' poverty. And it's the only one with an organised global movement behind it, whose years of campaigning have given the Mark huge recognition amongst consumers (eight out of ten people in Britain know about Fairtrade) – which in turn gives it great power to persuade traders and supermarkets to act. That's what gives Fairtrade its legitimacy and its strength and makes it so very special.

The nightmare scenario is that if products become more and more cluttered with different stamps, and if every company starts claiming to be very, very nice with their own different logo to prove it, the weary shoppers get first confused and then cynical about the whole lot of them – including Fairtrade.

That's the moral of the green washing-powder tale. Ecover long held the position as the environmentally friendly washing powder. Then in the 1980s with an upsurge of concern about the environmental impact of washing powders, many big brands started becoming 'environmentally friendly' with a plethora of claims on their products. The consumer had no way of telling what any of these meant. They became disenchanted and disengaged. The big-brand soap powders gradually, quietly dropped their environmental claims and the opportunity of consumer pressure really to change their practices was blunted and lost. That's why consumers need to show they know the difference – and keep on backing FAIRTRADE Mark products.

'Watch out,' one business leader warned me. 'There are those with a long-term plan to undermine and destroy Fairtrade.' It sounds almost too Machiavellian to be true, but we should never underestimate the degree to which, within some business circles, Fairtrade is challenging the status quo and provoking a reaction.

In other cases it has still not seriously flashed on to business' radar screen. I have had to sit firmly on my hands in workshops organised by leading multinational brands, where they have clearly spent thousands and thousands of pounds on consultants concocting trendy ideas about how 'to market sustainability', or how to involve HQ staff with their suppliers, or to give charity to the very communities that grow their products. Why, oh why, don't they just do Fairtrade, I think: the farmers do not want to go on needing charity; they just want a fair price for their goods and to be treated with respect.

Nor does anyone think for one minute that the battle is won, that companies have seen the light and reinvented themselves as agents of social change. They are doing Fairtrade because the public have made it commercially possible or even necessary. But all companies are under pressure to deliver more profit to their shareholders and as companies are taken over or go out of favour with City analysts, their one-time commitments can be axed or scaled back. Which is why it's so important that Fairtrade supporters everywhere keep on asking for Fairtrade and why we must ensure that Fairtrade gets better and better at delivering real change.

Then there are those bodies that we absolutely can and should partner more closely into the future. Key is the Ethical Trading Initiative, which the Foundation helped set up and encourages all companies to join, so they can do better on core standards for workers in factories across all their supply chains. That's the base; then on top they increase their commitment to Fairtrade products.

In Ireland, for example, Fairtrade has grown at a huge rate in recent years, but Fair Trade Mark Ireland Director Peter Gaynor also emphasises their work with those industry groups open to serious dialogue to raise minimum standards in sectors like coffee, including on large estates where Fairtrade certificates aren't available anyway.

'Our ambition in Ireland is to maximise sales on Fairtrade terms as the "gold standard" for people in developing countries. We'd like to see 100 per cent sold on Fairtrade terms. But while we seek to maximise volumes, we could also collaborate with organisations to ensure we raise the floor of minimum standards – as well as keeping on pushing at the ceiling with Fairtrade. Fairtrade has never been the only initiative. It's the most important and the best, but there are complementary initiatives which tackle the problems from different approaches.'

Other key partners for the future are the organic certifiers such as the Soil Association. We do not aim to create some kind of über-label that tries to cover all global issues under one enormous roof. Rather, keeping our distinct roles with the public – because organic and Fairtrade have different, if overlapping, missions – in the future we could work together more so producers do not have to deal with many different bodies.

People often complain that they find it hard when they have to choose: should I buy organic or Fairtrade? Or local? What about the carbon footprint of products from overseas – isn't that bad for climate change? The 'anxious' shopper is a symptom of our times – but it's also often an exaggerated worry when in practice most such initiatives are mutually supportive. For example, there are not many bananas grown in East Anglia yet, despite global warming; so people can buy local cheese or milk or meat and buy Fairtrade tea, oranges and pineapples. But when there are trade-offs, I believe each of us has to find what feels right for us – be the 'happy shopper'. As the Women's Institute slogan put it so neatly in one of their earliest Fairtrade campaigns, which was picked up in Garstang when it became the first Fairtrade Town: 'Buy local. Buy Fairtrade'.

Some people only ever buy local apples and good for them. I too glory in the early small, sour Coxes and misshapen, textured Russets (which, having been almost driven to extinction by the supermarkets' promotion of factory-farmed apples, are now making a comeback as expensive 'speciality' varieties). But if people do want apples when the European season is over, then isn't it best they buy South African Fairtrade fruit? (Which, by the way, have no chance of competing with English apples in season thanks to high duties, while European apples can enter South Africa tariff-free all year round.) On cut flowers, isn't it better to give Kenyan workers a chance to earn a decent income, than buy flowers grown in Dutch greenhouses which research has shown, in fact, release more carbon? [10] Of course, the overwhelming majority of Fairtrade goods come by boat.

The Fairtrade movement welcomes wholeheartedly the nation's belated waking up to climate change; indeed some Fairtrade farmers are reporting that their crops have been badly affected by changing weather patterns. Barry Coates, Vice-Chair of Fair Trade Association of Australia and New Zealand, says it is already spelling catastrophe for many farmers in the Pacific: 'Here nature is majestic and huge and climate change will render whole Pacific islands uninhabitable and is already doing so. We're seeing more storms, sea-levels are rising, people are moving inland or to other islands and we are starting to see environmental refugees from the Pacific already. So climate change is massive here.'

Of course companies should seek to limit the footprint of Fairtrade products. Interesting new research is showing that the largest impact on climate change is not at all with the producers but at this end – the processing, such as making instant coffee or the packaging or people driving to the shops. So we should reduce the carbon impact in these areas first while avoiding knee-jerk reactions that put a brake on poor farmers earning a living. We should consider 'fairmiles' as well as ' foodmiles', and look at a product's social footprint as well as its carbon footprint.

No one puts that better than John Kanjagaile. Once at a public meeting in London, he was asked about Fairtrade and global warming. His eyebrows shot up and smiling, he gently replied, 'In our villages, none of the farmers have fridges, or cars, or TVs or computers or air conditioning. They have never been to our capital city, let alone got on a plane. Don't ask these poor farmers to pay the price for the mess rich nations have made of the world.'

Powerful words I have never forgotten. There's so much we can do to clean up our mess, to own and consume less – while enabling those who need more to earn a decent livelihood. And often there are obvious win-wins: as when the Co-op launched shopping bags made with Fairtrade certified cotton to encourage people to get away from their addiction to plastic bags. Or when you buy Fairtrade brazil nuts from the nut company Liberation, you know you are enabling the farmers in Bolivia to live in harmony with the Amazon rainforest so they have a financial stake in protecting it, instead of being driven to cut down the trees to survive.

So I frequently stomp around the house when people assert on the morning radio that 'Climate change is now accepted as the greatest issue facing the world.' I, for one, do not accept that: I think there are three great issues facing the world today – conflict, poverty and climate change. All are killing poor people in poor countries; they are often interrelated and all three need companies and individuals to take action and governments the world over to show courage and vision in getting a grip on the problems.

To date, the EU and USA have failed to offer a fairer trade deal to developing nations. Quite the reverse. As the global talks have floundered, it looks as if these big players may pick off countries one by one for individual deals that will be as lopsided as their respective weights in the bargaining balance suggest. It's not an edifying sight and many in organisations like Oxfam and Traidcraft Exchange fear for the impact in countries such as the Windward Islands.

Against this backdrop of gathering trade storm clouds, Fairtrade supporters have queued up to lobby their MPs, arguing that the overwhelming public support for Fairtrade gives the British government and the EU a clear mandate to take the big, bold steps needed at international trade talks to ensure the rules are made fairer for developing countries. As the Foundation looks to the future, Bruce Crowther and many in the Fairtrade Towns movement are itching to get their teeth into more such lobbying. So, too, are some of the schoolchildren. When I met then trade minister Alan Johnson ahead of another attempt to restart the

Doha trade talks, he recounted how he'd had a postcard from a primary schoolboy urging him to 'make trade fair', with a PS at the bottom adding in his best handwriting, 'Could you come to our school assembly on Monday dressed as a Fairtrade banana, please'. Unfortunately ministerial engagements prevented him.

Barry, now in New Zealand, has a powerful pedigree of campaigning against forced liberalisation having made a name for himself as Director at the World Development Movement in the UK. When he first became my boss, he boasted a lovely little ponytail although that had gone under the knife by the time he became my boss again – this time on the Board of the Fairtrade Foundation, an experience which helped him when he moved back to his home country and got stuck into helping start Fairtrade there. Now as Director of Oxfam New Zealand, he's deeply concerned about the way the trade talks are going: 'These free trade deals being pushed on vulnerable nations would be devastating, absolutely devastating – leading to loss of government revenues, opening up to abuse of corporate power, pushing privatisation into small countries. . .' Barry's list goes on and on: 'That is why the relationship between Fairtrade and trade campaigning needs to become tighter – we have to build a deeper level of public education.'

Even *The Economist* magazine has recognised the role Fairtrade can play in this: 'The best thing about the spread of the ethical-food movement is that it offers grounds for hope. It sends a signal that there is enormous appetite for change and widespread frustration that governments are not doing enough to preserve the environment, reform world trade or encourage development.'[11]

Back at the Foundation, Mike Gidney is sober in the face of the enormity of the challenge to shift governments: 'The rules that govern international trade, and international businesses, need urgently to be reformed so that the most vulnerable people are protected from the brutality of the free market. Fairtrade is showing that it is possible to intervene successfully and manage markets, but governments are lagging behind the public in recognising this – and look more and more out of step. When there is so clearly a mandate to raise their game, no government has stood up and taken action to make trade rules work for development. As more people buy Fairtrade, more governments must start to listen. Consumers are voters, after all. To ignore them for too long would be a historic mistake.'

Not long ago, cotton specialist at the Foundation, Tamara Thomas went to a meeting with a major company to encourage them to use Fairtrade cotton in their clothing. Their chief buyer has a fearsome reputation as one of the hardest-nosed in the business, although there's quite a few competing for that title! He obviously thought he'd make mincemeat of the attractive, blonde Tamara, living up to his reputation by opening with a series of macho one-liners to the effect that her do-gooding pleas wouldn't cut any ice with him.

But Tamara is a tough cookie. She spent thirteen years as a buyer for high street retailers until she could no longer stomach having to negotiate lower and lower prices while witnessing what this meant for producers. She became convinced there must be a fairer way of trading and selling clothes and started as a volunteer in the Fairtrade Foundation, quickly proving her worth. It's a tribute to her tough, calm negotiating tactics, but also to the compelling evidence she presented that consumers were demanding Fairtrade cotton, and that it was making a difference to the producers, that by the end of the meeting 'The Difficult One' had agreed to buy all the Fairtrade cotton that could be sourced that season.

Increasingly, the Foundation is driving a tougher bargain. Where once, with campaigners' help, we just tried to persuade companies, please, to try one little Fairtrade product, now we ask and indeed expect much more. In the earliest negotiations on bananas, head honcho at banana importer Geest told the then Director of the Foundation Phil Wells: 'Get your tanks off my lawn.' Phil, checking over his shoulder, was surprised – we didn't have any tanks; our bargaining position was really quite weak then. Now we do have huge public support, a vibrant national network of campaigners and NGOs and a proven track record. So we can push for much deeper commitments from companies. We can encourage them to switch whole categories, or engage more with their suppliers or invest in enabling the poorest farmers to enter Fairtrade.

As Tamara says, 'We encourage companies to go from compliance to commitment – not just meeting the Fairtrade rules but really engaging with the spirit of Fairtrade, supporting the poorer growers, investing in their needs, informing consumers, undertaking major commitments not token one-offs, and really tackling the social and environmental issues right through their supply chains.'

At the party to launch Fairtrade Fortnight 2006, I didn't envy Marks & Spencer Chief Executive Stuart Rose. Sporting their new Fairtrade certified-cotton socks, he took to the podium after the most rousing call to action by Comfort Kwaasibea from Kuapa Kokoo who had had the audience chanting their co-op's trademark quality call – 'the best of the best'. It was a hard act to follow. Stuart pulled the focus back to the consumers. Their confidence to turn belief into action was, he said, because of the 'robust and transparent certification process' afforded by the FAIRTRADE Mark. But he continued:

'We cannot be complacent. Consumers are rightly becoming more demanding (and) . . . will carefully scrutinise what actions businesses are actually taking. Increasingly, they will not accept bland assurances. Fairtrade as a fig leaf will not wash with consumers – they want to see evidence of basic standards and ethical behaviour across everything businesses do.

'There are enormous opportunities to grow Fairtrade – we are at the start of a long and exciting journey. Although more and more retailers are getting behind Fairtrade, we, like many others, would welcome more competition on Fairtrade to help drive the pace of change.

'I see it as a virtuous circle – retailers changing their practices in response to growing consumer interest in Fairtrade. The Fairtrade Foundation will then be in a stronger position to work with a wider range of producers to satisfy the increased demand.'[12]

The Co-operative Group's major benchmark survey of consumer

attitudes on food and ethics in 1994, repeated again in 2004, found just such rising consumer expectations:

'Attitudes have hardened. Ten years ago, consumers were hungry for the ethical alternative and hungry for the information they needed to identify it. Now they are even hungrier. They are more prepared to use their purchasing power to support products that meet their standards – and equally prepared to veto those that don't. They increasingly want to play an active part in making these standards mainstream, using their influence to drive change.'[13]

Brad Hill at the Co-op is convinced that, 'The movement on the ground is driving Fairtrade forward and making it part of the fabric of our society. When we switched all our coffee to Fairtrade, we picked up on the Oxfam coffee campaign and told people what it was all about.' He himself has been involved with the Fairtrade Towns campaign in Salford and Manchester and the Co-op have worked closely with local supporters across the country, developing materials that have been used as far afield as France, Korea and Japan.

A dad himself, Brad is most excited by the new Fairtrade Schools scheme launched by the Fairtrade Foundation with a grand coalition of development education centres around the country in 2007, as that is clearly aiming at the future generations: 'When Brian Namata from the Kasinthula sugar co-op was over from Malawi, he explained to my son Matthew, who was just nine at the time, that the villagers no longer had to get water from the crocodile-infested river – that really made an impact. We organised a day at his primary school which involved workshops and a special Fairtrade assembly. It's a big school, around 300 children, and class by class they presented what Fairtrade meant to them through songs, poems and artworks. Then this little lad of nine or ten stood up in his football shirt and said he'd always had his team's latest shirt but he'd discovered that all this money his parents paid wasn't going back to the people who made it. And then and there, in front of all those children, he took it off.' Years later, Brad's voice still cracks at the memory.

Fairtrade brands are once again moving one step ahead. Traidcraft is considering how to add more value to products, for example, with Fairtrade tinned pineapple from a factory in Swaziland (instead of exporting them fresh), and undoubtedly new companies will come with new ideas. At the time of writing, Robin Murray has just overseen the latest launch from the TWIN stable – the nut company Liberation supplying brazil nuts from Bolivia, Brazil and Peru and peanuts from farmers in Malawi initially to Co-op and Tesco supermarkets. Indeed Tesco has given a huge opening to these very poor nut producers, with a quarter of all their brazils now Fairtrade. But Robin stresses that the pioneers need to keep opening up new areas – to remain distinct in the market and to keep innovating:

'The 100 per cent fair-traders do a hundred things differently. They are trying to establish a different kind of firm, a different way of business, a people to people trade. They are highly professional now while still deeply into economic innovation, putting social and political values into the heart of the economy, to show another way is possible based on the values of trust between consumers and producers.'

The Fairtrade movement, he says, always needs to keep focused beyond just the business of selling more chocolate or coffee, important though that is, to the ultimate objective which he sees as, 'about redistributing power and money from those where it is concentrated to those with much less. There is a pyramid that shows the concentration of money and power right at the top; that needs to be flipped over. So we should have much greater producer ownership of companies.'

Divine chocolate and Agrofair were among the first companies to be part-owned by the producers and in 2004 Cafédirect became a public limited company with shareholders including producer–partner organisations and a golden share for its founders. In 2004–5, Cafédirect put 86 per cent of its operating profits (£574,000) back into tailor-made support and training initiatives with the growers. The company is also looking to increase dramatically the number of farmers they reach, including through the first stage of its ambitious international plans with a move into selling its products in Hong Kong and Singapore. CEO Penny Newman, a sharp-minded strategist who learned her trade at The

Body Shop and has steered the company to the number six slot in the UK coffee market, is convinced that its continuing success will spring from its values.

'We must be driven by producers' needs, that's why we are unique. But we must adapt for the world as it will be in five, ten years' time with all the coming changes in agricultural practices, in commodity markets, and the rise of China and India. We must consider how Fairtrade could look differently in the future, and how Fairtrade companies will be raising the bar.'

Fairtrade Foundation's Chairman Mike is nodding to most of the Foundation's emerging future strategy so far. He agrees we need to reach a real breakthrough across the product range, push companies from compliance to commitment and develop strategies to work in the least developed countries. But he's also keen to discuss his vision of a 'Fairtrade lifestyle' for the public here so that millions more producers can participate. He readily agrees to the work in progress on new agricultural products, for example, to introduce Fairtrade lentils, jute, soya and Palestinian olive oil. Also in the pipeline are new areas, such as cosmetics using Fairtrade ingredients. In future we may move beyond certifying cotton and get involved with the manufacturing stages of textiles; and undertake new ventures such as seafood on which we are doing initial research with the communities in developing countries and where we'd want to link up with experts in sustainable fishing; and new departures into service enterprises like Fairtrade tourism, which are likely to be much further down the line.

One long held personal ambition is to be able to label Fairtrade handicrafts. This could bring benefits to thousands of handicraft producers and would unite FLO with the grouping of 100 per cent Fairtrade companies, the International Fair Trade Association (IFAT), who've long bought and sold everything from handmade paper to baskets and gifts, but until now have not labelled products. The first steps of a ritual dance to bring the schemes together are being played out, with the Fair Trade Association of Australia and New Zealand playing a lead role. There, both FLO and IFAT are joint-owners of the labelling initiative.

Each such step forward requires time and resources as we research how to ensure Fairtrade delivers change in each new area. First, we check if Fairtrade can make a difference to the producers, if it can stimulate development and bring greater justice into the trade, and if so how will it have to be framed and adapted? We look at which communities could be interested and which traders. We have to ask: Will it work in the market? What level should the price be set at? Do we need additional rules for this particular product? For example, cosmetics will mix Fairtrade cocoa butter or shea nut butter with chemicals and water, so we will need new rules on the percentages that have to be Fairtrade.

But when I gaze into my crystal ball on the future of Fairtrade, the new product that sparkles the most brightly is gold. Since that chance meeting all those years ago in Katharine Hamnett's basement kitchen, Greg Valerio has kept in touch, slowly chipping away at each obstacle to his vision of a best-selling gold wedding ring carrying the FAIRTRADE Mark.

A jeweller himself, he's teamed up with organised small-scale miners in Colombia who started developing 'green gold' to tackle the terrible environmental problems they face. But they quickly ran into a shortage of funds. How, they wondered, were they going to get more of the final selling price of gold so they could improve their lives and the environment? Greg, who'd been watching the rise of Fairtrade food, thought he had the answer. So began a partnership between FLO, the Association for Responsible Mining and the Fairtrade Foundation to explore whether Fairtrade labelling could make a difference to the miners' lives.

To find out more, Chris Davis, who leads on new product development at the Foundation, but previously worked on a project in South Africa helping people in handicrafts get better income from their products, visited Greg's partners in Peru and was shocked by what he saw: 'The most vulnerable people mining gold are getting ripped off; they earn absolutely nothing – and so work in the most appalling conditions. In one community I visited, the men go deep underground hacking out the ore. Kids as young as six then stand on a huge granite rock, rolling it over the ore mixed with water and mercury, which gradually absorbs the gold.

'Then these kids scoop it up with their bare hands into cut-off plastic bottles and take it to their homes. There, on their kitchen stoves, they evaporate the mercury, so releasing poisonous gases, to leave the gold. It's very dangerous, and totally unnecessary; there is a machine no bigger than a suitcase and costing less than $2,000 that can do it; but they can't afford it because they get so little for their gold.'

Yet read the papers and you only hear how gold prices are soaring to seventeen-year highs due to demand from India and China. Try telling that to the miners. It's a sobering reminder that without mechanisms in place, higher commodity prices often do not reach the vulnerable people at the beginning of the supply chains.

Debate has raged about Fairtrade going into such new and difficult ground, and some fear Fairtrade's reputation may suffer when the public learn how hard life is for the small-scale miners. 'There are risks,' says Chris, 'but we are here to create change for the most vulnerable people. The public can understand that if Fairtrade is involved with a community, that doesn't mean all is perfect. It's not perfection guaranteed; it's a better deal guaranteed. Some 100 million people depend on small-scale mining; what keeps them poor is that they are not getting a fair price. Fairtrade could help change that.

'In five or ten years' time, with Fairtrade prices, those children I saw could be in school, and the miners could be exploring other ways to supplement their incomes.'

Greg, whose shops see the scale of public interest in Fairtrade gold, especially in Ireland, has no doubt it will go down a storm. 'Unquestionably the demand is there for Fairtrade gold and gems. It's a total no-brainer. And once we have one film star on the red carpet flashing a Fairtrade ring, they'll all have to have it,' he laughs.

We're catching up outside a cinema where the London Fairtrade Campaign Group is hosting a film festival. Tonight, they're showing Blood Diamond, in which the gorgeous Leonardo di Caprio plays a tough South African diamond dealer in the tragedy that is Sierra Leone's mining industry.

It's shocking, but compelling, viewing and the audience is receptive to Greg telling true stories at the end: 'A small scale alluvial diamond miner in the north-east corner of Congo found an eight and a half carat red diamond. He sold it to a trader for $2,000. This same stone, because of its rarity – it's like finding an undiscovered Picasso in your loft – was bought in New York for $150 million. That's the scale of inequality we're up against. And we're going to change that.'

As we look to the future, one question we're so often asked is: will we create fair trade for UK farmers? We've considered this very carefully. Clearly, British farmers share much with their counterparts in developing countries: they are both at the end of what the Soil Association's Patrick Holden calls 'long fear chains'. Price cuts get passed down the line, stopping only with the person at the end: the farmer. That's why so many farmers in Britain, just as overseas, are going out of business, and why suicide rates among farmers are so high worldwide. In the United States, workers on the fruit and vegetable farms are often migrants from the very communities in Mexico or Nicaragua where Fairtrade is trying to make a difference.

With so much shared ground, the Soil Association asked us to consider working with them on fair trade for farmers in rich northern countries. But the more we researched, the more it didn't feel right. The conditions for farmers here are so different, the standards needed totally rewriting. The public reaction was mixed. Support for UK farmers, and in particular those most on the ropes such as Welsh hill farmers, is widespread. But people clearly associate the FAIRTRADE Mark with the relief of absolute poverty – with products grown by farmers who don't have clean drinking water or schools for their kids. It would be confusing to find the same Mark on carrots from English farmers in a very different position.

But the final word went to the Fairtrade producers. I knew they would welcome sharing ideas with British farmers, but I was nervous of putting a more ambitious proposition to the FLO international board meeting. Gilmar Laforga, the normally mild-mannered representative of the Brazilian orange growers, snapped his pencil in rage. 'The day', he fumed, 'that Europe's farmers no longer have subsidies and tax advantages, the day Europe lets us compete on a level playing field with fair international trade rules – that's the day we can apply the same FAIRTRADE Mark to US and European produce.'

And so, while the Foundation appreciates all that is shared in the positions of farmers here and overseas; and welcomes other organisations supporting British farmers' demands for fairer prices; and encourages groups to make connections like the WI 'Buy local. Buy Fairtrade' campaign, we ourselves are keeping our focus on tackling poverty in developing countries. Which, let's face it, means we have our work cut out.

An African colleague once told me a saying: 'If you want to go fast, go alone. If you want to go far, go together.' Putting to one side the problem that I want to go both fast *and* far, everyone in the Fairtrade movement has been building the networks to go far in the future. Producers have already formed three networks – the CLAC (Coordinadora Latinoamericana y del Caribe de Comercio Justo), the African Fairtrade Network and the Network of Asian Producers, which in 2007 officially became full members of FLO, thanks once again to the persistent work of our Ian in drafting endless documents. As Binod Mohan, Chair of the Asian Network said: 'The face behind the Fairtrade movement is the southern producer and the inclusion of producer networks in the FLO constitution is a welcome step towards further strengthening Fairtrade.'

Latin America and the Caribbean, where the first Fairtrade producers came together and still home to the biggest number of Fairtrade producer groups, have been networking as far back as 1996, and 300 organisations are members of the CLAC representing over a million growers. In Africa and Asia such co-ordination is newer, but growing fast especially in Africa. Supporting such networks is a vital building block for Fairtrade in the future.

FLO already has offices and staff across the world, monitoring and supporting groups, and we are exploring how FLO could devolve more and more to the South. It's not a straightforward debate – how to keep the global consistency and also allow flexibility for different contexts around the world. But it seems to me that as the system grows, we may need a simple set of core international principles, with more specific standards for different regions and products. One size does not fit all.

That would enable the regional organisations and producer groups to develop and ensure implementation of the standards. While the rigour of the Fairtrade standards and the global system of certification are central to the success of Fairtrade, they should never be a straightjacket either. Rather they should facilitate the aim of tackling poverty and promoting development. So it's right the standards are constantly updated, that we keep on pushing up the bar to increase the benefits Fairtrade can bring and push companies to do more – while also widening the net for the poorest producers to come into the system for the first time.

This is very much the vision of our colleagues in Australia and New Zealand too. Barry Coates says, 'In the future it's important we devolve more to an Asia–Pacific hub as this is where the future growth will be. Functions like certification need to have a closer link with people, to be more responsive to the issues of the region to developing training and sharing capacity. It is the logical next stage in the development of an international organisation like FLO – to position itself for the next stage.'

Barry is also passionate about Fairtrade strengthening its work with producers, and widening opportunities for new groups and new countries, 'In this part of the world, trading routes are very thin, there are not a lot of buyers out there offering deals and you lack competition so you get a lot of rip-off deals. So Fairtrade can be very important to the farmers. Yet, in the Pacific, there is only a handful of Fairtrade-certified groups. So we want to support more Pacific groups to gain Fairtrade certification – help build local organisations' understanding and engagement with the process.' In fact, they're talking to TWIN about how to do this.

As Barry outlines, we need an increased focus on the poorest growers in the poorest countries – in the future we should work in countries like Bangladesh, Cambodia, Mozambique, Congo where farmers have difficulty in getting even on to the first step of the trade ladder. As Noel Oettle, the Chair of Fairtrade South Africa, says, support is needed to 'develop the capacity of producers and workers to become effective entrepreneurs and to develop and maintain direct links to national, regional and international markets'.

Take for example some Indian cotton farmers who wanted to join the Fairtrade scheme. Firstly someone had to explain what Fairtrade is all about, the benefits and responsibilities. Then to receive the Fairtrade premium, the farmers' group needed to open a bank account – a new step for the farmers. When they went to the bank, they were asked for documents to prove they owned the land, as collateral. But, as so often, the farmers, many illiterate, did not have those documents. So they were stuck. It took outside help to negotiate with the bank manager, to track down the missing documents and file requests to the government for the right records. This can be a long process. Selling to developed nations may also mean that producers have to meet a panoply of complex food safety, quality and packaging standards required by governments and supermarkets.

So ensuring Fairtrade reaches disadvantaged farmers takes resources – resources we simply do not have. Three-quarters of the Fairtrade Foundation's income comes from the licence fee that companies pay for putting the FAIRTRADE Mark on their products; which is for all our core costs and means the system is sustainable. The last quarter of the pie comes from donors – ranging from generous individuals to trust funds and government sources – as we do not want our independence compromised by relying solely on company fees. These donor funds are focused on developing new products, raising awareness and supporting producers. But the development needs run way ahead of our bank balance.

As the 2005 Commission for Africa noted: 'Increased funding from developed countries would help increase the participation of producer groups in "fairtrade". The demand for products carrying the "fairtrade" mark is growing, but investment is needed in building the capacity of producer groups in Africa to meet the rigorous demands of developed country markets.'[14]

Their assessment was backed up by the cross-party International Development Select Committee of the House of Commons that held an inquiry in 2007. They recommended that Fairtrade should 'help the most disadvantaged producers in the poorest countries. We recommend that this pro-poor focus becomes a key area for future government funding for fair trade.'[15]

That's why the Fairtrade Foundation has been calling for a group of international donors to fund Fairtrade's next big steps to the tune of £50 million over five years. Setting the ball rolling, Comic Relief has already pledged £5 million to support Fairtrade in Africa. It's a flying start that we hope the UK government will follow.

In Ireland the rapid rise in public support for Fairtrade has encouraged the government to increase its support for producers through Irish Aid. Working with our international body FLO, they are helping Fairtrade farmers in Central America get the professional training they wanted in techniques for the more productive and environmentally sustainable use of soils, crop varieties and pest control. And there are plans to extend the work into Africa too.

Part of the future of Fairtrade in developing countries will be the growth of local Fairtrade markets so producers can gain Fairtrade terms selling locally or to other developing countries. So 2007 saw the launch of Fairtrade labelling in South Africa. It's one of a growing band, along with Brazil, India and the Philippines, interested in the sales of Fairtrade products within their own countries too – a path forged by Mexico.

In 2006 Mike and I attended the launch meeting of an initiative, backed by Traidcraft, to develop the Fairtrade label in India. Their research showed the huge potential of harnessing the rapidly rising consumer spending power of the middle class together with India's long involvement with Fairtrade.

Everyone at the meeting wanted to get Fairtrade on the road in India, and like Australia and New Zealand to work with both FLO and the 100 per cent fair trade organisations in IFAT. It seems crazy, they said, that we export Fairtrade tea and cotton when there are plenty of people in India who could and would buy them!

The meeting's official report concluded that, 'The celebrated 8 per cent growth rate has reduced poverty in India, and more people are better off today than a decade earlier. But the service-sector-led income and consumption growth is skewed – a very sharp rise in income and conspicuous consumption of an increasingly visible few – juxtaposed with the sense of being left out for the majority, especially in the agriculture sector in rural areas. The number of poor in India today, 440 million, far exceeds that of sub-Saharan Africa and income disparities lead to resentment towards the rich steamrollering the poor . . . In such conditions, Fair Trade could prove to be a beacon of hope for marginalised producers. . . However the Fair Trade markets in the West are not growing in proportion to the requirements of poor producers, and the need is to expand Fair Trade markets in the country by tapping the recent affluence.'

Of course, the major obstacles to developing Fairtrade in a country like India or South Africa cannot be underestimated, but building local and regional sales will be lynchpins of the future. I look forward to the day when Fairtrade in Britain, far from leading the world any more, is a minnow beside these giants.

When Comfort in Ghana weighed the farmers' cocoa on their huge iron scales, when in India Ganga's group invested their first premium in new digital scales for weighing their cotton, they were immediately taking more control over their goods. As this pattern is repeated a thousand-fold across the world, these scales are also hugely symbolic of how collectively the Fairtrade movement is starting to tip the balance. For centuries, weighing scales have been a symbol of justice (today they are the adopted logo of the Trade Justice Movement) and the Fairtrade Foundation is determined that over the coming five years we will scale up Fairtrade's reach and impact so we can touch more lives more deeply and thereby, ultimately, tip the balance of power in trade. As public opinion builds behind Fairtrade, we believe people will expect companies to commit more and more to Fairtrade, and certainly the explosions of interest in recent years augur well for the balance tipping in the future.

I dream that one day you will walk into a small independent health food shop, or the supermarket next door, and really have to search the shelves for products from developing countries that are not Fairtrade. You simply cannot find them. In the end, you ask the tired assistant, who cannot understand why anyone would be so wacky as to want those old-fashioned products. She points you to a dusty bottom shelf at the back of the shop where there's a sad collection of coffee, tea and sugar without the Mark.

This dream will come true if each of us makes it happen. Fairtrade has grown thanks to the power of people – thousands of miles apart across the globe – each deciding that they wanted to make a difference. And as we scale up and develop Fairtrade in new and exciting ways, the engine powering that change will still be people buying, campaigning and living Fairtrade.

People come to Fairtrade from a huge variety of perspectives, all with differing motives for taking action; that's part of its strength. For me, when I buy Fairtrade I am answering the call from millions of organised producers to give them a chance, to give them dignity, to bring about change, to protest against the brutal logic of the global marketplace, to create living justice.

I buy Fairtrade products because it is simply the right thing for me personally to do. I'm not on a moral high-horse. But, for me, Fairtrade is a way of taking up Gandhi's challenge I absorbed working in India as a young woman – to 'be the change you wish to see in the world'. Of course it's not enough, it's not the only or the total answer; of course it's not and we never claim that. But it is one part of the answer because you and I and everyone can so very easily buy and support Fairtrade – and so connect with farmers and workers across the world. With each purchase, we are helping build that living, more humane alternative. And, at the end of the day, I am a mother who wants mothers the world over to realise the same dreams for their children as I do for mine.

Victor Perezgrovas, manager of one of the earliest Fairtrade coffee co-operatives in Mexico, told me once how, when explaining to farmers how their small crop can be part of an international movement that makes a real difference, he quotes an ancient Indian saying that, 'Many little raindrops falling in the mountains make the mighty rivers flow'. So it's in all our hands to turn the stream of Fairtrade into a torrent.

What You Can Do: Ten Steps Towards Fairtrade

'But what can I do about it?' is one of the commonest responses we all have to the injustice and poverty in the world. The problems are so staggering in scale, so terrifying in their complexity that it is easy to feel completely overwhelmed. And to forget that every one of us can do a few practical things to start setting the world around us to rights. The story of Fairtrade is a story of how many people each took a few small steps and ended up covering a vast distance together.

It is inspiring to read about how much Fairtrade producers are achieving, how far Fairtrade has come in getting companies to act differently, and how this change has only been possible because thousands of individuals, families and communities have got involved.

The beauty of Fairtrade is, of course, anyone can support it. We can all spend those few extra seconds in the coffee aisle of our local shop, stick out our hand and suddenly we're part of the solution. We can all get together with other people in our communities, or at college or church or at work – and come up with any number of ideas of how to include Fairtrade in just about anything we do, anywhere.

And the bigger changes now needed to expand Fairtrade all depend on people like you and me continuing to take action. There are lots of ways we can all make a difference – here are just ten. They range from the immediate and simple, to the more time-consuming. You may already be doing some of them, or be ready to give a few others a go. Have fun.

Step One: Buy Fairtrade

For home

People choosing to buy Fairtrade products is the foundation of its success; the bottom line that makes everything else possible. The FAIRTRADE Mark was set up, after all, to make certified products easier to find. While the range and availability of products varies in different countries, there are now more Fairtrade products than ever before and they are becoming more and more widely available.

You can find a list of the Fairtrade products you can currently buy, and who stocks them, on the website of the Fairtrade Foundation and the other national Fairtrade organisations. You might sometimes have to search out the products in your town and not every supermarket or chain of shops will have the whole range of products. In which case, you just have to ask. Whatever happens, don't give up easily!

In the UK, from flowers to footballs, nuts to biscuits and spices, the Mark is now on over 4,500 different products that can be found in tens of thousands of shops up and down the country. You can find a wide range of Fairtrade products in all the major supermarkets, and some independent stores in particular wholefood shops. Keep your eyes peeled down at your local off-licence too as Threshers for example have a range of South African and Chilean Fairtrade wines.

Towns also have dedicated Fair Trade shops. Many of the products they sell carry the Mark; others, especially handicrafts, might not do but you can be sure that they have been traded fairly if the shop belongs to the British Association of Fair Trade Shops (BAFTS) – as Traidcraft do – or if the organisation is part of the International Fair Trade Association (IFAT).

Recently, products made with Fairtrade certified cotton have started to appear in clothes shops such as Next, John Lewis and Topshop and you can shop online through websites like Gossypium, Traidcraftshop or People Tree.

New companies are continually coming into the system, persuaded by public demand, bringing with them new and exciting products. The Fairtrade Foundation is always working to develop international standards for new lines of Fairtrade products. Much of this work is being done with fair trade organisations, such as Traidcraft.

Keep an eye on the websites of the Fairtrade Foundation and its partners in other countries (see the end of this chapter) for an updated list of products and where to buy them. In the UK you might also want to sign up to receive *Fair Comment*, the Foundation's quarterly newsletter, which will keep you up to date.

The comedian Lenny Henry, who was instrumental in Comic Relief, is a committed Fairtrade buyer: 'By buying Fairtrade products, you are ensuring that Third World farmers and workers are able to make a decent living, create new businesses and contribute to their communities. This has got to be a good thing – keep an eye out for Fairtrade products and know that when you are reaching for your wallet, you're actually reaching out to help someone who wants to be considered your equal.'

And away

When you're out and about, meeting up with friends or just having a break in a café, go to places that you know serve Fairtrade coffee and tea. These include chains which serve all Fairtrade coffee, such as Pret a Manger (who do not display the Mark), Progreso coffee shops, or AMT kiosks in stations (all Fairtrade coffee 'due to popular demand'), as well as others like Costa Coffee that offer it as an option. Many independent cafés around the UK and in other countries also serve Fairtrade hot drinks. If they advertise it, you just order Fairtrade; if they don't advertise it, make sure you ask. Pubs and bars also offer Fairtrade coffee, tea and wine, so make sure you check next time it's your turn to buy a round.

You can buy Fairtrade when you're away from home too. Whether you are in Brussels, Berlin or Paris you'll be able to find the Fairtrade products you've come to love – and others besides. Fairtrade is a worldwide movement and just about every country in Europe – as well as the US, Canada, Mexico, Australia, New Zealand and Japan – has an established FAIRTRADE Mark that can be found on products in supermarkets and specialist shops. The logo is the same in all countries (except the USA and Mexico), the guarantees are identical, so look out for them and don't hesitate to let friends and family living in other countries know what they can do to help producers by buying Fairtrade. Dunkin' Donuts offers 100 per cent Fairtrade expresso coffee in North America and Europe, while Insomnia Coffee Company serves only Fairtrade in all its outlets across the country.

In Brooklyn, New York, people even seem ready to move to a particular area to get good Fairtrade coffee: 'The fact that the coffee is fair trade is certainly more sustainable for the farmers, and having this coffeehouse also helps sustain our community,' said Willow Fodor, twenty-nine, a customer who said she moved to Ditmas Park because of the Vox Pop café. 'I just loved the vibe.'

Shopping list:

- Buy Fairtrade regularly: make it part of your lifestyle.

- If you're already a fan of Fairtrade coffee, try new products.

- Introduce your friends, family and work colleagues to buying Fairtrade.

- Look for the FAIRTRADE Mark when you are travelling abroad.

- Ask for Fairtrade drinks at your local café, pub or restaurant.

Step Two: Demand Fairtrade

If it's not already there, then ask for it. Your local store manager may not be convinced there is a demand in their particular town and therefore might not carry the range of products or particular product you are looking for. So although the product may be offered by the supermarket at national level, their local branch might not have it. There are suggestions boxes in most supermarkets and you can always get your message across by talking to a shop assistant or the store manager. It really does work as Asda or Morrison's supermarkets can tell you!

Point out that you shop there regularly (or will do if they offer the Fairtrade products you're looking for) and also tell them that you will spread the news about new Fairtrade products. Convince the shop, as the Channel 4 newsreader Jon Snow puts it, that, 'Finding fair-traded items on a shop shelf elevates the establishment on to another level for me. I am far more likely to shop in a place that displays "fair trade" products than one that doesn't.'

Fairtrade coffee and other products may sometimes be available on an optional basis in coffee shops, offices and other places. You may therefore have to ask for it specifically – so make sure you do! Always make a point of insisting on the Fairtrade option; and if a chain that says it offers Fairtrade but doesn't in a branch you visit, complain there and let their head office know about it.

Thousands of cafés and restaurants of course don't offer any

Fairtrade at all – yet! So keep asking, building up the critical mass that will convince them sooner rather than later that it's worthwhile for their business. Got a favourite pub, bar or restaurant? Ask them to change to Fairtrade. During Fairtrade Fortnight 2007 about forty restaurants signed up to the Switch a Dish campaign and used Fairtrade ingredients in their restaurants. Antony Worrall Thompson, owner of top restaurants in London and Henley, says: 'Choosing to switch to Fairtrade mangos in our restaurants means that together we are opening up more opportunities for producers like the mango farmers in Burkina Faso, one of the poorest countries in the world, for whom Fairtrade has brought a route out of poverty.'

Menu:

- Ask for the Fairtrade option wherever available.

- Drop a note in your shop's suggestion box requesting Fairtrade products.

- Talk to the manager of your local shop or supermarket about offering Fairtrade products or extending their range.

- Suggest that your local pub, café or restaurant serve Fairtrade drinks or use Fairtrade ingredients in their kitchen.

- Pack your local with your friends if it has Fairtrade wine or other products.

Step Three: Work Fairtrade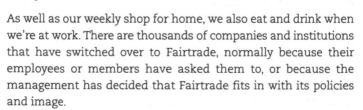

As well as our weekly shop for home, we also eat and drink when we're at work. There are thousands of companies and institutions that have switched over to Fairtrade, normally because their employees or members have asked them to, or because the management has decided that Fairtrade fits in with its policies and image.

For a small company, it can simply mean sitting down with your colleagues, suggesting they try a change and then deciding who is going to buy it from the local shop. At the other end of the spectrum, getting a larger company or organisation to purchase Fairtrade can be much harder work, requiring long negotiations with caterers and suppliers who might not yet offer Fairtrade lines. Good internal communications are essential to get employees to buy in to the idea, and if you have a trade union, they might back you too. Large companies generally have many different sites, which cause extra complications for them to source Fairtrade, and there are also questions of cost and of taste. But scores of examples of workplaces switching to Fairtrade show these can be overcome.

In the private and voluntary sector

Most of the largest companies listed on the London Stock Exchange have now implemented corporate social responsibility policies and report publicly on their activities. For many of them, offering Fairtrade forms part of their environmental and social sustainability agendas. A YouGov survey for the Fairtrade Foundation in September 2006 showed that 17 per cent of employees in the UK worked for companies that already offered Fairtrade products in the workplace, but 38 per cent felt that their employer should be making Fairtrade products available to their staff.

The Co-op Group is a pioneer in the area of sustainability. Co-operative Financial Services backs Fairtrade to the hilt. In 1997, the Co-operative Bank switched its vending machines to Cafédirect Fairtrade coffee – a world first. Faced with the problem of how to get Fairtrade coffee, and later hot chocolate, into the machines, CFS brought Cafédirect and Manchester Vending Services together to figure it out. Barry Clavin, CFS's Ethical Policies Manager, says: 'We could have said, "Well, it doesn't exist, so we'll do nothing about it." But the organisation's ethical goals led it to take a proactive approach.' Today, all hot beverages available to CFS's 14,000 staff and customers in branch offices, staff restaurants and vending machines are Fairtrade.

That, says Barry, adds up to 4 million cups and, when other Fairtrade certified products are included, they're spending £500,000 a year on Fairtrade goods – 'The business puts a lot of money behind Fairtrade, but the benefits certainly outweigh the costs – about a third of our customers join us because of our ethics. Staff response has been positive, customer perception has been positive and the cost isn't a barrier.' Since those early days, several specialist vending machine companies have sprung up to cater to the Fairtrade market. So that's another excuse out of the way.

Another large company to have made the switch is Arup, the global design and business consulting firm responsible for landmarks such as the Sydney Opera House, the City of Manchester Stadium and the Channel Tunnel Rail Link. Associate Director Andy Lawton recalls how the motivation to explore Fairtrade came from 'individual employees just going out on their own initiative to find out about it and bring it back to the office'. Each office organised blind trials and tastings, and collected employees' feedback through questionnaires. Staff clearly preferred the Fairtrade coffee and tea on the basis of taste. Once Fairtrade products were on offer, posters were placed around kitchens and offices as well as in meeting rooms to flag up to visiting clients the company's commitment to Fairtrade. Five years on, the company's 3,000 employees in London and Leeds drink about 2 million cups of Fairtrade coffee and tea per year.

'Fairtrade frequently crops up in office conversations as one of the positives about working for Arup. Clients who have similar attitudes to social responsibility see it as a positive thing that we are engaged with Fairtrade,' says Lawton. Likewise Umza Hamid of KPMG says that Fairtrade 'is just what we do. It's a culture now.' While in France, agnès b., the fashion label that epitomises French casual style, uses Fairtrade products in-house.

Francisco Rebollo is a Mexican pilot for Aurigny, an airline that flies to and from the Channel Islands, and he was one of the staff who persuaded the airline to serve Fairtrade coffee on all its flights.

Not-for-profit workplaces have also taken up Fairtrade enthusiastically – from the Youth Hostel Association to the Transport and General Workers Union. In March 2007 the UK's National

Council for Voluntary Organisations (NCVO) announced a switch to Fairtrade in all its operations – including its major conference facilities – as part of its 'Operation Green' to model the changes it was encouraging all voluntary organisations to adopt. The initiative was part of a wider government-backed Every Action Counts (EAC) drive to green the voluntary sector.

But just because you work or volunteer with a charity don't assume they're offering Fairtrade. An EAC researcher found that, 'On the whole within the charity sector, you would generally expect the ethos of most staff to be entirely favourable to the green agenda. They are, especially at junior staff level, but many were surprised at what needed to be done. . . In terms of awareness of sustainability issues, some [people] were much less aware than you would hope.'

In the public sector

Getting Fairtrade into public bodies has been varied – some great examples, but still much to be done. If you work in local government, then Fairtrade gives your council a very transparent, effective and practical means to show solidarity with developing countries and ties in with their commitment to the Local Agenda 21 initiative for sustainable development that came out of the 1992 Rio Earth Summit. It also helps to promote the many local companies that have become involved.

As a whole, the public sector spends about £2 billion a year in England alone, 13 per cent of our national wealth, on buying supplies. In 2003, then Prime Minister Tony Blair lent his support to the Public Sector Food Procurement Initiative (PSFPI), which aims to encourage government authorities to contribute to sustainable development through their food and drink procurement practices.

It's not easy for public authorities to switch to Fairtrade, especially if the size of the catering contract exceeds certain thresholds that require the calls for tender to be published in the official journal of the European Union. Such contracts must ensure 'value for money', but guidance from the Office of

Government Commerce (OGC) advises that procurement officials can state that companies responding to an invitation tender may include Fairtrade options in their offer. The same invitation to tender may say 'the FAIRTRADE Mark or equivalent is a helpful way of demonstrating that fair trade standards are being met'. The OGC guidance document also clarifies that value for money 'is not just about price'.

But the House of Commons all-party Select Committee on International Development's report on Fairtrade in 2007 urges the government to go further in ensuring that procurement guidelines support Fairtrade saying, 'If companies and public bodies are finding it difficult to interpret the Office of Government Commerce guidance [on Fairtrade], and if other EU member states are interpreting EC procurement rules differently, there is obviously a lack of clarity which the government must address.'

The Department for Environment, Food and Rural Affairs (DEFRA) is one of the organisations to show the way and it was Margaret Beckett, in her spell as Secretary of State, who threw her weight behind the change. In 2005, Fairtrade products, mainly hot beverages, were sold in their eleven staff restaurants in London, York, Guildford and Reading. Kevin Bates, in charge of the department's Strategic Procurement Group, says of managing the switch: 'Initially, due to the higher cost of Fairtrade beverages, the suppliers wanted to charge a premium for the supply of Fairtrade products, which would have had a negative effect on sales and benefited no one. However based on the volume, the good publicity and the subsequent reduction in procurement costs, it was agreed by all suppliers that the new products would be supplied cost-neutral, at least in the early days.'

The Department for International Development (DFID) funds various Fairtrade initiatives, including some support for the Fairtrade Foundation. Cafédirect is now the only coffee served on the department's London site and there is a range of Fairtrade confectionery, juices, teas and snacks. DFID currently subsidises the extra cost of Fairtrade to employees. 'We are really marketing Fairtrade,' says Steve Niblett who is responsible for managing the catering contract. His next aim is to ensure that every day there is a dish on offer that contains a Fairtrade ingredient such as rice.

All sorts of public bodies are now successfully making the switch. The Scottish Parliament and Welsh Assembly both serve Fairtrade and, when the Metropolitan Police Service moved to Fairtrade, we couldn't resist saying 'It's-a-fair-cop'.

Resources for companies and public authorities in the UK

- Various tools and advisory documents from DEFRA: www.defra.gov.uk/farm/policy/sustain/procurement/trade.htm
- Office of Government Commerce (OGC) Guidance on Fair and Ethical Trading: www.ogc.gov.uk/documents/Guidance_on_Fair_and_Ethical_T rading.pdf
- 'Buy Fair – A Guide to the Public Purchasing of Fair Trade Products', from the ICLEI (Local Governments for Sustainability): www.buyfair.org
- The Fairtrade Foundation's 'Fairtrade At Work' campaign website: www.fairtradeatwork.org.uk
- 'Buying into Fairtrade: Procurement in the Private and Public Sector' (Fairtrade Foundation, September 2006). Examines the opportunities, experiences and challenges of adopting Fairtrade products. Many of the above examples are drawn from this study. Order a hard copy or download at http://www.fairtradeatwork.org.uk/resources/buying_into_ fairtrade.pdf

Memo:

✐ Wherever you work, persuade your employer to go Fairtrade.

✐ If you're involved with a trade union or a charity, get them hooked.

✐ Ask your political representatives, local and national, to back public bodies switching to Fairtrade as a matter of policy.

Step Four: Play Fairtrade

We've never had as much leisure time and so many ways to spend it. It's easy to make Fairtrade a part of your activities and look out for Fairtrade products whenever you have a day out.

If you're the sporty type, how about asking your local leisure centre or swimming pool to serve Fairtrade drinks in their café or vending machines? If you're a member of your local sports club or team, then tell everyone about Fairtrade and look into how you might kit yourselves out in Fairtrade. There is a full range of sports balls (football, rugby, volleyball, basketball) available for your team to use, whether you play down at the local park or in a league. And, to go with the balls, there are now several companies who supply T-shirts and sweatshirts in Fairtrade cotton for your sporting events and other special occasions. Just ask the Fairtrade Foundation for contacts.

Cinemas, libraries, theatres, music venues and museums can also get involved in offering Fairtrade to their visitors. Edinburgh Zoo was the first zoo to serve only Fairtrade coffee, tea and hot chocolate to its visitors; other well-known landmarks that have changed to Fairtrade include Kew Gardens and Greenwich Maritime Museum. In the Netherlands, a small brewery called Gulpener has adopted Fairtrade coffee for its employees and is associated with The Critical Mass in Rotterdam, the country's first sustainable dance club where funky beats come with locally sourced, organic and Fairtrade drinks.

Many theatres serve Fairtrade drinks and in Canada there is even a Fair Trade Theatre Society, which describes itself as 'a group of local Vancouver bohemians with a penchant for theatre (and social consciousness)'. A recent performance was a play called 'Untold Crimes of Insomniacs'. Who finished the coffee, then?

If you're throwing a party, become a Fairtrade barman or woman and get in the Fairtrade rum, limes and sugar to make some mean mojitos! If it's a children's birthday party, then stock up on juices and bake that cake with some yummy Fairtrade chocolate. And that goes for the cakes you make for the local fete or coffee morning too – with Fairtrade sugar, chocolate, fresh and dried fruit, nuts and spices, the range of delicious treats you can make is almost endless.

In fact, every dinner party with friends can be an excuse to show off your cooking skills and show your guests what can be done with Fairtrade ingredients, all washed down with a glass (or several) of Fairtrade wine. Or indeed beer. For example, the traditional Westerham Brewery Co. found its William Wilberforce Freedom Ale, brewed in 2007 to commemorate 200 years since the passage of the bill abolishing slavery in the British Empire, outsold its most popular brew. Demerara sugar from Malawi – which was commonly used by brewers in Britain when they also owned slave-labour sugar estates in the Caribbean – is now Fairtrade and 'adds a fruitiness reminiscent of pear drops and sherbet lemons to the nose, dominated by biscuity malt and hop resins', according to one real ale buff. Or perhaps you could try the Mongozo Fairtrade banana beer brewed in Belgium in its tradition of fruit beers. The possibilities, it seems, are once again endless.

Of course, you can always imitate Ben Clowney, a charity worker with Tearfund, and make Fairtrade your life for a while! Ben, already thin, became Fairtrade Man for two weeks in 2007, eating only Fairtrade products and keeping everyone up-to-date on all his adventures on MySpace. He even had a date with Oxfam's Fairtrade woman. He told *New Consumer* magazine: 'The idea of my fortnight is to show that if you combine Fairtrade with locally produced food you can get by. I'm looking forward to experimenting. Lots of people have emailed in recipes, peanut curry . . . I thought it was just going to be rice and raisins '

But don't get too carried away with your cookery ideas. Two Frenchmen (who shall remain anonymous) were so worried about how badly fed some Colombian Fairtrade coffee producers looked in a photo they had seen, they felt they just had to act. They decided to contact the producers . . . and see about giving them a few proper cookery classes in French! The French Fairtrade organisation had to explain gently that this might not be so useful.

Step Five: Join Fairtrade

A great way you can help Fairtrade is to get involved with other like-minded people in a local group or campaign. There are currently Fairtrade groups all over the world, and lists are available on the Fairtrade websites (see end of the chapter). These local groups have often coalesced around development campaign groups like CAFOD, Oxfam, WDM or Traidcraft.

There are thousands of ways these groups promote Fairtrade – the only limit is your imagination. You might want to dream up an event specifically to talk about Fairtrade, host a Fairtrade party or just make it part of your faith group's service, your local summer fete or a school barbecue.

Fairtrade Towns

As described in Chapter 2, a central plank of promoting Fairtrade has been the Fairtrade Towns programme. From its beginnings in Garstang, a set of goals have been agreed which a town must show they meet before being granted "Fairtrade" status by the Fairtrade Foundation in the UK. The targets vary according to the size of the town or area (if it's a large city, of course, it needs to have more shops or restaurants offering Fairtrade than a village does) – but the overarching criteria are:

- The local council must pass a resolution supporting Fairtrade and agreeing to serve Fairtrade coffee and tea at its meetings and in its offices and canteens.
- A range of (at least two) Fairtrade products readily available in the area's shops and catering establishments.
- Fairtrade products are used by a number of local workplaces (such as estate agents, hairdressers, etc.).
- Attract media coverage and popular support.
- A local Fairtrade steering group is convened to ensure community-wide support and continued commitment to Fairtrade Town status.

'The whole Fairtrade Towns idea is inspirational,' says Rita Verity, who runs a Fairtrade shop in the Yorkshire village of Howarth, home of the Brontë sisters, and is a stalwart of the local group. 'It's a marketing tool that embraces people: they get a feel-good factor they can't really explain but which comes from doing the right thing. Do you know, I think we're pushers really – it's like a drug!'

Rita has certainly got the habit. She and her group of eight persuaded the council and local people to back the project in record time and Howarth became the first village to get Fairtrade status in 2002.

She remembers the occasion when pop mogul and steam railway enthusiast Pete Waterman came to town. 'He came to Howarth because *Songs of Praise* was being recorded, with a candlelit procession and all. The local railway was ready to announce Fairtrade status, so it fitted in nicely with our schedule. I talked about the importance of Fairtrade while Pete Waterman was presenting the certificate. During it he leaned over to me and said, "Love, you're a dreamer. People just want things as cheap as they can get them."' Dream on Rita, I say!

Inspired by the slogan 'Get the Fairtrade Habit', Rita gave out fourteen blank books around her village, to the school, the Brontë Parsonage, the hotel and the local MP, Anne Cryer. She asked people to write something about Fairtrade inside – and then pass the book on. 'I'm not quite sure where they are now. One was in Australia and another came back from Parliament with the signatures of Tony Blair, John Prescott and Gordon Brown in it. I even got the President of Dominica to sign it at the launch of Fairtrade Fortnight' Rita has even been out to Peru and managed to arrange for Howarth, one of the UK's tourist highlights, to be twinned with the world-famous Inca city of Machu Picchu.

Fairtrade Towns are spreading – with a programme to link up Fairtrade communities across Europe, especially in Ireland, France and Belgium where schemes are already well established.

In June 2006 the Pennsylvania town of Media ('Everybody's Hometown') declared itself the first Fairtrade Town in the United States, based on the UK criteria, with plans to set up a home-grown US-wide system of Fairtrade Towns. Elizabeth Killough, one of the driving forces behind the campaign in Media, was asked by a London-based journalist if it was true that she had bribed the business authority and borough council into becoming a Fairtrade Town with Fairtrade chocolate: 'I laughed myself silly! If only it was that easy. If on the other hand our committee's gift of chocolate to the powers-that-be did the trick, then I say bribery is a good thing!'

The Fair Trade Association of Australia and New Zealand has developed a programme of Fairtrade Communities, which is just what it says: any place where people live, work, play and hold religious services can meet a set of criteria based on promoting Fairtrade. Examples of such communities are Yarra in Victoria, Australia, Rangitoto College in Auckland, New Zealand, and a host of shops, schools and workplaces.

Ireland has taken up the idea with gusto since 2003 – with twenty-four at the last count. From Belfast in the north to Kinsale and Waterford in the South – in a very short time the movement has helped catapult public recognition of the FAIRTRADE Mark to over half of people by 2007 and driven a sharp rise in sales. The Irish government has also now pledged aid to support the development of Fairtrade, investing in Ireland and with producers in developing countries.

In fact one of the most remarkable stories of a Fairtrade Town comes from the Emerald Isle, in the shape of Newry, which straddles the border between Northern Ireland and the Republic. Catherine Mallon, a community worker and lecturer at Newry Institute, set out virtually single-handedly to obtain Fairtrade status for her hometown. No easy task, as the town is still divided along sectarian lines.

'Fairtrade was an excuse to bring people together, to think outside themselves about a subject on which there could be no disagreement. A simple jar of Fairtrade coffee became our political and moral compass, a means of renewing our community from the inside out. It was Fairtrade that made it possible for a Free Presbyterian minister and an ex-Republican prisoner to sit down and discuss together. About six members from the travelling community have also joined.'

Newry became the first town to gain simultaneous Fairtrade status from the UK and the Irish Republic in March 2005. It was a moment of great political symbolism and, later, Newry also chose to fly the Fairtrade colours – blue and green – at its Saint Patrick's Day parade.

For a town, village or island that has spent months or even years persuading and negotiating with local players to get Fairtrade status, the day the certificate comes through from the Fairtrade Foundation is a moment for celebration. It's an opportunity to get publicity for Fairtrade, and local groups have hatched a variety of different plans. For Windermere and Bowness's award, a boat took to Lake Windermere for a cruise with the local MP, the mayor and chairman of the local district council, and 500 revellers aboard . . . as well as local hero Benjamin Bunny swigging his mug of Fairtrade hot chocolate!

At school

You can help your school go Fairtrade too, often using materials produced by the Foundation's charity owners such as SCIAF or Cafod. In autumn 2007 the Fairtrade Foundation launched its new schools scheme and 2,000 schools had signed up by 2008.

John Dougan, a sixteen-year-old pupil at St Joseph's High School Business and Enterprise College in Workington, Cumbria, gives a great account of how enthusiastic pupils and staff can get about Fairtrade. His business studies and social enterprise teacher asked him to join the school Fairtrade group. 'There are about eighteen pupils – English, Scottish, Indian, Lithuanian, Slovak and Polish – and four teachers involved, in a school of six hundred. We started by organising coffee mornings and tasters for the pupils. The teachers came down from the staff room for their coffee as well – and they realised that the kids were not so nasty after all!

'We immediately decided we needed to go for Fairtrade School status, but when we first talked about it, some teachers were a bit shocked. We set up a steering group and made sure we promoted Fairtrade at every event: governors' meetings, parents' evenings, at the school production, by putting up posters in the staff room and the classrooms. In April 2006 we got Fairtrade products into the school canteen and they've sold well.

'Fairtrade is now part of our courses in religious studies, business studies, English, geography and even in art – they made the banner for Fairtrade Fortnight – and design and technology, where we worked on packaging for Fairtrade products. We were awarded Fairtrade status in March 2007. Fairtrade really changed the face of St Joseph's.'

Trewalynd V&A Primary School in Flintshire in Wales has developed an array of activities – presentations, songs, plays – around Fairtrade with its kids with obvious success. Six-year-old Ewan Fraser says, 'I look out for Fairtrade symbols in the supermarket when I go shopping with my mum.' It is obviously not only the pupils who appreciate the school's efforts: parents have written in saying things like, 'Making us aware of these issues has an impact on the way we think and act – thank you for helping us become more aware.'

The Young Co-operatives have a pioneering national scheme to encourage older kids to sell Fairtrade themselves and learn all about new ways of doing business along the way.

Resources for Fairtrade in schools
www.youngcooperatives.org.uk/
www.fairtrade.org.uk/schools

At university

Students are among the most active at pushing Fairtrade – so join in the fun to help spread the word on campus. In the UK they are often helped by People & Planet, a student network campaigning on poverty and the environment among UK sixth-form and university students, who have a Fairtrade campaign.

Oxford Brookes University was the first to achieve Fairtrade status in the UK in June 2003 and eighty-seven universities have now joined them. As Students' Union President Becca Mann put it when Brighton University went Fairtrade: 'Students at Brighton study in a privileged environment which is perhaps why so many want to make a difference in poverty-stricken countries.'

North East Wales Institute for Higher Education (NEWI) is a founder member of the Wrexham Fairtrade Coalition, just one example of student groups working with the wider community on Fairtrade. At a ceremony to mark his university becoming the first in Scotland to go Fairtrade, Will Garton, President of Edinburgh University Student Association (EUSA) said, 'Last year EUSA purchased over 1,700 kg of coffee and the university's accommodation services served around 300,000 cups of coffee a year to staff, students and commercial clients. A wide range of Fairtrade products are available and even Fairtrade wine is on the way to becoming the default option across the board.'

In the US, United Students for Fair Trade co-ordinates the actions of over a hundred affiliated student Fair Trade organisations and has rolled out training programmes on campuses across the country. They organise an annual convergence where student groups and other actors from the Fair Trade movement come together to discuss their activities – and what Fairtrade should look like in the future. The Canadian Student Fair Trade Network was set up in 2004 and has an active programme of campaigns, events, producer speaker tours and publications, including an e-newsletter called 'Synergy'. One great campaign was promoting Fairtrade chocolate around screenings of the film of *Charlie and the Chocolate Factory*. Increasingly there is close co-ordination between the student Fairtrade groups in North America.

Resources for student groups
In the UK: People & Planet – www.peopleandplanet.org
In the US: United Students for Fair Trade – www.usft.org
In Canada: Canadian Student Fair Trade Network – www.csftn-recce.org

In faith groups
If you are a member of a faith group, you should get a welcome response from your place of worship or linked community organ-

isations if you suggest they commit to Fairtrade products. By 2008 well over 4,500 churches had committed to Fairtrade, while thirty-eight synagogues and Jewish organisations in the UK have gone Fairtrade since 2006. The B'nai Jeshurun Congregation in New York City in the United States became involved with Fairtrade through part of its commitment to *tikkun olam* or repairing the world.

In Woking, the beautiful Shah Jahan Mosque, the longest established mosque in Britain, invented a new category, becoming the first Fairtrade Mosque when they announced it at the *mela*, or summer fete, in 2005 that brought together about 3,000 people. Mufti Liaquat, one of the imams at the mosque, was immediately interested in the idea. 'I first heard about Fairtrade from one of my colleagues who was teaching at the mosque. Fairness and justice with the poor are very important in Islam, and we wanted to be part of this. Of the Muslim community in Woking 80 per cent are from Pakistan and, although we promote all Fairtrade products, there is particular interest in the sports balls because they are made in Pakistan. People in our community feel a sense of pride and well-being through helping developing countries where many of them originally come from.'

Action list:

- Persuade your village, town, borough, island or county to go for Fairtrade status.

- Convince your school or university to go Fairtrade.

- Work with your church, mosque, temple or synagogue to go Fairtrade.

Step Six: Celebrate Fairtrade

There are now special times of the year to promote and celebrate Fairtrade in many countries. In Britain and in Ireland you can get involved in each country's Fairtrade Fortnight, usually held at the beginning of March each year. There were over 10,000 events in 2008 in Britain – so it's getting hard to miss even if you try. In Australia and New Zealand there is also Fairtrade Fortnight in April/May each year. While in Canada there are the National Fair Trade Weeks in the first two weeks of May. In the United States, October is Fair Trade Month, with lots of information on what you can do on the Transfair US website, as well as in your local community. And there are Fairtrade weeks, fortnights and months in a growing number of countries across Europe.

Of course, there are a huge range of types of events and initiatives across countries and local communities. You can help your local group organise tastings, discussions, plays, art competitions, fashion shows and film screenings. You can use the focus to persuade your local shops to promote Fairtrade products. Make your town a hotbed of Fairtrade activism with days of coffee and chocolate-fuelled madness each year. Bring along the local press as you should have lots of juicy stories for them to get their teeth into.

How about some of these wild ideas for inspiration? In Australia, Elena Katz-Chernin, a famous Australian pianist-composer, unveiled an original piece called 'Road to Harvest' inspired by Fairtrade producers at the Fairtrade Fiesta, and again while chef Kylie Kwong cooked for journalists in Billie Kwong, her Sydney restaurant. Back in Europe, people dressed up in labelled banana suits have swept through Scandinavia, and mayors and celebrities in the Netherlands donned backpacks that looked like a cross between spacesuits and a petrol pump to serve coffee to passers-by in town centres. Firemen from Besançon in eastern France have sewn the Fairtrade logo on to their clothes to run the Paris, New York and Mont Blanc marathons.

But it's important to keep on promoting Fairtrade all year round. Sports and games are always a powerful draw and football is a good vector for a fair play message. Up till now, the highest-profile game to publicise Fairtrade in Britain was between Derby FC and Burnley FC during Fairtrade Fortnight 2006, when the ball boys wore special bibs displaying the Fairtrade logo. There was also a penalty shoot-out at half-time using Fairtrade balls. Two teams from the University of Derby Students' Union played a match symbolising a world of two halves: the girls' team desperately tried to score in a tiny toy goal as they hobbled around the field tied to each other, while the lads, in pristine kit, could run rings around them. Aston University hosted a similar type of netball game during Fairtrade Fortnight, only a bit more hardcore as one team was handcuffed!

Contact any local celebrities: they can give much-needed media exposure to Fairtrade by endorsing it or going on trips such as the one Harry Hill, a self-styled celebrity volunteer, made to Ghana. Gail Porter visited farmers in Uganda and Oz Clarke has been to Rwanda, Chile and South Africa. So if you happen to be a celebrity, Fairtrade needs you. And if you know a celebrity, persuade him or her to get in touch with the Fairtrade Foundation.

It doesn't always work of course. Rita Verity, of Fairtrade Haworth group fame, has been appearing as an extra on the soap opera *Coronation Street* for thirty years. A couple of years ago, during Fairtrade Fortnight, while one of the episodes to be broadcast was being shot, she went on set with some Fairtrade posters. 'Granada Studios promote Fairtrade and I thought that Roy and Hayley were the type of people who should and would go for Fairtrade. I went to see the props manager, the set dresser and finally the director, but I wasn't allowed to put the posters up anywhere.' Better luck with the product placement next time!

The Haworth group did however get Yorkshire-based Joanne Harris to come to see the film based on her best-selling novel *Chocolat* in the company of two Fairtrade cocoa farmers from Ghana . . . and delicious chocolate muffins made by Leeds Catering College.

The Cumbria Fairtrade Network brought together fifteen Fairtrade bodies throughout the county. Their activities took on a regional and then an international dimension. 'Being a network gave us the ability to present ourselves as an "agent" to the county council and, with the help of a councillor who took care of getting cross-party support for Fairtrade, the council passed a resolution on Fairtrade unanimously. One specific aspect of the resolution is that it sets Fairtrade alongside a policy of local purchasing,' says Joe Human. The council and Fairtrade volunteers set up a contact group to hold the council accountable and offer support.

The network even went to visit Ethiopian Fairtrade coffee farmers and now Keswick 'the birthplace of pencils' has set up an active link with Choche in Ethiopia, 'the birthplace of coffee', and home to a Fairtrade coffee co-operative. Joe says of this direct contact: 'The primary schoolteacher who went to Ethiopia now gives a day's work a week on Fairtrade in primary schools and we estimate we have talked to 5,000 people locally since we visited Choche.'

Campaign programme:

- Join your local Fairtrade group or committee.

- If you'd like some ideas, then the Fairtrade Foundation has resources online at www.fairtrade.org.uk/get_involved/fairtrade_fortnight/fairtrade_fortnight_2009/default.aspx

- Then let your imagination run riot!

- Get the local press and local radio to cover events.

- Promote Fairtrade in your shop, library, school, community centre, etc.

Step Seven: Offer Fairtrade

It goes without saying that if you run, work in or have close contacts with a company that trades or sells products from developing countries that could become Fairtrade certified, then see if you can interest the company in exploring how Fairtrade could become an integral part of your business. It's what thousands of businesses have done already – and they have all reported positive customer feedback and wider benefits to the business. Often it has been driven at first by one person.

Sell it

Fairtrade is an open system and your company – importer, wholesaler, supermarket, shop or caterer – can get involved. Just contact the Fairtrade Foundation or your national Fairtade labelling initiative and consult their website for further information about the range of products covered by Fairtrade standards and the products that carry the Mark. Fairtrade organisations are interested in any enquiry, be it to sell existing products or to develop completely new lines.

Fiona Mitchell has more difficulty than most in ordering Fairtrade products for her shop, given that she lives on Fair Isle, two-and-a-half hours by boat from the Shetland Islands. Fiona estimates that just about every household on Fair Isle (70 inhabitants) has one or more Fairtrade products in the cupboard. As she puts it, 'Fair Isle can relate easily to communities in the South; here too we have to operate collectively to achieve things and to survive.'

Of course, you don't have to be a company to sell Fairtrade. Many people are reps for Traidcraft or have market stalls and, for example, the Isle of Man group set up a shop on the main street in Douglas for a day during Fairtrade Fortnight. Members of student campaign People & Planet at Thomas Tallis Sixth Form College in Greenwich formed a Fairtrade Co-operative. Chaired by Neha Duggal, the co-operative made a bid for Enterprise Pathfinder funding from their local educational and business partnership on behalf of ten Greenwich Borough schools. With the funds, they converted an old Portakabin. Lucy Craker, from the group, says: 'There can't be too many seventeen year olds who can say they helped start and run a business. What I like is that while I'm picking up this experience and developing my skills, I am also making a difference out there – that's important to all of us.'

Serve Fairtrade

Your bed and breakfast, hotel or café can also offer Fairtrade products. Keswick in the English Lake District, population 5,000, has about 30,000 beds and attracts between half a million and a million tourists per year. There are now seventy guesthouses and two dozen restaurants that serve Fairtrade coffee, tea and chocolate, most of them exclusively. The Keswick Fairtrade group has joined the local tourism association, which flags up Fairtrade providers on their website on the basis of a set of criteria developed locally. These include having Fairtrade coffee and tea (as a minimum) on offer, making sure that customers can see they are on offer and having Fairtrade literature available.

'Some people do come and stay with us because we do Fairtrade,' says Helen Farquharson of Allerdale House B&B. 'Compared to normal coffee, Fairtrade only costs £1 more per week. There's no reason not to do it and we get lots of comments that the fresh coffee is nice.' Allerdale House also has a liquor licence and serves two Fairtrade wines.

The 200 Youth Hostels across the UK have progressively converted to Fairtrade products – and others worldwide have gone down the same path, such as the one in Nîmes in the south of France, which serves a full Fairtrade breakfast while Scandic and Hilton, one of Sweden's major hotel chains, announced in October that it would switch all its coffee to Fairtrade.

The Isle of Man Fairtrade group worked with one of the island's largest employers, the Isle of Man Steam Packet company, to make sure it could offer holidaymakers Fairtrade products in the cafés and gift shops on all its sailings. More and more travel companies are offering Fairtrade on the move from Via Rail, Canada's national rail service, to Ryan Air, Virgin Trains and Virgin Atlantic airlines.

Shopping list:

🍂 Ask your supplier about their range of Fairtrade products.

🍂 If you would like to develop your own Fairtrade products, contact your national Fairtrade organisation to become a licensee.

Step Eight: Campaign for fairer trade

Fairtrade cannot change world trade or fight world poverty on its own – it is just one small part of the many solutions needed. There need to be major changes in the world trade system to protect developing countries from cheap subsidised farm goods produced in developed countries undercutting local farmers, give poor Southern producers fair access to international markets and allow developing countries to protect their vulnerable economies.

The success of Fairtrade shows the public support for governments and international organisations to change their policies to the benefit of countries, producers and communities in the South. So, to carry the fight for trade justice further, take part in some of those campaigns too.

In the UK the Trade Justice Movement (TJM) – www.tjm.org.uk – brings together eighty organisations with 9 million members from all parts of civil society. TJM campaigns for trade justice – rather than free trade – to ensure that everyone benefits from trade and that the rules are tilted towards people in developing countries, those in the greatest need. TJM targets politicians at national, European and international level, mobilising its members and the general public on issues such as the unfair trade deals being promoted through the EU's Economic Partnership Agreements (EPAs) with poor countries in Africa, the Caribbean and the Pacific. The TJM's members also run their own individual campaigns such as Oxfam's campaign that forced Starbucks to recognise Ethiopia's intellectual property rights over its speciality coffee brands Harar, Sidamo and Yirgacheffe.

There is also the long-running campaign to Make Poverty History (www.makepovertyhistory.org) that led to the reduction of the debt burden on the world's poorest countries but needs you to keep on campaigning to make progress on trade.

You can find the full lists of the groups involved on websites mentioned below.

Campaigning list:

⊘ Support trade justice and anti-poverty campaigns.

⊘ Petition your representative in Parliament or Congress and your government for fairer trade rules.

⊘ Join one of the organisations that campaigns for fairer trade rules.

Step Nine: Invest in Fairtrade 🌐

Banks often advertise about being concerned with getting your money to work for you – but what if your money could also work for a better world, including Fairtrade?

Thankfully, the ethical banking sector is growing daily as more and more people look for a way of making sure that their bank doesn't lend their money to companies involved in sectors they do not support on principle, like the arms trade. Increasingly, however, people also want their savings to help grow sustainable business initiatives.

There are four main possibilities open to savers who want to support Fairtrade with their money:
- Opening a current account that invests in Fairtrade
- Lending through a share account
- Buying shares in Fairtrade companies
- Donating to support the development of Fairtrade

Triodos Bank was established in the Netherlands in 1980 with a mission of making environmental, social and cultural objectives a part of day-to-day banking. It only finances enterprises in areas that add sustainable value, such as renewable energy, social housing, organic farming and fair trade.

James Niven of Triodos Bank UK in Bristol says citizens can contribute to Fairtrade in two different ways by banking with Triodos: 'Money deposited in our regular account supports all the projects we finance, including Fairtrade. But we also run a Fairtrade Saver Account jointly with the Fairtrade Foundation. Not only do we invest the money in this account exclusively in fair trade businesses – some examples are Cafédirect and Zaytoun, which imports fair trade olive oil from Palestine – but we also donate 0.25 per cent of the average balance deposited in the account to the Fairtrade Foundation each year. And our customers can choose to donate a proportion of their interest to the Foundation as well.'

In 2006, Triodos managed around £2.4 million worth of deposits in the Fairtrade Saver Account, generating £27,000 for the Fairtrade Foundation's work. The account works in the same way as a classic current account.

Or put your money to work for producers directly. Shared Interest Society Ltd (SI), based in Newcastle, runs a share account rather than a bank account. It was set up in 1990 to provide long- or short-term loans to Fairtrade producer organisations and to the importers who work with them. Over 8,400 members have joined SI and lend between £100 and £20,000 each. In 2005, SI financed more than £27 million worth of Fairtrade orders. Jenny Hamilton, an SI investor and Council Member puts her motivation for joining thus: 'I wanted to join Shared Interest to "put something back". . . It takes private investment and uses it creatively to establish a partnership with developing countries.'

You can also invest in Fairtrade companies directly. Cafédirect made a highly successful share issue in 2005 to raise £5 million for its development and expansion, including into markets other than the UK. One of the most innovative aspects of the share issue was that it was advertised on packets of coffee and tea on supermarket shelves. Cafédirect's shares are not listed on an exchange, but

Triodos Bank manages Ethex, a matched bargain system, which facilitates contacts between buyers and sellers of Cafédirect's shares. Traidcraft also welcomes investors and, like Cafédirect, its registrars are Brewin Dolphin in Manchester.

Making a donation to the organisations that seek to take Fairtrade forward is another way of backing the movement. In Britain these include two organisations that are part owners of the Fairtrade Foundation: the Shared Interest Foundation, an international development agency whose current programmes involve providing training to Fairtrade producers in East Africa and sponsoring the Fairtrade Foundation's producer tour as part of Fairtrade Fortnight; Traidcraft Exchange, the UK's only development charity specialising in making trade work for the poor, which campaigns on trade issues, leads regional development programmes and assists producers in gaining access to the market; and, of course, the Fairtrade Foundation itself to fund awareness raising and the development of new Fairtrade products.

For more information:
- Triodos Bank UK: www.triodos.co.uk (investment offers given are subject to change but correct at the time of publication)
- Shared Interest Society Ltd: www.shared-interest.com
- Shared Interest Foundation: foundation@shared-interest.com
- Cafédirect:www.cafedirect.co.uk/our_business/inves torrelations/
- Traidcraft: www.traidcraft.co.uk
- International Association of Investors in the Social Economy (INAISE): www.inaise.org
- The Ethical Investment Group (www.ethicalinvestors.co.uk) provides specialist financial advice to people who want to know how to invest their money with social and environmental concerns in mind.

Step Ten: Read about Fairtrade

With the boom in interest in Fairtrade, there are a lot of new developments to keep up with. So you'll find a list of titles, publications and websites below that will help you find out more about world trade, how to make it fairer . . . and a few tasty Fairtrade recipes for good measure!

About Fairtrade

Books

Jacqueline DeCarlo, *Fair Trade: A Beginner's Guide* (Oneworld Publications, 2007)

Daniel Jaffee, *Brewing Justice: Fair Trade Coffee, Sustainability, and Survival* (2007)

Miles Litvinoff and John Madeley, *50 Reasons to Buy Fair Trade* (Pluto Press, 2007)

Alex Nicholls and Charlotte Opal, *Fair Trade: Market-Driven Ethical Consumption* (Sage Publications, 2005)

David Ransom, *No-Nonsense Guide to Fair Trade* (New Internationalist, 2006)

Laura Raynolds, Douglas Murray and John Wilkinson, *Fair Trade: The Challenges of Transforming Globalization* (Routledge, 2007)

Recipe books

Vicky Bhogal, *A Fair Feast, 70 Celebrity Recipes for a Fairer World* (Simon & Shuster, 2005)

Linda Collister, *Divine Heavenly Recipes with a Heart* (Absolute Press, 2007)

Sophie Grigson, *The Fairtrade Everyday Cook Book* (Dorling Kingsley, 2008)

Sophie Grigson and Oxfam, *Oxfam Forward Cookbook* (Cassell Illustrated, 1997)

Lucas Rosenblatt, Judith Meyer, Edith Beckmann and Andreas Thumm, *Cooking with Coffee: 60 Recipes Using Fair Trade Coffee* (New Internationalist, 2003)

Troth Well, *Vegetarian Main Dishes: From Around the World* (New
    Internationalist, 2004)
Troth Well, *Salads and Side Dishes: From Around the World* (New
    Internationalist, 2004)
Troth Well, *The Bittersweet World of Chocolate* (New
    Internationalist, 2006)

About International Trade and Development
Resources
• Oxfam's 'Make Trade Fair' website (www.maketradefair.org)
  has analysis and examples of what is wrong with the state of
  world trade today, what needs to be done to make trade a
  force for good, and how to go about it.
• Oxfam's Cool Planet website (www.oxfam.org.uk/coolplanet)
  has material and resources on Fairtrade and development in
  general for children and schoolteachers.
• The UK's Department for International Development (DFID)
  publishes a free, readable and well-illustrated quarterly
  magazine, *Developments*, www.developments.org.uk
• One World Online (www.oneworld.net) has easy-to-read
  guides and views on development, environment and fair
  trade issues.

Books
Maggie Black, *The No-Nonsense Guide to International Development*
    (New Internationalist, 2002)
Joseph E. Stiglitz and Andrew Charlton, *Fair Trade for All: How
    Trade Can Promote Development* (Oxford University Press, 2007)

About Ethical Shopping
Books
Duncan Clark, *The Rough Guide to Ethical Shopping* (Rough
    Guides, 2004)
Melissa Corkhill, *How to Be an Ethical Shopper: The Practical Guide
    to Buying What You Believe In* (Impact, 2007)

Organisations and resources
- **Bananalink** (www.bananalink.org.uk) campaigns on the banana trade to get a fair deal for growers and workers.
- **The Ethical Trading Initiative** (ETI) (www.ethicaltrade.org) is an alliance of companies, non-governmental organisations (NGOs) and trade union organisations that exists to promote and improve the implementation of corporate codes of practice which cover supply chain working conditions. ETI's ultimate goal is to ensure that the working conditions of workers producing for the UK market meet or exceed international labour standards.
- **Labour Behind the Label** (www.labourbehindthelabel.org), and the international campaign to which it is affiliated, the **Clean Clothes Campaign** (www.cleanclothes.org), work to improve working conditions in the international garment industry.
- **The New Economics Foundation** (www.neweconomics.org) is an independent 'think-and-do' tank which 'believes in economics as if people and the planet mattered'. Its website gives access to a large range of publications, including *The Ethical Consumerism Report 2005* in association with the Co-operative Bank and The Future Foundation.

Fairtrade Worldwide

Australia and New Zealand

Fairtrade Labelling Australia and New Zealand (FLANZ)
P.O. Box 306, Flinders Lane PO, 8009 Victoria, Australia

tel. + 61 (0)396 622919

fax. + 61 (0)396 633482

email aust@fta.org.au (Fairtrade Labelling Australia);
and info@fairtrade.org.nz (Fairtrade Labelling
New Zealand)

websites www.fta.org.au
www.fta.org.nz

FLANZ is the FLO member for both Australia and New Zealand.
It is the labelling arm of the Fair Trade Association of Australia
and New Zealand (FTAANZ), founded in 2003, with which it
shares a secretariat.

Founder members (2005)
Oxfam New Zealand – www.oxfam.org.nz
Oxfam Australia – www.oxfam.org.au
Christian World Service New Zealand – www.cws.org.nz
Friends of the Earth Australia – www.foe.org.au

Other key actors in Fairtrade
Trade Aid Importers – www.tradeaid.org.nz

Fairtrade products available
Coffee, tea/herbal tea, cocoa and chocolate (widely available);
rice and quinoa, sports balls, sugar, cotton products (limited
availability).

Where to buy
Australia
- Supermarkets: Coles, Woolworths, IGA's
- Fairtrade shops: Oxfam Trading
- Wholefood shops: Macro Wholefoods

- Coffee shops: Starbucks
- Online/mail-order: Trade Winds

New Zealand
- Supermarkets: Woolworths, Countdown, Foodtown
- Fairtrade shops: Trade Aid Importers
- Coffee shops: Starbucks, Esquires
- Online/mail-order: Trade Winds

Approximate Fairtrade retail sales value in 2006:
A$11.9 million

Canada
TransFair Canada
328 Somerset West, Ottawa ON K2P OJ9, Canada

tel.	+1 613-563-3351
fax.	+1 613-563-1462
toll-free	1-888-663-FAIR
email	info@transfair.ca
website	www.transfair.ca

TransFair Canada is a member of FLO and the Fairtrade labelling organisation for Canada.

Founder members (1994)
Individuals

Other key actors in Fairtrade
Canadian Student Fair Trade Network – www.csftn-recce.org
Engineers Without Borders – www.ewb.ca
Equiterre – www.equiterre.qc.ca
Oxfam Canada – www.oxfam.ca
World University Service of Canada – www.wusc.ca

Fairtrade products available
Coffee, tea, cocoa and chocolate, bananas, cotton products, rice and quinoa, sugar, spices, flowers, sports balls, wine.

Where to buy
- Supermarkets: Costco, Loblaws, Loeb, Metro, Sobeys, Thriftys Foods
- Fairtrade shops: Ten Thousand Villages, the Marquis Project (Brandon, Manitoba)
- Natural health food shops: Choices Market, the Natural Food Pantry (Ottawa), Herbs and Spices (Ottawa), Planet Organics Food Market, the Big Carrot (Toronto)
- Coffee shop chains: Bridgehead, Van Houtte, Starbucks

Approximate Fairtrade retail sales value in 2006:
C$80.5 million

Ireland
Fairtrade Mark Ireland
Carmichael House, North Brunswick Street, Dublin 7, Ireland

tel.	+353-1-475 3515
fax.	+353-1 873 2114
toll-free	1-888-663-FAIR
email	info@fairtrade.ie
website	www.fairtrade.ie

Fairtrade Mark Ireland is a member of FLO and the Fairtrade labelling organisation for Ireland.

Founder members (1992)
Individuals and the main development charities in Ireland.

Other key actors in Fairtrade
Amnesty International – www.amnesty.ie
Comhlámh – www.comhlamh.org
Trocaire – www.trocaire.org
Concern – www.concern.ie
Action Aid, Ireland – www.actionaidireland.org
Irish Congress of Trade Unions – www.ictu.ie
Self Help – www.selfhelp.ie

Fairtrade products available
Coffee, cocoa and chocolate, tea, bananas, cotton products, rice and quinoa, sugar, sports balls, wine and beer.

Where to buy
- Supermarkets: Centra, Dunnes Stores, Londis, Marks & Spencer, Superquinn, SuperValu, Spar, Tesco
- Fairtrade shops: Trade Fair Ireland ,Oxfam, Trocaise
- Natural health food shops: National Organic Products, Munster wholefoodsconatural Limited
- Coffee shop chains: Bewley's, Coffee Perfection, Java Republic, Starbucks

Approximate Fairtrade retail sales value in 2006:
€11.6 million

United Kingdom
The Fairtrade Foundation
3rd Floor, Ibex House, Minories, London, EC3N 1DY

tel.	+ 44 (0)20 7405 5942 (general)
	+ 44 (0)20 7440 7676 (resources order line)
fax.	+ 44 (0)20 7977 0101
email	mail@fairtrade.org.uk
website	www.fairtrade.org.uk

Members
Banana Link – www.bananalink.org.uk
CAFOD – www.cafod.org.uk
Christian Aid – www.christian-aid.org.uk
Methodist Relief and Development Fund – www.mrdf.org.uk
Nicaragua Solidarity Campaign – www.nicaraguasc.org.uk
National Federation of Women's Institutes – www.nfwi.org.uk
Oxfam UK – www.oxfam.org.uk
Scottish Catholic International Aid Fund – www.sciaf.org.uk
Shared Interest – www.shared-interest.com
Tearfund – www.tearfund.co.uk

Traidcraft Exchange – www.traidcraft.co.uk
United Reform Church – www.urc.org.uk
World Development Movement – www.wdm.org.uk

Other key actors in Fairtrade
British Association of Fair Trade Shops (BAFTS) –
www.bafts.org.uk
IFAT – www.ifat.org.uk
TWIN Trading – www.twin.org.uk

Fairtrade products available
Coffee, teas, cocoa and chocolate, bananas and other fruit,
cotton products, sugar and confectionery, rice and quinoa, fruit
juice, herbs and spices, honey, nuts and snacks, preserves and
spreads, flowers, sports balls, beer, wine and spirits

Where to buy
- Supermarkets: Asda, Budgens, Booths, Londis, The Co-op,
  Marks & Spencer, Morrisons, Sainsbury's, Somerfield, Spar,
  Tesco, Waitrose
- Fairtrade shops: Oxfam, members of British Association of
  Fair Trade Shops, Bishopston Trading
- Wholefood shops: Fresh and Wild, Holland and Barrett,
  independents
- Wholesalers: Suma
- Other independent shops: Stokes, National Union of Students
  (NUS) shops
- Coffee shop chains: AMT, Costa Coffee, Greggs, Marks &
  Spencer Café Revive, Pret a Manger, Starbucks
- Shops with clothes and other items made from Fairtrade
  cotton: Accessorize (bags), Co-op (bags), Debenham's
  (including men's wear), Marks & Spencer (wide range of
  clothing), Next (children's, men's and women's clothes),
  Sainsbury's (wide range of items in the TU brand), Topshop
  (also including People Tree at Topshop), Tesco (wide range of
  clothing)
- Online retailers: Traidcraftshop, Ethical Shopper, Goodness

Direct, Greenol, New Consumer Shop, Simplyfair, Bishopston Trading, Epona, Gossypium, Hug, People Tree, Ralper, Ascension, Oxton

Approximate Fairtrade retail sales value in 2006:
£290 million

United States
TransFair USA
1500 Broadway, 4th Floor, Oakland, CA, 94612-2002, USA
tel. + 1 (0)510 663 5260
fax. + 1 (0)510 663 5264
email info@transfairusa.org
website www.transfairusa.org

TransFair USA is a member of FLO and the Fairtrade labelling organisation for the United States.

Founder members (1996)
Institute for Agriculture and Trade Policy – www.iatp.org
Equal Exchange – www.equalexchange.com
Global Exchange – www.globalexchange.org
Fair Trade Federation – www.fairtradefederation.com
Food First – www.foodfirst.org
Headwaters International/Peace Coffee
Paul Rice/Independent Coffee Consultant

Other key actors in Fairtrade
Catholic Relief Services – www.crsfairtrade.org
Co-op America – www.coopamerica.org
EcoLogic Finance – www.ecologicfinance.org
Fair Trade Resource Network – www.fairtraderesource.org
Oxfam USA – www.oxfamamerica.org
United Students for Fair Trade – www.usft.org

Fairtrade products available
Coffee, tea and herbs, cocoa and chocolate, bananas and other
fresh fruit, sugar, rice, vanilla and flowers

Where to buy
- Supermarkets: Carr's, CostPlus World Market, Dominick's
  Finer Foods, Fred Meyer, Guenardi's, Gian, H-E-B Grocery
  Stores, Harris Teeter, Nordstrom, Publix, Quality Food Centers,
  Randall's, Safeway, Sam's Club, Shaws Supermarkets, Stop 'n'
  Shop, Target, Tops, Trader Joe's, Vons
- Fairtrade shops: 10,000 Villages
- Wholefood shops: Whole Foods, Wild Oats,
- Coffee shop chains: Bruegger's, Caribou, Dunkin' Donuts,
  Peet's Coffee and Tea, Seattle's Best Coffee, Starbucks

Approximate Fairtrade retail sales value in 2006:
US$690 million

The Global South
Fairtrade labelling initiatives
There are a number of emerging Fairtrade labelling initiatives
in developing countries, following the example set by Comercio
Justo Mexico, with producers joining forces with civil society to
promote sales of their Fairtrade produce on the domestic
market. FLO has received enquiries from traders in sixty
countries, particularly in the Middle East and South East Asia,
to join Fairtrade.

Brazil
The first Fairtrade labelled coffee was launched in August 2007
in the Brazilian supermarket chain Pao de Acucar. This was the
first time a purely smallholder coffee had been sold
countrywide.
For information on the Brazilian labelling initiative: Veronica
Rubio, v.rubio@fairtrade.net

India

India not only contains a vast number of farmers and farm workers – including Fairtrade-certified tea, rice, coffee, cotton, vanilla, nut and spice producers – but also a growing middle class that is interested in socially and environmentally responsible purchasing.

International Resources for Fair Trade (India) and Traidcraft (UK) are leading a project entitled Promoting Fair Trade in India (PROFIT) to set up a Fairtrade labelling initiative.
www.profit.org.in

South Africa

South African Fairtrade smallholder organisations and plantations have joined together to create the Fair Trade South Africa Trust in order to provide producer support and found a Fairtrade labelling initiative for the domestic market, which was launched in 2007.
www.fairtrade.org.za

Selected Fairtrade Producers

Ever wondered where your Fairtrade product comes from? You can now take a look with Google Earth.
www.transfairusa.org/content/certification/producer_profiles_google.php
Many Fairtrade producers also have websites where they tell their own stories. Here are a few that you might like to take a look at.

UCIRI – Mexico

The story of the very first Fairtrade certified coffee producers' organisation in the heart of the state of Oaxaca in the south of Mexico. The story of how the idea of an international Fairtrade system was born – and the background on the products they grow today.
www.uciri.org

Stellar Organics Winery – South Africa

Stellar Organics was the first organic winery to be Fairtrade certified and is situated in the world's only semi-arid biodiversity hotspot in the world, between Cape Town and the Namibian border.
www.stellarorganics.com

Kuapa Kokoo – Ghana

Kuapa Kokoo was one of the very first Fairtrade-certified cocoa co-operatives, owns and supplies the cocoa used in Divine chocolate.
www.kuapakokoogh.com

Makaibari Tea Estate – India

Makaibari is a longstanding organic and Fairtrade-certified tea estate in the foothills of the Himalayas in Darjeeling.
www.makaibari.com

Oromia Coffee Farmers Co-operative Union – Ethiopia

Oromia is a union of over 100,000 coffee farmers in the birthplace of coffee.
www.oromiacoffeeunion.com

Kagera Co-operative Union (KCU) – Tanzania

KCU is a coffee co-operative in Tanzania with 90,000 small-scale coffee farmers organised in 124 village co-operatives working together.
www.kcu-tz.com/

Prodecoop – Nicaragua

Prodecoop is located in the state of Esteli, Nicaragua, and has a membership of forty coffee-growing co-ops and 2,300 member producers.
http://transfairusa.org/pdfs/profiles/Prodecoop-Nicaragua.PDF

International
Fairtrade Labelling Organizations (FLO) International
Bonner Talweg 177, 53129 Bonn, Germany
tel.	+ 49 (0)228 949230
fax.	+ 49 (0)228 2421713
email	info@fairtrade.net
website	www.fairtrade.net

Fairtrade Labelling Organizations International (FLO), established in 1997, is an umbrella organisation that unites twenty labelling initiatives in twenty-one countries and three producer networks representing fairtrade certified producer organisations in Central and South America, Africa and Asia. FLO-Cert – www.flo-cert.net – is an independent international certification company set up by FLO to offer Fairtrade certification to producers and companies trading in Fairtrade products.

National labelling initiatives
Australia and New Zealand – www.fta.org.au
Austria – www.fairtrade.at
Belgium – www.maxhavelaar.be
Canada – www.transfair.ca
Denmark – www.maxhavelaar.dk
Finland – www.reilukauppa.fi
France – www.maxhavelaarfrance.org
Germany – www.transfair.org
Ireland – www.fairtrade.ie
Italy – www.fairtradeitalia.it
Japan – www.fairtrade-jp.org
Luxembourg – www.transfair.lu
Mexico – www.comerciojusto.com.mx
Netherlands – www.maxhavelaar.nl
Norway – www.maxhavelaar.no
Spain – www.sellocomerciojusto.org
Sweden – www.rattvisemarkt.se
Switzerland – www.maxhavelaar.ch

United Kingdom – www.fairtrade.org.uk
USA – www.transfairusa.org

Producer network members
Africa Fairtrade Network (AFN) – www.2can-consult.com/afn
Coordinadora Latinoamericana y del Caribe de Comercio Justo
(CLAC) – www.claccomerciojusto.org
Network of Asian Producers (NAP)

Other Fair trade networks
International Fair Trade Association (IFAT) – www.ifat.org
Network of European Worldshops (NEWS!) –
www.worldshops.org
The Association of Responsible Mining –
http://www.communitymining.org/

Notes

1. Banana Battles

1. Names have been changed to protect the identities of workers and because legal proceedings to secure compensation continue.
2. Except on pineapple plantations in Hawaii. World Development Movement (WDM), *DBCP Legal Action*, 1997, WDM.
3. WDM, *DBCP Legal Action*, 1997, WDM
4. WDM, *Saying Yes to the Best – Justice for Banana Workers*, 1997, WDM
5. Associated Press, 5 November 2007; *Los Angeles Times*, 6 November 2007. See also www.iht.com/articles/ap/2007/ 11/06/ business/NA-FIN-US-Banana-Workers.php
6. WDM, *Saying Yes to the Best – Justice for Banana Workers*, 1997, WDM
7. At the time, Del Monte's perspective on the core issue of union recognition was that the company-backed worker-management associations, the *solidarista* groups, provided representation for workers, and they were happy with them and didn't need to join the normal trade unions. However, the International Labour Organisation (ILO) regards such groups as an obstacle to the workers realising their rights to form independent trade unions. Indeed, when the workers were later given the chance to join the proper union, they did so in large numbers
8. *Check Out Fresh* magazine, November 1997
9. Human Rights Watch, *Tainted Harvest: Child Labor and Obstacles to Organizing on Ecuador's Plantations*, April 2002
10. http://www.fairtrade.net/el_guabo_equador.html
11. 'Banana Gate' in *New York Times*, 26 March 1997
12. http://www.flexnews.com/pages/6607/Tesco/ tesco_market_share_rises_314_uk_grocery_market_dj.html

13. Fairtrade Foundation, *Fairtrade Bananas Impact Study: Dominica, Windward Islands*, June 2004
14. FLO, Annual Report 2006
15. *The Age*, 26 March 2006

2. You'll Never Make it Work

1. BBC *News* magazine, 2 February 2007
2. Saul Alinsky, *Rules for Radicals*,1971, Vintage
3. *Guardian*, 26 February 2003
4. Gordon Brown, *Britain's Everyday Heroes: The Making of the Good Society*, Community Links, 2007
5. TNS Omnibus Survey Results April 2007. See also surveys commissioned by DEFRA and BOND
6. Clive Barnett and Paul Cloke, *Governing the Subjects and Spaces of Ethical Consumption*, ESRC, 2007
7. Dragon Brand Agency, *Inspire: Consumer Understanding of Fairtrade*, 2005. Mintel, *Attitudes Towards Ethical Food – UK*, August 2006
8. *The Grocer*, 16 December 2006
9. FLO *FLO Annual Report 2006/07*
10. You can find a more detailed account of the Green & Black's story in a chapter by Craig in Simon Wright and Diane McCrea (eds.), *The Handbook of Organic and Fair Trade Food Marketing*, Blackwell, 2007
11. David Croft, 'Corporate Social Responsibility from a Supermarket Perspective: Approach of the Co-operative Group', in Stephanie Barrientos and Catherine Dolan, *Ethical Sourcing in the Global Food System*, 2006, Earthscan
12. The Co-operative Group, *Chocolate: A Campaign for Fairtrade Chocolate and an End to Exploitation*, 2002
13. David Croft, 'Corporate Social Responsibility from a Supermarket Perspective: Approach of the Co-operative Group', in Stephanie Barrientos and Catherine Dolan, *Ethical Sourcing in the Global Food System*, 2006, Earthscan
14. BBC *Money Programme*, 5 October 2004
15. 'Memorandum Submitted by Marks & Spencer', in House of

Commons International Development Select Committee, *Fair Trade and Development: Seventh Report of the Session 2006–07 – Written evidence*

16. House of Commons International Development Select Committee, *Fair Trade and Development: Seventh Report of the Session 2006–07 – Written evidence*

3. To Hell and Back

1. Frontline World: Rough Cut, *Seeds of Suicide: India's Desperate Farmers*, 26 July 2005, http://www.pbs.org/frontlineworld/rough/2005/07/seeds_of_suicide.html

2. Brink Lindsey, *Grounds for Complaint? 'Fair Trade' and the Coffee Crisis*, Adam Smith Institute, 2004

3. International Fund for Agricultural Development (IFAD). They have an excellent overview of facts and issues on rural poverty and agriculture at http://www.ruralpovertyportal.org

4. Fairtrade Foundation, *Redressing a Global Imbalance: The Case for Fairtrade-Certified Cotton*, November 2005

5. Oxfam, *'White Gold' Turns to Dust: Which Way Forward for Cotton in West Africa?*, March 2004

6. Oxfam, *'White Gold' Turns to Dust: Which Way Forward for Cotton in West Africa?*, March 2004

7. John Baffes, *Cotton and Developing countries: A Case Study of Policy Incoherence*, World Bank, 2003

8. Oxfam, *Cultivating Poverty: The Impact of US Cotton Subsidies on Africa*, 2002

9. Oxfam America http://www.oxfamamerica.org/whatwedo/campaigns/agriculture/news_publications/fields_of_hope/feature_story.2006-07-05.9382851456

10. Oxfam America. See previous note for link

11. And this is out of a total global fibres market that has grown threefold since 1960. The world grows over 26 million tonnes of cotton a year – double what it did in 1980. See UNCTAD, Cotton Info Comm,

http://r0.unctad.org/infocomm/anglais/cotton/uses.htm
12. US aid to Africa is pledged to rise but latest OECD figures show a total of $3,899 million in 2005.
http://www.oecd.org/dataoecd/42/30/1860571.gif
13. For an overview of a number of the key studies see Overseas Development Institute, *Developed Country Cotton Subsidies and Developing Countries: Unravelling the Impacts on Africa*, ODI Briefing Paper, July 2004.
14. Oxfam, *Cultivating Poverty: The Impact of US Cotton Subsidies on Africa*, 2002
15. Republican debate in West Columbia, South Carolina, 7 January 2000
16. Oxfam, *Cultivating Poverty: The Impact of US Cotton Subsidies on Africa*, 2002.
17. IMF, *World Economic Outlook*, September 2005
18. Quoted in Oxfam, *Cultivating Poverty: The Impact of US Cotton Subsidies on Africa*, 2002
19. *Los Angeles Times*, 17 December 2005
20. US actions had only amounted to about a 10 per cent cut in their subsidies, according to an Oxfam analysis. *Financial Times*, 29 September 2006
21. *Financial Times*, 5 February 2007
22. Fairtrade Foundation, *Cotton: A Guide for Certification of Cotton Products*, June 2006
23. Interview with Lynn Barber, *Observer*, 15 April 2007
24. *Telegraph*, 28 September 2007
25. Andrew Mold, *Tackling the Commodity Price Problem: New Proposals and Revisiting Old Solutions*, UN Economic Commission for Africa [no date]
26. FAO, *The State of Agricultural Commodity Markets*, 2006
27. *Scotsman*, 25 July 2007
28. *DailyIndia.com*, 29 March 2007
29. Addressing the Twenty First Summit for the Heads of State of Africa and France, February 2003
30. OECD, OECD.stat. Based on GDP in real terms national currency
31. See http://www.statistics.gov.uk

32. UNDP, *Human Development Report 2005*, OUP
33. Oli Brown, 'Supermarket Buying Power, Global Commodity Chains and Smallholder Farmers in the Developing World', Human Development Report Occasional Paper, UNDP, 2005
34. *Financial Times*, 20 September 2006
35. *Financial Times*, 2 August 2004
36. *Economist*, 16 September 2006
37. *Economist*, 16 September 2006
38. UNDP, *Human Development Report 2005*, OUP
39. UNDP, *Human Development Report 2005*, OUP
40. The deal says payment levels will fall by 35 per cent over four years – though this will still leave them a good way above world prices.
41. *Financial Times*, 14 July 2006
42. Quoted in Oxfam, *Rigged Rules and Double Standards: Trade, Globalisation and the Fight Against Poverty*, 2002
43. *Financial Times*, 21 July 2006.
44. For more on TJM's current campaigns; as well the provisions of the Company Act 2006, see http://www.tjm.org.uk
45. *Newsweek*, 5 November 2001.

4. Swimming with Sharks

1. Interview for HaveFunDoGood blog, 24 April 2007 http://havefundogood.blogspot.com/2007/04/fair-trade-certified-interview-with_24.html
2. Fairtrade Foundation, *Spilling the Beans on the Coffee Trade*, 2002
3. Inter Press Services, 8 August 2003
4. Inter Press Services, 23 August 2003
5. See http://insidecostarica.com/specialreports/nicaragua_march_for_hungry.htm
6. Fransisco van der Hoff Boersma, 'The Urgency and Necessity of a Different Market: From the Perspective of the Producers Organized Within the Fairtrade Market', speech to Canadian Association for Studies in Cooperation, June 2006
7. Fransisco van der Hoff Boersma, see previous note

8. Fransisco van der Hoff Boersma, see previous note
9. The name 'Max Havelaar' is taken from the nineteenth-century literary hero of the book of the same name by Edward Douwes Dekker alias Multatuli. It relates a Dutch official's attempts to protect indigenous people's rights in the Dutch East Indies colonies.
10. FLO, *FLO Annual Report 2007*
11. FLO, *FLO Annual Report 2007*

5. Many Raindrops Make Mighty Rivers

1. http://www.thandi.com
2. Ronnie Morris, 'Poor Farm Workers Pose Challenge for Wine Industry', *Business Report*, 25 July 2007
3. *Telegraph*, 28 March 2006
4. *Capespan Courier*, December 2003
5. Johann Hamman, 'The Variety of Land Reform and Empowerment Projects in Commercial Agriculture', *Fairtrade South Africa*, 2005
6. Sara de Villiers, *South African Wine News*, 12 December 2005
7. http://news.bbc.co.uk/1/hi/magazine/6611447.stm
8. Mintel, *Attitudes Towards Ethical Food – UK*, August 2006
9. *Scotsman*, 25 July 2007
10. Cornelis Vringer, *Analysis of the Energy Requirements for Household Consumption*, University of Utrecht 1996
11. *Economist*, 9 December 2006
12. Speech for launch of Fairtrade Fortnight, February 2006
13. Co-operative Group, *Shopping with Attitude*, 2004
14. Africa Commission, *Our Common Interest: Report of the Commission for Africa*, Penguin 2005
15. House of Commons International Development Committee, *Fair Trade and Development Seventh Report of Session 2006–07*, HMSO, 2007

Take the Ten Steps Fairtrade Challenge

Step 1   **Buy Fairtrade** ☐
Look for the FAIRTRADE Mark whenever you're out shopping or travelling. Search out Fairtrade products from across the whole range available in your country.

Step 2   **Ask Fairtrade** ☐
If a Fairtrade product is not already there, then go ahead and ask for it.

Step 3   **Work Fairtrade** ☐
Why not ask for Fairtrade tea, coffee and other items to be served in your workplace.

Step 4   **Play Fairtrade** ☐
Check if Fairtrade products are on offer at your local leisure centre, cinema or library and swap to a Fairtrade football next time you go to the park.

Step 5   **Join Fairtrade** ☐
Find out if your town, local school, university or place of worship has a local Fairtrade and join up.

Step 6   **Celebrate Fairtrade**   ❑
Thousands of events are held every year so
why not get involved or organise an event in
your area? It's often a lot of fun.

Step 7   **Offer Fairtrade**   ❑
Do you sell or serve products from develop-
ing countries that could be Fairtrade?
Explore whether you could switch to a
Fairtrade.

Step 8   **Campaign for Trade Justice**   ❑
Get involved with campaigns like the Trade
Justice Movement to win the major changes
to make trade fairer.

Step 9   **Invest in Fairtrade**   ❑
Your savings could directly support Fairtrade.
Check out the options and put your money
where your mouth is.

Step 10   **Read about Fairtrade**   ❑
Gen up on how Fairtrade is changing lives by
checking out the publications and websites
on Fairtrade.

A Short History of Fairtrade

1940s
- Oxfam in the UK, and the US organisations Ten Thousand Villages and SERVV, lay the foundations for the Fairtrade movement by starting to sell goods made in projects amongst disadvantaged communities in war-devastated Eastern Europe and Puerto Rico.

1959
- A boycott of South African goods is launched in Britain in response to a call from the African National Congress (ANC). Part of a growing movement against apartheid, it shows how consumer power can be mobilised in support of justice and social change at an international level.

1960s
- The UN Commission on Trade and Development (UNCTAD) is created in 1964, helping coin the slogan 'trade not aid' as a focus for development efforts.
- In 1964, Oxfam creates the first fair trade organisation and shop.
- In 1967, Fair Trade Original is established as the Netherlands' first fairtrade importer.

1979
- Traidcraft, a pioneer alternative trade organisation, is set up in Britain to demonstrate 'the Christian principles of love and justice in international trade' selling only fairly-traded foods and handcrafts via churches, stalls and mail order.
- The Sandinistas overthrow the Somoza dictatorship in Nicaragua. Solidarity movements around the world support the newly-established coffee co-operatives of the new government, including selling 'solidarity coffee'.

1986
- The Mexican coffee farmers' co-operative UCIRI starts discussions with the Dutch NGO Solidaridad about selling coffee as Fairtrade.

1988
- International Coffee Agreement collapses, the world coffee market is liberalised and prices plunge.
- The Max Havelaar Foundation is founded in the Netherlands to label products as Fairtrade.
- The world's first Fairtrade-labelled product, coffee, is presented to the Dutch Prince Claus and Fairtrade quickly starts to take off.

1990
- Max Havelaar Belgium is established as the idea of Fairtrade labelling spreads.

1991
- The first major Fairtrade coffee brand, Cafédirect, is launched in the UK.

1992
- Fairtrade labels are born in France, Switzerland and in Germany, quickly followed by Austria and Luxemburg.
- The Fairtrade Foundation is set up to take Fairtrade-labelling onto the high street in Britain.
- In Switzerland, the two dominant supermarket chains, Migros and Coop, simultaneously introduce their own brand Fairtrade coffee.

1994
- The FAIRTRADE Mark is launched on its first UK product, Green & Black's Maya Gold chocolate, soon followed by Clipper tea and Cafédirect coffee.

1997
- The British House of Commons switches to Fairtrade coffee for all its refreshment outlets.
- TransFair is launched in Canada, taking Fairtrade into North America.
- Fairtrade Labelling Organizations (FLO) International is founded to co-ordinate standard-setting, certification and producer-links work internationally.

1998
- TransFair USA is launched: the world's largest coffee market discovers Fairtrade.
- The first Fairtrade bananas (from Ghana and Ecuador) hit shops in the Netherlands.

1999
- The first Fairtrade label gets started in a producer country: Comercio Justo México.
- Annual Fairtrade sales in the UK are now £22 million.

2000
- The first Fairtrade bananas in the UK are available in 1,000 Co-op stores, along with Sainsbury's.
- TransFair USA signs a national agreement with Starbucks.

2001
- Garstang in Lancashire proclaims itself the world's first 'Fairtrade Town'.
- Fairtrade blossoms as the world's first Fairtrade roses from East Africa go on sale in Switzerland.
- World market coffee, banana and cocoa prices drop to historically low levels. The need for Fairtrade has never been greater.

2002
- Co-op supermarkets switch all their own-brand chocolate to Fairtrade in the UK.
- Sandwich chain Pret a Manger offers customers 100% Fairtrade filter coffee in all its branches.

- FLO's national members start to replace their different symbols with one common international Mark.
- The first Fairtrade rice is launched in Switzerland and France.

2003
- FLO wins the prestigious King Badouin International Prize for Development.
- The first plantations and farmer groups are certified in South Africa.
- The company FLO-Cert is set up by FLO to guarantee impartial, independent certification services to Fairtrade producers and importers.

2004
- As the Fairtrade Foundation celebrates its tenth birthday, annual Fairtrade sales reach £141 million.
- Tesco, the UK's largest retailer, unveils an own brand range of Fairtrade products.
- Co-op Switzerland switches all its bananas to Fairtrade, the first supermarket worldwide to do so.
- The value of combined international Fairtrade retail sales crosses the $1 billion threshold

2005
- Cotton farmers join the Fairtrade system for the first time.
- 658 McDonalds restaurants in the northeastern United States start selling Newman's Own Organic Fair Trade coffee.
- The Fair Trade Association of Australia and New Zealand joins FLO, bringing the number of labelling countries to 21.

2006
- In July, the European Parliament adopts a resolution recognising the benefits of Fairtrade.
- In the UK, annual Fairtrade sales running at £290 million. Marks & Spencer converts 100 per cent of its retail coffee and tea to Fairtrade.
- Discount supermarket Lidl launches a range of Fairtrade products in Germany.

- Dunkin Donuts, Ryanair and Scandic & Hilton hotels (Sweden) all adopt 100 per cent Fairtrade coffee policies.
- Worldwide Fairtrade retail sales top $2 billion.

2007
- Worldwide, 2,000 companies now sell Fairtrade products.
- There are now 569 producer organisations representing 7 million farmers, workers and their families in 57 countries.
- In October, Sainsbury's announces it is converting all of its own brand tea and coffee to Fairtrade – set to triple UK Fairtrade tea sales to £1 in £10 of all tea sold. Earlier in the year, it has converted 100 per cent of its bananas to Fairtrade, as has supermarket chain Waitrose.
- Sainsbury's converts all of its own brand tea and coffee to Fairtrade and, with Waitrose, it converts 100 per cent of its bananas to Fairtrade.
- The African, Asian and Latin American Fairtrade producers formally become co-owners of FLO.

2008
- Tate & Lyle switch all their retail pure cane sugar to Fairtrade, bringing Fairtrade premium worth £2 million to 6,000 producers in Belize.
- Starbucks announce that by the end of 2009 they will double their global purchases of Fairtrade coffee, and all espresso-based drinks served in their UK branches will carry the FAIRTRADE Mark.
- Tipping the Balance, the Fairtrade Foundation's ambitious strategy for 2008-2012 is launched.
- A new Fairtrade labelling initiative is launched in South Africa; Fairtrade products such as coffee and tea are now available to shoppers in South Africa.
- London becomes the largest Fairtrade City in the world.
- The Fairtrade Foundation launches country partnerships with Malawi, Mozambique and Madagascar to deepen its engagement with producers in those nations.
- Liberation, the world's first 100% Fairtrade nut company, begins trading.

From Crop to Cup: the Fairtrade route vs. the conventional route for Coffee

The conventional coffee route

In conventional markets, large producers and transnational corporations have access to markets, capital and technology, while small coffee farmers and plantation workers are isolated from the market and unable to gain the full benefits their efforts deserve.

SMALL FARMERS ▶ **PROCESSING MILL** ▶
Over 50 per cent of the world's coffee is grown by small family farmers with less than 10 acres. They are often trapped by circumstances in a cycle of poverty and debt.

Processing of coffee is generally carried out on large farms or in coffee mills.

▶▶▶ **LOCAL MIDDLEMEN**
Small farmers usually sell to local intermediary traders who have a virtual monopoly over local transport and credit facilities, and are therefore able to determine the price at which the farmers have to sell. ▶▶▶

ESTATE WORKERS ▶ **COFFEE ESTATES** ▶
Millions of people are employed as workers on large coffee plantations or estates; many of them are migrants. Low wages and poor living and working conditions prevail.

Plantations/estates vary in size and can cover thousands of acres. Many of them are highly mechanised.

The Fairtrade coffee route

Fairtrade enables co-operatives of small farmers to bypass middlemen and sell directly to importers at fair prices.

FARMERS
There are some 600,000 members of co-operatives that sell to Fairtrade importers throughout the world. Farmers in Fairtrade are able to earn 3 to 5 times as much as on the conventional market. ▶▶

The conventional coffee route cont.

▶ **EXPORTERS**
Exporters are either independent companies or subsidiaries of multinational corporations that export coffee beans to importers in other (generally developed) countries. They aim to buy coffee at the lowest price and resell it for the highest profit, whilst satisfying their clients' quality requirements.

▶ **BROKERS**
Brokers buy and sell on commission for importers and exporters. They don't own the coffee beans they trade.
Multinational corporations have their own brokers and they have the power to speculate and influence prices on the New York and London coffee exchanges.

▶ **IMPORTERS**
Importers purchase green coffee of different origins from brokers or exporters and sell it on to roasters.

The Fairtrade coffee route cont.

▶ **CO-OPERATIVES**
Co-operatives enable farmers to work more efficiently and to strengthen their negotiating position. There are 250 democratically organised Fairtrade-certified coffee co-operatives or associations in 29 producer countries. They usually process their coffee with their own equipment and export directly to importers.

▶ **IMPORTERS**
Importers buy directly from certified co-operatives and pay the Fairtrade minimum price and premium (US$ 1.31/lb; US$ 1.51/lb for organic) or higher. If requested, the 450 importers registered with FLO-Cert (see below) must provide credit to the co-operative.

▶ **ROASTERS**
Roasters buy from importers certified by FLO-Cert and roast and package coffee for retail sale. They sign a contract with the national labelling body (e.g. Fairtrade Foundation in the UK) to be able to use the Fairtrade label on their product. ▶

▶ **ROASTERS**
Most roasters buy their coffee from importers based in their own country. After roasting and packaging the coffee, roasters then sell either to wholesalers or to supermarkets and caterers.

▶ **RETAILERS/ CATERERS**
Retailers and caterers are supermarkets, restaurants, cafés, companies and institutions that sell coffee to the final consumer.

▶ **CONSUMERS**
Most coffee is bought in supermarkets. Consumers generally receive no information about the conditions in which the coffee was produced and traded.

▶ **FAIRTRADE CERTIFICATION**
National labelling organisations such as the Fairtrade Foundation in the UK, and FLO-Cert* – their international Fairtrade certification body – inspect co-operatives, importers and roasters to check compliance with Fairtrade standards.

▶ **RETAILERS/ CATERERS**
Retailers and caterers, supermarkets, cafés, restaurants and other outlets that sell Fairtrade coffee directly to the consumer. Fairtrade coffee is currently being sold in some quarter of a million retail locations worldwide.

▶ **CONSUMERS**
Consumers are the engine driving the Fairtrade movement by creating and sustaining demand for Fairtrade coffee and other products.

(Based on an original diagram by Oxfam America – www.oxfamamerica.org)

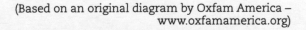

Tipping the Balance

The Fairtrade Foundation's Vision for Transforming Trade 2008–2012

Over the next five years as part of our goal of transforming trade, The Fairtrade Foundation will aim to tip the balance by:

1. Increasing Fairtrade's impact on producers' lives
2. Shifting public opinion and consumer lifestyles to make Fairtrade the norm
3. Expanding business engagement with Fairtrade from just compliance to deeper commitment
4. Growing Fairtrade's share of key markets to propel sales to a new level
5. Scaling up and developing the Fairtrade system

INDEX